WHY AUSTRALIA SLEPT

Why Australia is in danger of sleepwalking into the future

WHY AUSTRALIA SLEPT

Why Australia is in danger of sleepwalking into the future

Peter Hendy

Connor Court Publishing

Connor Court Publishing Pty Ltd

Copyright © Peter Hendy 2018

ALL RIGHTS RESERVED. This book contains material protected under International and Federal Copyright Laws and Treaties. Any unauthorised reprint or use of this material is prohibited. No part of this book may be reproduced or transmitted in any form or by any means, electronic or mechanical, including photocopying, recording, or by any information storage and retrieval system without express written permission from the publisher.

PO Box 7257
Redland Bay QLD 4165
sales@connorcourt.com
www.connorcourtpublishing.com.au

ISBN: 9781925501940

Cover design by Maria Giordano

Cover illustration: "Lost" (1907) by Frederick McCubbin
Wikimedia Commons

Printed in Australia

CONTENTS

Preface ix

Acronyms xi

1: Introduction
Why write this book? 1
Why Australia slept 5
Conclusion 8

2: Federation and the Rise and Fall of the Australian Settlement
Introduction 11
A brief history of Australian Federation 12
The economic case for Federation 20
The rise and fall of the Australian Settlement 29
"New Protection" re-labelled 30
The validity of the Australian Settlement concept 45
Social Liberalism shaped Australia 55
The demise of the Australian Settlement 59
The Australian Settlement 2.0: "The neo-liberal consensus"? .. 65
Conclusion 69

3: What Led to the Australian Settlement 2.0?
Introduction 71
The economic and political context 72
The Gorton and McMahon Governments (1967-1972) 79
The Whitlam Government (1972-1975) 80
The Fraser Government (1975-1983) 86
The Hawke and Keating Governments (1983-1996) 93
The creation of the Business Council of Australia 95
The New Right 99

Business argues for tariff reform 116
Business changes industrial relations policy 123
Business groups consolidate their voice for reform 126
The Howard Government (1996-2007) 134
An assessment: who fathered the Australian Settlement 2.0? ... 138
What has happened 2007 and beyond? 143
Conclusion 148

4: How Do We Sustain the Australian Settlement 2.0?
Introduction 149
Where to start? 150
The Washington Consensus versus the Beijing Consensus 157
The economic reform agenda 162
Democracy Paradox 165
Conclusion 168

5: Parliamentary Reform
Introduction 171
Reforming the Constitution 172
Fundraising reform 176
Conclusion 181

6: Tax Reform Part A (The Reform Agenda and Company Tax)
Introduction 183
State of play on tax reform 184
Recent tax "reform" picture 186
Prioritising tax reform 187
Prospects for the passage of company tax cut legislation 192
Reforming company tax rates 194
More radical change to company tax 197
Other areas for reform 200
Conclusion 201

7: Tax Reform Part B (Personal Income Tax Reform and GST)
Introduction 203
How personal income tax rates compare 204
Reforming personal income tax 208
Indexing the tax brackets (or thresholds) 210
Abolishing or lowering the Tax Free Threshold 210
Helping to pay for personal income tax reform without a GST increase 213
The scope for more comprehensive tax reform with an increase in the GST 214
Increasing GST collections 215
Increasing the GST rate 216
Broadening the GST base 217
Comment on a GST package 218
Reforming the Capital Gains Tax 222
Conclusion 224

8: Tax Reform Part C (Federation Tax Reform)
Introduction 227
Federal-State relations reform shouldn't be about raising tax levels 228
Conclusion 235

9: Industrial Relations Reform
Introduction 237
Setting the context for reform 238
Where to from here?' 245
Conclusion 249

10: The Country-City Compact
Introduction 251
Regional policy 252

High speed rail and the Very Fast Train 254
Conclusion 257

11: Trade Deals
Introduction 259
Setting the context 260
The benefits of freer trade and the threats of its demise 262
What needs to be done 267
Conclusion 272

12: International Relations and Defence
Introduction 273
The strategic setting 274
Overview 274
Government White Papers 279
China 283
Russia 292
Terrorism 295
North Korea 298
A more independent foreign policy? 300
Increased spending 301
Missile defence 304
Nuclear submarines 306
Nuclear weapons 308
The Quadrilateral Dialogue 311
New Colombo Plan 312
Immigration and population size 313
Conclusion 317

13: Conclusion 319

Index 325

PREFACE

This book examines the policy challenges that confront Australia in the second decade of the 21st century. In doing so it also discusses the political constraints imposed on those people who are trying to wrestle with these problems. It therefore also addresses the related question "Is our democracy broken?"

Part of the book looks at the history of Australia over the course of some 200 years and discusses the economic and political framework that existed. I believe that it is important to understand where we have been if we are to adequately confront the problems of today.

The book therefore looks at the rise and fall of the "Australian Settlement" during the period 1901-2007. In particular the study focuses on the principal economic framework of the Australian Settlement – a policy known as "New Protection". This policy linked high levels of tariff protection with a heavily regulated centralised wage fixing system operated through Federal compulsory arbitration of industrial relations processes. However, it also goes beyond that to look at parliamentary reform and key international relations and defence issues.

As with almost all books it is the product of many years of research.

It also has some genesis in the PhD thesis I wrote to get my doctorate in Government from the University of Canberra. As such I wish to particularly acknowledge the great assistance of my PhD supervisor Associate Professor Gwyn Singleton. Over the years I have also had to rely heavily on records held at the Australian National University, Flinders University, the National Library of Australia and the State Library of NSW. I would like to thank the staff of these institutions who gave me assistance.

Lastly I would like to thank Bronwyn, Caroline and Patrick who demonstrated great patience with me over the years while I wrote up the thesis, both in Australia and while we lived in the Kingdom of Bahrain and then more recently while I have written this book. The book is dedicated to them.

Peter Hendy
Sydney NSW
Autumn 2018

ACRONYMS

ACAC	Australian Conciliation and Arbitration Commission
ACCA	Associated Chambers of Commerce of Australia
ACC	Australian Chamber of Commerce
ACCI	Australian Chamber of Commerce and Industry
ACEF	Australian Council of Employers Federations
ACMA	Associated Chambers of Manufactures of Australia
ACTU	Australian Council of Trade Unions
AFE	Australian Federation of Employers
AIRC	Australian Industrial Relations Commission
ANU	Australian National University
BCA	Business Council of Australia
CAI	Confederation of Australian Industry
CCAC	Commonwealth Conciliation and Arbitration Commission
CCCA	Commonwealth Court of Conciliation and Arbitration
CCEA	Central Council of Employers of Australia
IMF	International Monetary Fund
IPA	Institute of Public Affairs
NFF	National Farmers' Federation
OECD	Organisation for Economic Co-operation and Development
PC	Productivity Commission
PMV	Passenger Motor Vehicle industry
TCF	Textile, Clothing and Footwear industries
UAP	United Australia Party
WTO	World Trade Organisation

1
INTRODUCTION

Why write this book?

In Australia in the 21st century, in some senses, we have never had it so good.

But few would know it.

There is an intense anxiety – a malaise in fact – that has settled over the land that is hard to explain. It is not unique to Australia. We have seen it in the US, the UK and in Europe as well.

Over my long career in public policy there was a similar period at an earlier time. That was when I started out. That was back in 1979 when, as a fresh faced youth, I first went off to university to study economics and law.

Australia at the end of 1970s was suffering from "Stagflation" which was an unholy combination of high inflation and high unemployment that led to a stagnant economy. I will speak more of that in later chapters.

This twin evil was defeated by a lot of hard work from policy makers. Not necessarily uncontroversial nor popular, the policies were often extremely hard to implement not least because the population at the time had developed a mindset that it might be all too hard to fix.

Does that sound familiar?

The saving grace now is that while there is also a malaise today we aren't in the economic pickle we were in in the 1970s and 1980s. As I said, in recent times the economic fundamentals have been sound.

However we are coasting as an economy and people are in fact correct to feel a sense of anxiety.

To use an analogy, it is like we have previously been paddling hard up the face of a huge wave and we have stopped paddling as we coast up to and momentarily sweep along the peak. What happens next, whether we continue to control our trajectory to the next wave and quickly get to subsequent peaks or we plunge into the trough between waves and stay wallowing, is up to us.

So why write this book? The answer to the question is simple. I'm offering up some policy solutions based on my experience over many years.

The topics covered in this book are all ones I know well.

I have had a blessed career. I have had an enviable mix of a private sector, public service and political career. Many people will condemn me for doing any one of these by themselves, let alone all three. People always have a reason to complain.

All politicians are crooks, they say.

All public servants are fat cats feeding off the poor taxpayer, they say.

All business people are fat cats feeding off the poor customers, they say.

However, I believe each has been a noble pursuit and has contributed to the Australian community in different ways.

I have built up a considerable amount of experience over the years, which I hope gives me some credibility when it comes to writing this book.

I am a former Chief Economist in the Office of the Australian Prime Minister. In addition I have been the Assistant Minister for Finance, Assistant Cabinet Secretary and Assistant Minister for Productivity in the Australian Government, during the time I was the Federal Member for Eden-Monaro between 2013 and 2016.

Introduction

The bottom line is that I am an economist by profession and have a PhD in Government. Indeed some of this book is based on my PhD thesis on Australian economic history. My economic career started with an early stint in the Australian Treasury Department. Much later, in 2003, I was awarded a Centenary Medal by the Governor General for "service to Australian society in business leadership". In 2006, I was honoured to have been commissioned by then Treasurer, Peter Costello, to co-author the landmark *International Comparison of Australia's Taxes* report, which lay the groundwork for meaningful long-term taxation reform on retirement benefits and income tax in Australia. In 2008, Melbourne University Press published my book *Captains of Industry,* which is a historical study of some of Australia's greatest business people.

All that, at the very least, should cover-off on economic policy.

As to international relations and defence policy, immediately prior to entering Parliament I was the Principal Advisor (Foreign Affairs and Trade) for Julie Bishop, who subsequently became the Australian Foreign Minister. Previously I had been the Chief of Staff to the Australian Minister for Defence. And for a time I worked in the Middle East and was an Executive Director (Deputy Secretary-level) with the Bahrain Economic Development Board responsible for tasks such as reforming their budget processes. And I was at one stage a national director of the Australian Institute of International Affairs.

However, besides these more "pointy-headed" pursuits I note that I also have a commercial background.

In those terms I was very fortunate indeed to be a former chief executive officer of the Australian Chamber of Commerce and Industry (ACCI) and have been in the corporate sector, being a member of the board of directors of a number of organisations and also chairman. Added to that I am a former chairman of the

International Chamber of Commerce (Australia). I was a vice president (designate) of the Confederation of Asia Pacific Chambers of Commerce and Industry (CACCI) and also the chairman for around six years of their Joint Policy Committee and a council member of the Business and Industry Advisory Committee (BIAC) of the Organisation of Economic Cooperation and Development (OECD). And I am proudest of the fact that I have also run my own small business as an economic consultant.

And let's not forget politics.

When I spoke in the House of Representatives for the very first time in 2013 I was not unfamiliar with the surroundings having sat in the advisors' boxes many times in the past.

My political journey started when I joined the Young Liberals in 1979. I joined the Liberal Party because I believed it genuinely encourages people to be the best they can be, not telling them what to be. However, I in no way disrespect those in other parties, particular the Labor Party. My father's family were very strong Labor supporters (going back to the time of the foundation of that party) with various uncles and cousins standing as Labor candidates or holding important jobs in Labor head office or Labor Cabinet Ministers' offices.

I first formally worked in politics for Andrew Peacock, the then Member for Kooyong as a newly recruited economist from the Federal Treasury. Part of the remit was to do a bit of economic tutoring for the then shadow treasurer. I knew from the first meeting that we would have a longer road than originally envisaged when Andrew, as the former Minister for Foreign Affairs, better recognised the word NAIRU as possibly being a Pacific island (ie Nauru) – made up mostly of bird droppings – rather than the economic acronym for the "non-accelerating inflation rate of unemployment". Be that as it may, Andrew Peacock's time as shadow treasurer was a success that eventually led him to return to the leadership of the party.

I was also there when the former Leader of the Opposition Professor John Hewson employed a young media adviser and talented wordsmith who later became the Member for Warringah and subsequently Prime Minister. Of course I'm talking of Tony Abbott. Many of us on staff copped regular tongue lashings from Dr Hewson. I did. So, as I recall, did Tony. We were often reminded that "we wouldn't know if our arses were on fire". And at least one of us – not me thankfully – were sacked because of questionable economic competence. However, we endured and the team collectively produced the Fightback! package which set the blueprint for economic reform for Australia in the following 20 years.

But this is not a memoir of my career. Certainly if I were to write my memoirs – especially of my time in Parliament – they would be very interesting and probably a tad controversial. However, I don't want to burn my bridges like Mark Latham and some other diarists over the years. I'll leave that to my dotage when, by then, I won't care so much who I offend.

Why Australia slept

To understand Australia's economic and other policy challenges of today it is important to understand how we have got to where we are. I think it is vitally important to understand Australia's economic history and appreciate the policies that have been tried before if we want a fuller understanding of the current debates on economic and other policy.

As part of this analysis I will spend quite a bit of time examining the rise and fall of the so-called "Australian Settlement". The reason for using this policy framework is determined by the centrality of the Australian Settlement to government policy over more than 80 years, until quite recently.

The concept of the Australian Settlement is much older than the term itself. Journalist and popular historian Paul Kelly coined the term in his 1992 book *The End of Certainty*[1] to describe a principally, economic framework that had been developed late in the 19th century. While having no formal definition, it is usually defined as a policy framework consisting of: industry protection; wage arbitration; state paternalism; a White Australia (or a restricted immigration policy); and imperial benevolence.[2] Kelly described the Settlement as "an achievement second only to the creation of Australian democracy, and its operation within that democracy has offered for most of [the 20th] century the best definition of nationhood".[3] Indeed, it put the bones on the flesh of the Commonwealth Constitution. As Professor Greg Melleuish[4] of the University of Wollongong states "it is arguable that the Australian Settlement was more fundamental in the shaping of Australian political culture than the institutional union of Federation or the rules for its Constitution". I will examine the Australian Settlement in detail in the next chapter.

However, suffice it to say in this introductory chapter, as a consequence of this policy Australia ended up sleepwalking through the decades. What do I mean by that?

This book's title is unashamedly a lift of the name of John F. Kennedy's book, originally published in 1940, called *Why England Slept*[5] in which he debated "why was England so poorly prepared for the war? ... What had England been doing while Hitler was building up [the] tremendous German army?" Kennedy went on

---

[1] Paul Kelly (1992), *The End of Certainty: The story of the 1980s*, Allen and Unwin, Sydney.
[2] Ibid., 1-2.
[3] Ibid., 1.
[4] Gregory Melleuish (2004), "From the 'social laboratory' to the 'Australian Settlement'", in Paul Boreham, Geoffrey Stokes and Richard Hall (eds) (2004), *The Politics of Australian Society*, 2nd edition, Pearson Education Australia, French's Forest, 84.
[5] John F. Kennedy (1962), *Why England Slept*, Mayfair Books, London, (originally 1940), 7.

to say: "About two years ago Winston Churchill published a book entitled *While England Slept*. This book is an attempt to explain *why* England slept. I have started with the assumption that there is no short-cut to the answer to this problem".

In England's case Kennedy came to the conclusion that:

> At times it may appear that I have tried unjustifiably to clear the leaders of responsibility. That is not my view. But I believe, as I have stated frequently, that leaders are responsible for their failures only in the governing sector and cannot be held responsible for the failure of a nation as a whole.
>
> So long as England was a democracy, a democracy with a Parliamentary system, so long as the leaders could have been turned out of office at any time on any issues, Parliament, and hence those who elect the Parliament, must all bear their share of the responsibility.[6]

Saying that everyone shared responsibility foreshadowed what Kennedy was to famously exhort in his presidential inauguration speech: "Ask not what your country can do for you, ask what you can do for your country".[7]

When I use such a phrase as "sleepwalking through the decades" in the context of Australia's economic history I am alluding to the fact that by the 1970s Australia was suffering from chronic economic problems. This was after, according to some research, Australia had the highest income per capita in the world at the time of Federation in 1901.[8]

Australia was falling behind other OECD nations. It was subject to chronically high unemployment and inflation. Economic

---
[6] Kennedy 1962, 169.
[7] John F. Kennedy (1961), "Inaugural Address", Washington DC, 20 January
[8] Ian W. McLean (2013), *Why Australia Prospered: the shifting sources of economic growth*, Princeton University Press, Princeton, 11.

stagnation or "stagflation" was the order of the day. As described in subsequent chapters, many groups, particularly in the business community, argued for a neo-liberal policy revolution. In the end this actually happened during the subsequent decades.

Depending on which authors are consulted the end of the Settlement began either as early as the Menzies Government, or the latter half of the Hawke-Keating Government; or indeed even the beginning of the Howard Government in 1996. Nonetheless, there is a consensus view that over the last two decades there was a demise of the Australian Settlement when it was replaced by a neo-liberal consensus[9] or what is termed in this study: the Australian Settlement 2.0. That, in my opinion, was a very good thing.

As we will see in chapters 2 and 3 the business community were critical in all these policy developments. If Australia is to sustain the Australian Settlement 2.0 it will again require the business community to be front and centre in arguing for the reforms that are needed.

Conclusion

In summary the first part of this book looks at how Australia sleep-walked through decades of ignorance. It squandered its starting point at the end of the 19th century of being the wealthiest country, by population, in the world.

In the end however, it woke up to itself and was able to again become the envy of the world.

The second part of the book looks at the very dangerous future Australia faces in a new bout of sleepwalking.

---

[9] See for example Kelly 1992, 13; Geoffrey Stokes (2007) "Australian Settlement" in Galligan, Brian and Roberts Winsome (eds) (2007), *The Oxford Companion to Australian Politics*, Oxford University Press, Melbourne, 56-57; Brian Galligan (2007), "Liberal party predecessors", in Galligan and Roberts 2007, 320; Melleuish 2004, 88-90.

Introduction

There has in recent years been much recidivism. Unfortunately it looks like that recidivism is growing and there is a real danger that it is becoming the new consensus. There is much talk of a return to protectionism and greater government intervention in the economy. On one side of the world we have an American president saying that tariff barriers should be raised and on the other side of the world a Chinese president who is extolling the virtues of State intervention in the market place.

This is potentially very dangerous for Australia. It flies in the face of the magnificent gains in prosperity that Australians have benefited from over many decades. It would be more than a great shame, but an absolute travesty, if such gains were squandered.

No-one should be under any illusions that this is possible. Those great gains can disappear in a flash and it will take decades to win them back – if indeed there is a collective will to even try and win them back. It should not be forgotten that it took Australia some 20 years to get back on an even keel after the short sharp shock of the economically disastrous Whitlam Government in the early 1970s.

These periods of stagnation can be distressingly long. After once before shaking a bout of sleepwalking Australia can ill afford to become a zombie nation afflicted with another bout.

While I think that to really come to grips with Australia's economic and other policy challenges it is important to understand its economic history, many readers will not want to plough through that history (and I admit it can be a bit academic in parts) but instead get straight to the meaty policy proposals. In that case they should just skip chapters 2 and 3. They can then go to the substance of the policy solutions that I address in chapters 4 to 12 inclusive. In particular the proposed changes to Parliament and the taxation system are I think vital for the future prosperity of the nation.

2
FEDERATION AND THE RISE AND FALL OF THE AUSTRALIAN SETTLEMENT

Introduction

As noted in the introduction to this book this chapter explores the rise and fall of the Australian Settlement. It will investigate the initial creation of this policy framework and how it developed over a number of decades. It then looks at the creation and implementation of the "Australian Settlement 2.0", which is a set of neo-liberal policies. This was a watershed change in Australia's policy framework.

I should state at this point that I am using the term "neo-liberal" for the sake of convenience. I personally strongly support such policies. They derive from the liberal tradition of philosophical thought and are rooted in the view that individualism is not just an accurate explanation of human activity but is a good thing and is something to be protected at all costs. Many left-leaning commentators use the word neo-liberal as a term of abuse. My attitude is the exact opposite.

Britain's Adam Smith Institute[1] has adopted the same attitude as myself – adopting a term that the Left use as a slur because it is something worth strongly defending. It is worth noting that the Institute defines the word neo-liberal to mean adherents who are:

- Pro-markets
- Pro-property rights

---

[1] Sam Bowman (2016), *Coming out as Neoliberals*, Adam Smith Institute, London, 11 October. See also Madsen Pirie (2014), *Looking at the World through Neo-Liberal Eyes*, Adam Smith Institute, London, 20 August.

- Pro-growth
- Individualistic
- Empirical and open-minded
- Globalist in outlook
- Optimistic about the future
- Focuses on changing the world for the better

There will be a lot of references to neo-liberalism in this chapter and be warned that the discussion can in parts be very academic and dry as I am seeking here to get to grips with Australia's economic and social history.

While it is not necessary for the purposes of this study to give a comprehensive, fully detailed history of Federation, I believe it helps to provide a brief history, setting out the key milestones, noting the main driving motivations for Federation and acknowledging that from the start Australia was handicapped with a heavily restrictive economic policy. And so that is where this chapter starts.

As I forewarned just above this chapter can at times be very dry and academic. If you are interested in the contemporary policy debates please feel free to skip to chapter 4 and beyond.

A brief history of Australian Federation

The Federation movement in Australia did not long follow the formation of the various colonies.[2] And indeed the first serious

---

[2] Unless otherwise noted this historical summary relies on a number of sources including: Bob Birrell (2001) *Federation The Secret Story*, Duffy and Snell Grove, Sydney; John Hirst (2000), *The Sentimental Nation: The making of the Australian Commonwealth*, Oxford University Pres, Melbourne; Brian Matthews (1999), *Federation*, Text Publishing, Melbourne; W.G. McMinn (1994), *Nationalism and Federalism in Australia*, Oxford University Press, Melbourne; L.F. Crisp (1990), *Federation Fathers*, Melbourne University Press, Melbourne; C.M.H. Clark (1981), *A History of Australia*, (6 volumes), Melbourne University Press, Melbourne; Ernest Scott (1929), *A Short History*

deliberations on Federation were made by the Secretary of State for the Colonies, Henry Grey – the 3rd Earl Grey – as early as 1847 when considering options for self-government. Not without a great deal of prescience, he was concerned that a fragmentation of self-government, without a central overarching government, would create serious quarrels.[3]

He referred the matter to a UK Parliamentary Committee of Trade and Plantations in 1849. It recommended that: "in addition to establishing Legislatures in the various colonies, the Governor-General should have the power to convene a body to be called the General Assembly of Australia. It was to consist of a single House, named the House of Delegates, whose members were to be elected, not by the people but by the Parliaments; and it was to have certain powers entrusted to it affecting the common interests of all Australia. It was to take charge of customs and excise, postal business, roads and railways, lighthouses, weights and measures; it was to set up a general Supreme Court to act as a court of appeal from colonial courts; and it was to have power to make laws on any subject which might be referred to it by the Parliaments of all the colonies".[4]

Interestingly, the powers proposed were centred on economic issues and omitted defence.

Earl Grey accepted these recommendations and he incorporated them in the self-government legislation he submitted to the Imperial Parliament in 1850. Nonetheless, his draft gained little support in the Australian colonies and the relevant clauses were struck out in the House of Lords.

---

of Australia, Oxford University Press, Melbourne; , Alexander Sutherland and George Sutherland (1911), *The History of Australia and New Zealand from 1606 to 1901*, Longmans, Green and Co., Melbourne; and Wood, F.L.W. (1943), *A Concise History of Australia*, Dymock's Book Arcade Ltd, Sydney.
[3] Matthews 1999, 36.
[4] Scott 1929, 298.

This was obviously an opportunity lost.

The British settlements in Australia, up until 1829 consisted solely of New South Wales, which covered the general landmass except for the area of today's Western Australia. In 1829, Western Australia was formally settled by the British, but governed separately.

In 1851 New South Wales was divided up administratively to establish the separate colonies of Victoria, South Australia and Tasmania. Not long after, these particular colonies received self-government in the years 1855 and 1856. A self-governing Queensland was separated from New South Wales in 1859 and it was not until 1890 that Western Australia gained self-government from Britain.

There developed a genuine lack of cooperation across the colonies. Serious arguments developed over issues surrounding the use of the Murray River that bordered three States (i.e., New South Wales, Victoria and South Australia), such as irrigation and the regulation of trading ships.

However, as historian Professor Frederick Wood puts it: "the most serious trouble was in connection with customs duties"[5], and further stated that "at times they quarreled so bitterly that some men thought there might some day be civil war".[6]

So what was this all about? One of the key causes was that successive Victorian Governments, from 1866 onwards, implemented a policy of high protective tariffs. As New South Wales implemented a free trade policy and the other colonies only had low, revenue raising tariffs the Victorian policy was the source of clashes and irritations over customs duties, especially on the Murray River border. Further, according to Wood, "the Victorian tariff at one time practically ruined Tasmania, and was a serious problem

---

[5] Wood 1943, 208.
[6] Ibid., 206.

to the wheat farmers of South Australia; but neither South Australia nor Tasmania could persuade the Victorians to lower their tariff".[7]

There had been a practical accommodative agreement between New South Wales and Victoria to assist inter-colonial trade in the late 1860s but this broke down in 1873.

Earlier, men like W.C. Wentworth, Deas Thompson and Reverend J.D. Lang from New South Wales, and Charles Gavan Duffy from Victoria, had sought to garner support to discuss these cross border issues but they failed.[8]

However, as time progressed a second critical issue besides customs issues gained greater prominence. This related to foreign policy and defence. There were gathering Australian concerns about French imperial encroachment in the Pacific Islands like New Caledonia (which led to the Australian colonies successful lobbying to have the British Government, reluctantly, annex Fiji); and German designs in New Guinea (where a preemptive annexation of part of the area by Queensland in 1883 eventually led to a British protectorate and, from 1888, annexation).

As former Prime Minister Alfred Deakin, a prominent Victorian politician, noted himself years later:

> The federal impulse of 1880 was in the first place a reaction from the ultra-Protectionist policy of 1878-9 some of whose imposts, and the Stock Tax in particular, being directly aimed at intercolonial imports, naturally provoked great bitterness of feeling upon the border. The completion of the connection between the New South Wales line to Albury and the Victorian line to Wodonga in 1883 afforded occasion for an outburst of sentiment in favour of union, though the way had been prepared for this and the chief

---

[7] Wood 1943, 208-209.
[8] Ibid., 209.

stimulus given by the threatening aspect of affairs in the Pacific in the immediate neighbourhood of Australia.[9]

The first formal move to Federation followed a speech by then Premier of New South Wales, Sir Henry Parkes (the 'Father of Federation'),[10] who as early as a speech in Melbourne on 16 March 1867 stated that "I think the time has arrived when these colonies should be united by some federal bond of connexion".[11] In 1881 he called for the creation of a Federal Council to coordinate various policies across the colonies.

This call was strongly supported by Premier James Service's Victorian Government and Premier Samuel Griffith's Queensland Government, which jointly took a leadership role on the issue. An Australasian Inter-Colonial Conference was convened in Sydney on 26 November 1883. It discussed defence issues, the annexation of New Guinea, and recommended the creation of a Federal Council.

In 1885 this eventuated in a *Federal Council of Australasia Act* being passed by the Imperial Parliament. However, this turned out to be a weak coordinating body and only had five members, viz: Victoria, Queensland, Western Australia, Tasmania and Fiji. Most importantly, New South Wales and South Australia (except briefly in 1889) did not join. Nor did New Zealand join. Nonetheless it lingered and it met biennially until January 1899.[12]

The issue was given further impetus when on 9 October 1889, Major General Sir Bevan Edwards of Britain, who had been invited

---

[9] Alfred Deakin (1944), *The Federal Story*, Robertson & Mullens, Melbourne, 9.
[10] Although this is not a view held by everyone, see Matthews 1999, 38-41.
[11] Henry Parkes (1876), *Speeches on Various Occasions Connected with the Public Affairs of New South Wales 1848-1874*, George Robertson, Melbourne, 256.
[12] Crisp 1990, 371-372.

by the Australian colonies to formally advise them on their defence preparedness, stated that they should federate in terms of their defence arrangements.

The next big push for federation came soon after with a watershed speech from Sir Henry Parkes in an address in Tenterfield, NSW, on 24 October 1889 calling for the convening of a new conference to advance the cause. Unsurprisingly, a principal theme of his argument was defence considerations.[13]

Following this a Conference on Federation was held in Melbourne on 6 February 1890. All the colonies, including New Zealand attended and after long discussion it was decided that the time had come to advance the cause of federation and it was agreed that a convention of representatives chosen by the respective parliaments should be held.

It was at the banquet preceding the conference that Sir Henry in front of a gathering that Professor Manning Clark tells us included "Premiers, bankers, presidents of chambers of commerce, mayors, [and] officers of the armed forces", stated his memorable phrases that they were all there "to drink of this water of national life" and that "the crimson thread of kinship runs through us all".[14]

The First National Australasian Convention was convened in Sydney on 2 March 1891. It initially dealt with various drafts of a possible constitution for a federated Australia, principally two drafts – one by Andrew Inglis Clark, Attorney-General of Tasmania[15] and one by Charles Cameron Kingston, former Premier of South Australia.[16]

---

[13] Crisp 1990, 372.
[14] Clark 1981, 32.
[15] Marcus Haward and James Warden, (1995) (eds) *An Australian Democrat: The Life, Work, and Consequences of Andrew Inglis Clark*, Centre for Tasmanian Historical Studies, University of Tasmania, Hobart, 3.
[16] L.F. Crisp (1984), *Charles Cameron Kingston, Radical Federationist*, pamphlet, Canberra.

The Convention commissioned a drafting team led by Sir Samuel Griffith to produce a final text for a constitution. This was debated and accepted by a reconvened Convention on 9 April 1891. However the constitution was rejected in the New South Wales Parliament and Queensland and Western Australia stayed on the sidelines without commitment, and so the momentum collapsed.

It is important to note here what the stumbling block was in New South Wales. In the context of this study it is noteworthy that it was not defence or other issues, but in fact the perennial question of tariff policy that had initiated the beginnings of talk of federation and which were central to the interests of the business community. As Wood notes: "The other colonies waited for New South Wales to lead the way, but New South Wales did nothing. A strong party led by George Reid argued that Federation would make New South Wales give up the free trade policy under which she had grown prosperous".[17]

Renewed momentum was initiated by the Australian Natives' Association which convened a Federation Conference in Corowa on 31 July to 1 August 1893, where it was decided that the way forward was the greater involvement of the population. This took the form of a motion by Dr John Quick, on the suggestion of Sir Henry Parkes, to seek a popularly elected convention (not as before from parliamentary delegates) to meet to resolve a constitution.[18]

At a Federal Council meeting held in 1895 this procedure was supported and during the course of late 1895 through to 1896, the various colonies, except for Queensland, passed enabling acts to support the holding of a convention.

The Adelaide session of the Second National Australasian Convention was held between 22 March and 23 April 1897 and

---

[17] Wood 1943, 212-213; also see Crisp 1990, 1-49 and McMinn, W.G. (1989), *George Reid*, Melbourne University Press, Melbourne.
[18] Sutherland and Sutherland 1911, 188-189.

with some amendments it recommended the 1891 draft constitution and sought colonial parliaments' comments.

At a reconvened Sydney session a large number of amendments were considered between 2 and 24 September 1897. The proposed constitution was finalised at a Melbourne session between 20 January and 17 March 1898.

In the subsequent referendums, New South Wales, Victoria, and Tasmania (on 3 June 1898) and South Australia (4 June 1898) secured a majority 'yes' vote. Queensland and Western Australia did not participate. However, the Parliament of New South Wales had previously stipulated that that colony would only support Federation if the 'yes' vote totalled at least 80,000 votes. They actually fell short with only 71,595 votes.

Premier George Reid of New South Wales took advantage of this result to push for some more amendments in favour of his constituency. Again, of importance to this study one of these changes related to the treatment of tariffs in the Constitution (ie Section 87). Other amendments related to the site of the future Federal Capital and the treatment of deadlocks between the House of Representatives and the Senate. These were agreed at a Premiers' Conference on 29 January-2 February 1899.[19]

The amended constitution was again put to the populace between April and September 1899 (although not in Western Australia) and finally agreed to.

The draft was put to the British Government which, with some of its own amendments, secured passage through the Imperial Parliament during 1900, by which time after a referendum on 31 July 1900, the Western Australians decided to participate. Royal proclamation occurred on 17 September 1900 and the Commonwealth came into being on 1 January 1901.

---

[19] Crisp 1990, 19.

The economic case for Federation

It is important to understand that a major impetus for Federation came from the business community and that a large motivating factor was an attempt to resolve economic issues. To fully appreciate this I think it is worth noting the views of the business community and the heavy involvement that leaders of the business community played as participants in the federal conventions themselves.

This is all relevant as it was during this time that the Australian Settlement was actually agreed between participants and indeed became the "flesh on the bones" of the Constitution.

It is rarely taught in Australian schools today but the business community played a significant role in the emergence of the Australian Federation and the associated issue of the tariff. For example prior to the federation of the colonies in 1901 to form the Commonwealth of Australia a number of continent-spanning gatherings of business leaders constituted a network to develop policies and strategies to influence government policy. The first of these gatherings was the 'Inter-colonial Conference of Chamber of Commerce Representatives' in Sydney on 3 May 1869,[20] where resolutions were passed in favour of a customs union, an economic arrangement involving free-trade between the participating states and the implementation of a common, uniform tariff against other non-member States. As J.B. Cooper[21] notes: "This was an historical conference, wherein Federation was spoken about as a coming necessity to the Commonwealth, a union of Customs, a union of national ideas, and aims, the beginning in fact of Australian nationhood".[22]

---

[20] *Intercolonial Conference of Chamber of Commerce Representatives* (1869), Report of the Proceedings of the Commercial Conference, held in Sydney on 3 May.

[21] J.B. Cooper (1934), *Victorian Commerce 1834-1934*, Robertson & Mullins, Melbourne, 171-172.

[22] See also H.G. Viney (1936), *A century of Commerce in South Australia*,

At the initiation of the Victorian Chamber of Manufactures (VCM) a series of a further three 'Inter-colonial Conferences of Free Trade between the Australian Colonies' were held to discuss these issues, beginning with a meeting in Adelaide on 5-7 October 1887 and followed by subsequent meetings on 6-8 June in Sydney and 14-16 November 1888 in Melbourne. The president of the meetings was Emil Steinfeld who was the then Victorian Chamber president.

The principal resolution of the first of these conferences was that: "it is desirable that free-trade amongst the colonies of Australia should be established on the basis of a Customs Union with a uniform tariff".[23] The following year, the second conference[24] began by passing a very similar motion, viz: "it is desirable that free trade amongst the Australian colonies, based on a Customs Union with a uniform tariff, should be established".[25] And very importantly the conference also passed the following resolution: "it is desirable that the Australasian colonies should be Federated upon a wide and comprehensive basis, embracing all measures that can only be dealt with by federal action and authority".[26] Each of these steps marked a significant milestone in the Australian business communities' collective support for Federation, well beyond support for simply unifying the tariff. As C.R. Hall[27] notes:

> In plain terms it was support for the notion of the Federation of the Colonies and the removal of all tariff barriers between them. Put another way, it was free-trade within Australia and a uniform tariff against the rest of the world – protection for Australian industry on a national basis.

1836-1936, Adelaide Chamber of Commerce, Adelaide, 76.
[23] *Adelaide Register* (1887), 7 October.
[24] *Daily Telegraph* (1888), 8 June.
[25] *Sydney Morning Herald* (1888), 8 June.
[26] *Daily Telegraph* (1888), 9 June.
[27] C.R. Hall (1971), *The Manufacturers: Australian Manufacturing Achievements to 1960*, Angus and Robertson, Sydney, 62.

By the third conference in November 1888 similar resolutions were again passed[28] and A.D. Nelson of the Chamber of Manufactures of NSW noted in debate that they were "aimed at the federation of the whole Australian groups, and the consummation of a great Australian nation".[29] Further, John Hack of South Australian Chamber of Manufacturers stated that: "Australian unity and Federation was a grand and glorious object to work for. Federation once accomplished, Australasia would become one of the great nations of the world".[30]

The other organisations that constituted the business community at the time had similar views. For example, Victorian Chamber's some-time rival, sometime-partner, the Melbourne Chamber of Commerce organised a 'Congress of Australasian Chambers of Commerce' to coincide with the Australian centenary celebrations held in Melbourne on 31 October-2 November 1888 that resolved that "free-trade amongst the Colonies of Australasia should be established on the basis of a customs union, with a uniform tariff".[31] It is not clear what direct influence such calls had on politicians at the time. However, in further attempts to influence policy, almost a decade later, a subsequent 'Conference of Chambers of Commerce of Australasia' to foster fraternal relations between the chambers of commerce and to debate important inter-colonial issues was held in Sydney in May 1897.[32]

As the push for Federation achieved momentum during the late 1890s the various Chambers of Manufactures (and some of the Chambers of Commerce) convened a number of 'Inter-colonial Tariff Conferences of Chambers of Manufactures' to maximise busi-

---

[28] The *Argus* (1888), 15 November.
[29] Ibid.
[30] Ibid.
[31] Hall 1971, 83-84.
[32] Melbourne Chamber of Commerce (1897), Annual General Meeting minutes, 22 April.

ness input into what type of tariff regime would be implemented by the soon to be convened Federal Parliament. The fact that the various Chambers of Manufactures had varying views on the type of protection policy they supported – ranging from low to very high rates of protection – was the precursor of what was to be a divisive issue for the business community in the post-Federation period.

The draft Australian Constitution (that had been agreed to by popular vote during the course of 1899) incorporated the clear implication that some-type of protectionist policy would be utilised by the Federal Parliament because the primary source of revenues for the new legal entity that was to be the Commonwealth of Australia would be tariff revenues. The debate therefore became not one between complete free-trade versus protection, but a policy spectrum between a very low level of protection, that would collect some level of revenues, and high levels of protection.

Two important indicators of the business community's development into a more cohesive lobbying entity were evident from the proceedings of the three inter-colonial tariff conferences held on 8-15 November 1899; on 22-26 May; and on 8 October 1900, where agreement was reached on a combined Chambers of Manufactures' view of a desirable tariff level to be recommended to the incoming federal government and a call was made for the establishment of a national body to represent their interests. At the first conference Victorian Chamber president and chairman of the proceedings, Frederick Derham, defined what his organisation regarded as an acceptable protection policy: "It seemed to him, when considering whether there should be some limit to the federal policy of protection, that they should remember that the object of protection was to furnish employment to the people, and that, therefore, the amount of protection to be afforded in any article should not be in excess of the proportion of wages expended in the production of the article".[33] While this was not a view held by all protectionists it articulated the majority view at the time and became known as the policy of New Protection. The third conference also passed a resolution recommending that manufacturers adopt the eight-hours-of-work-a-day principle. This linkage between industrial relations and tariff policy became an important factor in the approach of the business community to the tariff post-Federation. As Derham stated on moving the motion, it: "was not intended that legislation be introduced on the subject. They preferred to see the principle carried out voluntarily. Already it was generally adopted by manufacturers, and there were very few firms where it was not already in force".[34] Incidentally, this conference also passed a resolution calling for the establishment of a more permanent federal manufacturers' body, viz: "a Federated Chamber of Manufactures".[35]

The consolidated tariff schedule that had been compiled during the course of the three conferences provided an important instrument for establishing the credentials of the business community as an important and significant source of advice to government. It is known that Derham presented it to the inaugural Minister for Trade and Customs in early 1901.[36] Hall[37] notes:

> The document gave the first Commonwealth Government, charged with the duty of more or less creating something out of nothing, a picture of manufacturing industry in Australia as it was at the turn of the century and as manufacturers believed it could be developed, and it was in analytical detail.

---

[33] *Proceedings of the First Conference of Inter-colonial Chambers of Manufactures to Prepare a Federal Tariff* (1899), Edward Lee & Co, Sydney, 8-15 November, 4.
[34] *Daily Telegraph* (1900), 12 October.
[35] *Daily Telegraph* (1900), 9 October.
[36] Hall 1971, 137-138.
[37] Ibid.

In his history of Federation, Professor John Hirst[38] noted that a "step-by-step approach to a customs union would not work" as the nature of parliamentary democracy at the time was one where 'party', in the modern sense, did not exist and the necessary discipline to overcome sectional interest groups was almost impossible to muster. He concluded that "the merchants and manufacturers were opposed to the federal movement because they thought federation was too difficult. The politicians who talked of federation were wasting everyone's time; they would not achieve it, and meanwhile the immediate benefits that could be secured by a customs union were being lost. These men were, as they boasted, practical men, and they wanted results".[39] However, Hirst's conclusion is not supported by the facts as presented above. While it is true that elements of the Chamber movement wanted to put the implementation of a customs union before Federation (e.g., Benjamin Cowderoy and the Melbourne Chamber of Commerce) to conflate this as opposition of the general business community against Federation is wrong. Indeed, Cowderoy, as Melbourne Chamber president, successfully initiated a resolution calling for the creation of a customs union *and* Federation at the crucial Corowa Conference in 1893.[40]

Professor Bob Birrell also incorrectly dismisses the tariff debate and the business community's support for Federation as an important part of the move to nationhood, when compared to nationalism.[41]

---

[38] Hirst 2000, 58-59.
[39] Ibid., 60-61.
[40] R.S. Parker (1964a), "Australian Federation: the Influence of Economic Interests and Political Pressures", in J.J. Eastwood; and F.B. Smith (1964), *Historical Studies: Selected Articles*, First series, Melbourne University Press, Melbourne, 176-177; see also *Official Report of the Federation Conference, Corowa* (1893) 31 July to 1 August 1893, James C. Leslie, Printer, Free Press Office, Corowa, 38-39.
[41] Birrell 2001, 93.

Certainly nationalism and defence were crucial factors in the push for Federation[42], but tariff issues were also a key factor.[43] Within the business community there was genuine support for greater federal integration, going well beyond the call for a customs union.[44]

As Geoffrey Serle[45] states: "Proceedings at these [chamber] conferences show to what extent businessmen in all the colonies, with the notable exception of the Sydney merchants, were recognising the need for federation." Serle's reference to the Sydney merchants would appear to relate to the Sydney Chamber of Commerce's sporadic participation in the various intercolonial conferences. Nonetheless many Sydney merchants did support Federation.

Indeed, the business community's heavy involvement in the Federation debates, its influence over tariff schedules and the interest in establishing a national body to represent the manufacturers (and other organisations) created the context for the business community's future dealings with the federal government.

The lists of colonial representatives who participated in the various formal Federation conferences included many prominent businessmen who were either Chamber presidents or otherwise active Chamber members.

Thus for example, from New South Wales, Sir William McMillan, who was the Sydney Chamber of Commerce president in 1886 attended with Sir Henry Parkes the 1890 *Conference on Federation* held in Melbourne. Further, along with Parkes, Edmund Barton and others he attended the 1891 *First National Australasian Convention* in Sydney, and finally, again with Barton, George Reid

---

[42] See Parkes 1876, 256 and Deakin 1944, 9.
[43] Scott Bennett, (ed) (1971), *The Making of the Commonwealth*, Cassell Australia, Melbourne, 3-18.
[44] See also Parker 1964a.
[45] Geoffrey Serle (1971), *The Rush to be Rich, A history of the colony of Victoria 1883-1889*, Melbourne University Press, Melbourne, 315.

and others, the all important 1897-98 *Second National Australasian Convention*. He was New South Wales Treasurer and Deputy Leader in 1889-91. Upon Federation he was the first member for the House of Representatives seat of Wentworth and was deputy leader of the Free Trade Party from 1901 to 1903.[46]

From Queensland, John Donaldson, who was the president of the Brisbane Chamber of Commerce in 1888-90, represented the colony along with Sir Samuel Griffith and others at the 1891 *First National Australasian Convention* in Sydney. He was Queensland Treasurer in 1889-90, as well as holding a number of other portfolios over the years. He was also Leader of the Opposition in 1890-91.[47]

From Western Australia, Sir Henry Briggs, who was the secretary of the Western Australian Chamber of Commerce in 1883-95, represented the colony along with Sir John Forrest and others at the 1897-98 *Second National Australasian Convention*. He was president of the Western Australian Legislative Council from 1906 to 1919.[48]

From Tasmania, Sir Philip Fysh, who was the president of the Hobart Chamber of Commerce in 1878 and 1882-83, represented the colony along with Andrew Inglis Clark and others at the 1891 *First National Australasian Convention* in Sydney; attended the 1897-98 *Second National Australasian Convention* along with Sir Edward Braddon and others; and also was a member of the delegation led by Edmund Barton to London in 1900. He was Premier of Tasmania in 1877-78 and 1887-1892. He was also Treasurer between 1873 and 1875 and again between 1894 to

---

[46] A.W. Martin (1986), "McMillan, Sir William (1850-1926)", *Australian Dictionary of Biography*, volume 10, Melbourne University Press, Melbourne, 342-344.
[47] Mary O'Keefe (1972), "Donaldson, John (1841-1896)", *Australian Dictionary of Biography*, volume 4, Melbourne University Press, Melbourne, 83-84.
[48] Toby Manford (1979), "Briggs, Sir Henry (1844-1919)", *Australian Dictionary of Biography*, volume 7, Melbourne University Press, 414-415.

1898. Upon Federation he was the first member for the House of Representatives seat of Denison and was Minister without Portfolio in 1901-03 and Postmaster-General in 1904. Fysh also attended the Chamber-organised 1900 *Third Inter-colonial Tariff Conference of Chambers of Manufactures*.[49]

Also from Tasmania was William Burgess who was the president of the Hobart Chamber of Commerce in 1891. He also represented the colony at the 1891 *First National Australasian Convention*. He was Tasmanian Treasurer in 1884-87.[50] And yet another from Tasmania was Charles Grant who was the president of the HCC in 1896-1901 and attended the 1897-98 *Second National Australasian Convention*. He was also a Minister without Portfolio in the Tasmanian Government of Henry Dobson between 1892 and 1894.[51]

In addition Sir Simon Fraser, who represented the colony of Victoria along with Alfred Deakin and others at the 1897-98 *Second National Australasian Convention* was a strong participant in his local Chamber of Commerce. He was also a Minister without Portfolio in the Munro Victorian Government in 1890-92 and a Senator for Victoria between 1901 and 1913. He was also the grandfather of Prime Minister Malcolm Fraser.[52]

Sir John Cockburn who represented the colony of South Australia along with Charles Kingston and others at the 1897-98

---

[49] Quentin Beresford (1981) "Fysh, Sir Philip Oakley (1835-1919)", *Australian Dictionary of Biography*, volume 8, Melbourne University Press, 602-603.

[50] E.R. Pretyman (1969), "Burgess, William Henry (1847-1917)", *Australian Dictionary of Biography*, volume 3, Melbourne University Press, Melbourne, 299-300.

[51] Scott Bennett (1983) "Grant, Charles Henry (1831-1901)", *Australian Dictionary of Biography*, volume 9, Melbourne University Press, 74-75.

[52] Elizabeth M. Redmond (1972), "Fraser, Sir Simon (1832-1919)", *Australian Dictionary of Biography*, volume 4, Melbourne University Press, 216.

Second National Australasian Convention was involved in the Chamber of Commerce movement and at the end of his career was chairman of the Australasian Chamber of Commerce in London. He was also Premier of South Australia 1889-90 and Minister for Education between 1885 and 1887.[53]

Lastly, Adye Douglas from Tasmania, who as a member of the Launceston Chamber of Commerce attended the Chamber-organised *Second Inter-colonial Conference on Free-Trade between the Australian Colonies*, represented the colony at the 1891 *First National Australasian Convention* in Sydney and the 1897-98 *Second National Australasian Convention*.[54]

So the conclusion from all this is that while it is undeniable that federation was about nationalism and matters like defence the whole project was nonetheless underwritten by a heavy dose of what some might call boring economic necessity.

The rise and fall of the Australian Settlement

Many authors have noted that the Australian Constitution, as a document, is dry and uninspiring.[55] It does not contain anything like the stirring words at the beginning of the Constitution of the United States of America. Big deal! Virtually no country emulates what the Americans genuinely had at its foundation. Most countries have never had a genius philosopher or wordsmith like Thomas Jefferson to help draft their constitution. Samuel Griffith, Alfred Deakin and Edmund Barton, to name a few, while highly talented

---

[53] John Playford (1981), "Cockburn, Sir John Alexander (1850-1929)", *Australian Dictionary of Biography*, volume 8, Melbourne University Press, Melbourne, 42-44.

[54] *Daily Telegraph* (1888), 7 June and Crisp 1990, 380.

[55] For example, W.K. Hancock (1961), *Australia*, Jacaranda Press, Melbourne; Clark 1981; Stuart Macintyre (1999), *A Concise History of Australia*, Cambridge University Press, Cambridge; and Paul Kelly (1992), *The End of Certainty: The story of the 1980s*, Allen and Unwin, Sydney.

individuals probably didn't reach Jefferson's heights. Instead as with most countries there is more to their foundation than just their constitution. As noted in the last chapter the Australian Settlement put the bones on the flesh of the Constitution.

There has been a debate in the Australian academic community about the validity of the Settlement concept. Some people, particularly academics,[56] have argued against journalist and historian Paul Kelly's analysis as they are concerned that it is in effect a *straw-man* construct, used to subsequently legitimise the implementation of neo-liberal policies (which they are opposed to). I will briefly examine that below before going on to a discussion on the implementation of the policy.

"New Protection" re-labelled

The concept of "the Australian Settlement" is much older than the term itself. As noted in chapter 1, in 1992 Paul Kelly coined it in his book *The End of Certainty*[57] as a term to describe a principally, economic framework that had been developed late in the 19th century.

As I also noted in the last chapter, the Australian Settlement,

---

[56] Jill Roe (1998), "The Australian Way, in Paul Smyth and Bettina Cass (eds) (1998), *Contesting the Australian Way: States, Markets and Civil Society*, Cambridge University Press, Cambridge, 69-80; Maddox 1998; Paul Smyth, (1998), "Remaking the Australian Way: The Keynesian Compromise" in Smyth and Cass 1998, 81-93; Tim Battin (1998), "Unmaking the Australian Keynesian Way", in Smyth and Cass 1998, 94-107; Marian Sawer (2000), "The Ethical State: Social Liberalism and the Critique of Contract", *Australian Historical Studies*, vol. 31, no. 114, 67-90; Marian Sawer (2003), *The Ethical State? Social Liberalism in Australia*, Melbourne University Press, Melbourne; and Marian Sawer (2004), "Comment: The Australian Settlement Undone", *Australian Journal of Political Science*, Vol 39, No 1, March, 35-37; MacIntyre 1999 and Stuart Macintyre (2004b), "Comment: An Historian's Perspective", *Australian Journal of Political Science*, Vol 39, No 1, March, 31-33.
[57] Kelly 1992.

while having no formal definition, is usually defined as a policy framework consisting of: industry protection; wage arbitration; state paternalism; a White Australia (or a restricted immigration policy); and imperial benevolence.[58] And it is worth repeating that Kelly described the Settlement as "an achievement second only to the creation of Australian democracy, and its operation within that democracy has offered for most of [the 20th] century the best definition of nationhood".[59]

However, while Kelly has gained a great deal of attention for this exposition of the Settlement, it is hardly new. His legitimate claim to fame is giving the policies it includes a new contemporary title that stuck with a wider audience than that of just historians and economists.

Academic, Dr Richard DeAngelis[60] from Flinders University argues that the concept described by Kelly actually originates with the work of a leading Australian academic Frank Castles in the 1980s. He particularly points to the concept developed by Castles labelled 'domestic defence'.[61] This is also noted by diverse authors such as Paul Smyth; Brian Howe; and John Warhurst. Stokes in addition refers to earlier work by Humphrey McQueen.[62]

---

58 Ibid., 1-2.
59 Ibid., 1.
[60] Richard DeAngelis (2004), "A Comment of the 'Australian Settlement' Symposium", *Australian Journal of Political Science*, Vol 39, No 3, November, 657.
[61] Francis G. Castles (1985), *The Working Class and Welfare: Reflections on the Political Development of the Welfare State in Australia and New Zealand*, Allen & Unwin, Sydney; and Castles, Francis G. (1988), *Australian Public Policy and Economic Vulnerability: A Comparative and Historical Perspective*, Allen & Unwin, Sydney.
[62] Smyth 1998, 81-84; Brian Howe (2001), "Economic growth and the ethical state: refashioning an Australian settlement", in John Nieuwenhuysen; Peter Lloyd; and Margaret Mead (2001), *Reshaping Australia's Economy: Growth with Equity and Sustainability*, Cambridge University Press, Cambridge, 99-

However, even this genealogy is very narrow and is actually incorrect. In the 19th century when the policy framework was actually being formulated it had a different nomenclature. In this case it was the more accurately descriptive policy label of "New Protection".

New Protection encapsulates three crucial parts of Kelly's Australian Settlement, viz: tariff protection; centralised wage fixing and restricted immigration policies – and easily accounted for the two other verities of the framework – i.e., significant State intervention in the operation of the markets and what Kelly describes as imperial benevolence.

The concept of New Protection was well documented in seminal histories of Australia by authors[63] such as Sir Keith Hancock, Edward

100; and John Warhurst (2004), "Patterns and Directions in Australian Politics over the Past Fifty Years", *Australian Journal of Politics and History*, Vol 50, No 2, 163-177, 163; Geoffrey Stokes (2004), "The 'Australian Settlement' and Australian Political Thought", *Australian Journal of Political Science*, Vol 39, No 1, March, 8 and H. McQueen (1980), "What's Wrong with Australia", in H. Mayer; and H. Nelson (1980), *Australian Politics: A Fifth Reader*, Longman Cheshire, Melbourne.

[63] W.K. Hancock (1930), *Australia*, Ernest Benn, London & Hancock 1961, Edward Shann (1930), *Bond or Free? Occasional Economic Essays*, Angus & Robertson, Sydney & Shann, Edward (1948), *An Economic History of Australia*, Cambridge University Press, Melbourne; F.W. Eggleston (1932), *State Socialism in Victoria*, King, London; Gordon Greenwood (ed) (1955), *Australia: A Social and Political History*, Angus & Robertson, Sydney; and Clark 1981. Also see W.A. Sinclair, (1976), *The Process of Economic Development in Australia*, Longman Cheshire, Melbourne, J.P. Nieuwenhuysen; and P.J. Drake (eds)(1977), *Australian Economic Policy*, Melbourne University Press, Melbourne; E.A. Boehm (1979), *Twentieth century Economic Development in Australia*, 2nd edition, Longman Cheshire, Melbourne; McIntyre 1986a; Alan L. Lougheed (1988), *Australia and the World Economy*, McPhee Gribble/Penguin Books, Melbourne; Kenwood, A.G. (1995), *Australian Economic Institutions Since Federation*, Oxford University Press, Melbourne; Geoffrey Brennan and Francis G. Castles (2002), *Australia Reshaped: 200 years of institutional transformation*, Cambridge University Press, Cambridge, 25-52; Geoffrey Brennan; and Jonathan Pincus (2002), "Australia's Economic Institutions", in Brennan and

Shann, Frederick Eggleston, Gordon Greenwood, Manning Clark and was described by any number of historians and economists in these terms up until the 1990s and beyond, including by Castles and Kelly themselves.

Eminent Federation historian J. A. La Nauze[64] notes that the term New Protection began to first appear in 1899. His research found that the term was originally coined by Victorian hat manufacturer Samuel Mauger (later a member of the first Federal Parliament representing Victoria and a cabinet minister in Alfred Deakin's 1906 – 1908 administration) who introduced the term at various conferences of manufacturers which met in 1899 and 1900. Indeed, these were the Inter-colonial Tariff Conferences of Chambers of Manufactures referred to earlier in this chapter.[65] In printed form the term first gained widespread currency when it appeared in the Age editorial of 8 November 1899.[66]

The policies were advocated by liberal politician Alfred Deakin who was Prime Minister on no less than three occasions (i.e., between 1903-1904; 1905-1908; and 1909-1910). As the principal architect of the Settlement Deakin "became recognised as Australia's greatest prime minister" according to Kelly.[67] And although Kelly and others attributed a negative connotation to the final outcomes of these policies, at the time the policies were seen as positive and are even seen by some commentators as such

---

Castles 2002, 53-85; John Uhr (2002), "Political Leadership and Rhetoric", in Brennan and Castles 2002, 261-294; and Judith Brett (2004), "Comment: The Country and the City", *Australian Journal of Political Science*, Vol 39, No 1, March, 27-29.

[64] J.A. La Nauze (1979), *Alfred Deakin: A Biography*, Angus & Robertson Publishers, Melbourne, 411.

[65] Also see John Lack (1986), "Mauger, Samuel (1857-1936)", *Australian Dictionary of Biography*, Vol 10, Melbourne University Press, Melbourne, 451-453.

[66] La Nauze 1979, 411.

[67] Kelly 1992, 1.

today. For example, MacIntyre[68] notes that "Deakinite liberalism set limits on the operation of the market to nurture a particular kind of nation-building social solidarity that would promote both equity and efficiency". The other principal, early architects of the policy framework were Charles Kingston (former Premier of South Australia and cabinet minister in Deakin's government) and Henry Bourne Higgins.[69]

Specifically, the five part framework can be explained in the following detail.

Industry protection

Kelly[70] noted that the "bedrock ideology" of the new nation was protection. And Hancock[71] stated that "Protection triumphed in Australia because it appealed irresistibly to the most ardent sentiments of Australian democracy and to the interests which lurked behind the sentiments".

As was noted above in this chapter, the early years of Federation were dominated by a debate between the opposing economic policies of free trade and protectionism through high tariff walls and other non-tariff protective devises like bounties and subsidies. Indeed, the principal political parties in addition to the Labor Party were the Protection Party and the Free Trade Party. The latter two have been generically divided into "liberal" Protectionists and "conservative" Free Traders, however there were liberals and conservatives in both camps (as in obverse there were free traders and protectionists in the Labor Party). Of the first seven Federal administrations, four were Protectionist; two Labor; and one Free

---

[68] Stuart Macintyre (2000), "Alfred Deakin", in Grattan, Michelle (ed) (2000), *Australian Prime Ministers*, New Holland, Sydney, 49.
[69] Bob Catley (2005), *The (strange, recent but understandable) triumph of liberalism in Australia*, Macleay Press, Sydney, 51.
[70] Kelly 1992, 2.
[71] Hancock 1961, 64.

Trade. And by the time of the amalgamation, or "fusion", of the Protectionist and the Free Trader parties in 1909 to form what was to be called the Liberal Party, the debate had been comprehensively won by those arguing for tariff protection.

Indeed, Ian Marsh[72] noted that the formation of the two party system of government at the time of the "Fusion" was an integral part of the Australian Settlement.

From 1901, the protectionists began building a "Fortress Australia" or what Professor Stephen Bell[73] calls a "Domestic Defence Model" that relied on the argument that Australian manufacturing industry had to be protected to allow it to build the necessary economies of scale to survive in a ferocious world market place and in parallel allow for a substantial increase in the population. As Deakin argued: "No nation ever claimed national greatness which relied upon primary industry alone".[74]

The initial tariff passed by Parliament in 1902 was a compromise between the Free Traders and Protectionists that provided lower levels of protection than the first administration of Prime Minister Edmund Barton sought but the necessary levels of revenue needed for the administration of the new Federation. However, with the amendments to the tariff in 1908-1911, tariff schedules were nearly doubled and had reached genuinely protectionist levels.[75] This was to remain government policy whichever party was in government for the next 80 odd years as tariffs were continuously raised in 1914, 1920, 1925, during the Great Depression of the 1930s, and remained high for subsequent decades.

---

[72] Ian Marsh (1995), *Beyond the Two Party System*, Cambridge University Press, Cambridge.
[73] Stephen Bell (1997), *Ungoverning the Economy: The Political Economy of Australian Economic Policy*, Oxford University Press, Melbourne, 65-69.
[74] Quoted in Kelly 1992, 6.
[75] Shann 1930, 397-400.

There was some reduction of tariffs during the Lyons Government before World War II. However, high protection levels were maintained during the Menzies years (followed by the Governments of Holt, Gorton and McMahon) despite Australia joining the General Agreement of Tariffs and Trade (GATT).[76] In fact, to an extent import quotas (as opposed to tariffs) significantly raised effective protection during the 1950s and 1960s and in relative terms by 1970 Australia had the highest manufacturing tariffs amongst industrial nations bar New Zealand.[77]

---

[76] Tom Conley (2007b), "Trade Policy", in in Galligan and Roberts 2007, 595.
[77] A general overview of developments over this period in Australian industry policy can be found in Peter Loveday (1982), *Promoting Industry, Recent Australian Political Experience*, University of Queensland Press, St Lucia; F.G. Davidson and B.R. Stewardson (1979), *Economics and Australian Industry*, 2nd edition, Longman Cheshire, Melbourne; Sinclair 1976; Kenwood 1995; Nieuwenhuysen and Drake 1977; Lougheed 1988; Jenny Stewart (1995), "Trade and Industry Policies", in Scott Prasser, J.R. Nethercote and John Warhurst (1995), *The Menzies Era: A Reappraisal of Government, Politics and Policy*, Hale & Iremonger, Sydney, 185-201. For a more detailed look at tariff policy see W.M. Corden (1971), *The Theory of Protection*, Oxford University Press, Oxford; W.M. Corden (1974), *Trade Policy and Economic Welfare*, Oxford University Press, Oxford; A.J. Reitsma (1960), *Trade Protection in Australia*, University of Queensland Press, Brisbane; R.G. Gregory and J.J. Pincus (1982), Industry Assistance", in L.R. Webb and R.H. Allan (eds) (1982), *Industrial Economics: Australian Studies*, George Allen & Unwin, Sydney, 113-162; Leon Glezer (1982), *Tariff Politics: Australian Policy-making 1960-1980*, Melbourne University Press, Melbourne; C. Bulbeck (1983), "State and capital in tariff policy", in Brian W. Head (1983), (ed) *State and Economy in Australia*, Oxford University Press, Melbourne, 219-237 and Ann Capling and Brian Galligan (1992), *Beyond the Protective State: The Political Economy of Australia's Manufacturing Industry Policy*, Cambridge University Press, Cambridge; Richard H. Snape, Lisa Gropp and Tas Luttrell (1998), *Australian Trade Policy 1965-1997: A Documentary History*, Allen & Unwin, St Leonards; and Tom Conley (2007a), "Australian Trade Policy: From Multilateralism to Bilateralism", in Giorel Curran and Elizabeth van Acker (eds) (2007), *Globalising Government Business Relations*, Pearson Education Australia, Sydney, 165-192 and Conley 2007b.

Wage arbitration

Allied to protection was a system of wage arbitration. Indeed the difference between "old protection" and what was labelled New Protection relies on a discussion of wage arbitration.

Old protection was simply the act of protecting the local manufacturer by the use of tariffs on imported goods. New Protection, in contrast, was a policy that sought to impose upon employers who were assisted by tariff protection a legal obligation to provide "fair and reasonable" wages and working conditions for their employees. This obligation was also to be extended to cover the employees of businesses that enjoyed other forms of assistance such as bounties on production and the restriction of coastal trade to Australian vessels.[78]

To use Deakin's own words: "The 'old' Protection contented itself with making good wages possible. The 'new' Protection seeks to make them actual ... Having put the manufacturer into a position to pay good wages, it goes on to assure the public that he does pay them".[79] Indeed Deakin's legislative and policy program has been described as an early version of what in recent years has been called "mutual obligation".[80]

When introducing an earlier draft of the Conciliation and Arbitration Bill in 1903, Deakin called it "a new phase of civilisation" that would establish the "People's Peace".[81] Provisions provided for conciliation between employers and unions and, if the situation deteriorated, compulsory arbitration in the form of an "award" settling the industrial dispute, to be made by a new Commonwealth Court of Conciliation and Arbitration.

---

[78] La Nauze 1979, 410.
[79] Quoted in Hancock 1961, 64.
[80] Uhr 2002, 282.
[81] Commonwealth Parliamentary Debates (1903), House of Representatives, 30 July, 2864.

The legislation was finally passed by Parliament in 1904 (ironically under the administration of Free Trade Prime Minister George Reid, who had originally been opposed to the Bill. He did so as part of a power sharing deal to secure parliamentary support for his minority government).

It was also initially proposed that legislation would provide that those companies that paid "fair and reasonable" wages would be afforded an additional benefit where its products would be exempt from excise duties imposed by new Excise Tariff Acts passed in 1906. For example, under the *Excise Tariff (Agricultural Machinery) Act* an excise duty equivalent to the customs duty on imported machinery was imposed upon Australian-made agricultural machines, but waived if the manufacturer met with conditions laid down by the Arbitration Court.[82]

This critical role for the Court has led Castles[83] to note that: "If the architect of the New Protection was Deakin, its presiding genius was Mr Justice Higgins, President of the Australian Commonwealth Court of Conciliation and Arbitration from 1907 to 1920".

In the Harvester judgement of 1907 the Court sought to determine a "fair and reasonable "wage that would be based on 'the normal needs of the average employee, regarded as a human being living in a civilised community'".[84] The judgement was based on an unskilled worker supporting a wife and family of five. It was based on social justice criteria rather than any eye to business productivity. This led to the development of a minimum wages regime that was subsequently called "the basic wage".

---

[82] Souter, Gavin (1988), *Acts of Parliament: A Narrative history of the Senate and House of Representatives Commonwealth of Australia*, Melbourne University Press, Melbourne, 99.

[83] Castles 2002, 43.

[84] H.B. Higgins (1922), *A New Province for Law and Order*, Constable and Company, London, 3.

However, the High Court ruled that the provisions exceeded the Commonwealth's constitutional authority and the relevant Excise Acts were struck down. Nonetheless, subsequent governments linked the provision of protection to the creation of the centralised wage fixing system and required the passing on of a share of the benefits of protection to ordinary workers.

For the sake of completeness it is worth noting that in 1911 the Labor Government of Andrew Fisher pursued a referendum to alter the Constitution to implement the original version of New Protection (the Attorney General of the time, William Morris Hughes was the principal advocate for the referendum). While Deakin's Liberal Party obviously continued to support New Protection, the referendum proposal was an "all or nothing" package of Constitutional amendments seeking powers not only with respect to New Protection, but also a massive widening of the Commonwealth's powers with respect to arbitration, the nationalisation of monopolies, and other aspects of trade and commerce. Deakin and his party opposed the referendum as being an unacceptable centralising of power to the Commonwealth. The amendment was decisively defeated in every State except for Western Australian.[85]

A repeat performance by the Fisher Government in 1913 was again to fail. Indeed some commentators attribute the Referendum push as a major contributor to Fisher's loss in the May 1913 Federal election.[86]

A subsequent referendum to alter the Constitution put by the Bruce Government in 1926 sought to also transfer exclusive powers to the Commonwealth. This failed and led to the opposite policy proposal being put by the same government in the 1929 election. This subsequent proposal was to transfer the role of industrial

---

[85] La Nauze 1979, 613-615.
[86] Doug Aiton and Terry Lane (2002), *Digest of Australia's Federal Elections Since 1901*, Pennon Publishing, Essendon, 21.

relations exclusively to the States except for the maritime industry. It was also (spectacularly) lost in the election fallout and was a major factor in entrenching the system for the best part of the next six decades. Two referenda in the 1940s, one each by the Curtin and Chifley Governments, also failed to win support for a further centralisation of power under the federal government.

Nonetheless, Kelly[87] noted that arbitration was "the greatest institutional monument to Australian egalitarianism and its quest for social order", and that "its longevity is a tribute to its ability to incorporate its opponents".

This system stayed in place for decades, only seriously being altered during the 1990s with Howard Government legislation.[88]

White Australia (or a restricted immigration policy)

Kelly described the support for White Australia as "the foundation idea" of the Australian Settlement. He noted that it was "the unique basis for the nation and the indispensable condition for all other policies".[89]

Indeed, after setting up the machinery provisions for the

---

[87] Kelly 1992, 9.

[88] For a more detailed overview of industrial relations developments during this period see Braham Dabscheck (1983), *Arbitrator at Work: Sir William Raymond Kelly and the Regulation of Australian Industrial Relations*, George Allen & Unwin, Sydney; Stuart Macintyre (1989),"Neither capital nor labour: the politics of the establishment of arbitration", in Stuart Macintyre and Richard Mitchell (eds) (1989), *Foundations of Arbitration: The origins and Effects of State Compulsory Arbitration 1890-1914*, Oxford University Press, Melbourne, 178-200 and Stuart Macintyre (2004a), "Arbitration in Action", in Joe Isaac and Stuart Macintyre (2004) (editors), *The New Province for Law and Order: 100 Years of Australian Industrial Conciliation and Arbitration*, Cambridge University Press, Cambridge, 55-97; Macintyre and Mitchell 1989, 135-155; Tim Rowse (2004), "Elusive Middle Ground: A Political History", in Isaac and Macintyre 2004, 17-54; and Paul Boreham (2007), "Industrial relations", in in Galligan and Roberts 2007, 272-275.

[89] Kelly 1992, 2.

operation of the new Parliament, the first substantive legislation to be passed by the Commonwealth in 1901 were the *Immigration Restriction Act* and the *Pacific Island Labourers Act*, both with the intent of regulating and restricting the sources of immigration.[90]

Kelly's focus on White Australia, however, to some extent skimmed over the more essential feature of the policy which was the fact that a key part of the Settlement was an active and large immigration program as exemplified by the old catch-phrase "populate or perish".

As Marsh[91] notes a central argument put in favour of New Protection was that "without protected manufacturing development, population growth could not be sustained at desired levels".

Nonetheless, this is not to deny the importance of the White Australia Policy which became a "creed" that was the "essence of Australian nationalism, and more importantly, the basis of national unity".[92]

The policy was abandoned in 1966 by the Holt Government, and while this was the principal point of departure with the past another watershed event in this area was the Fraser Government's acceptance of Vietnamese refugees in the late 1970s and the adoption of "multiculturalism" in the early 1980s.[93]

State paternalism

Kelly[94] describes "state Paternalism" as "individual happiness through government intervention". He is referring to the historically strong reliance by Australians on government intervention.

---

[90] Souter 1988, 62-65.
[91] Ian Marsh (2001), "The Federation Decade", in J.R. Nethercote (ed)(2001), *Liberalism and the Australian Federation*, The Federation Press, Sydney, 70.
[92] Kelly 1992, 3.
[93] Keith Windschuttle (2004), *The White Australia Policy*, Macleay Press, Sydney; and Kelly 1992, 4.
[94] Kelly 1992, 9.

Kelly notes that it also has its origins in political and social development as represented by the successful advance of political rights and the demand for economic benefits from the State for the common man.[95]

Indeed its roots go back to earliest colonial times in Australia and Professor Noel Butlin and others have described it as "colonial socialism".[96] Colonial governments were heavily involved in commercial activity from the beginning of White settlement. This is hardly surprising when it is recalled that New South Wales began as an institutionalised prison system. However, as time moved on government involvement was seen as crucial in the building of infrastructure across a continent dominated by vast distances. Government was involved in the provision of railways, roads, water supply, electricity, banking, agricultural services, ports, forests, banking, and many more activities.[97] As Davies[98] noted, Australians have a genius for bureaucracy.

And around the time of Federation, the term commonly used to generically describe various components of government intervention in the economy was "state socialism". Deakin used the term and on more than one occasion stated that experience "justified certain forms of state socialism".[99] And [Sir] Frederick Eggleston documented the policy program in detail in his work *State Socialism in Victoria* and although being a supporter of both

---

[95] Kelly 1992, 10.
[96] N.G. Butlin, A. Barnard and J.J. Pincus (1982), *Government and Capitalism: Public and Private Choice in Twentieth century Australia*, Allen & Unwin, Sydney.
[97] Eggleston 1932.
[98] A.F. Davies (1958), *Australian Democracy*, Longmans, Green & Co., Melbourne, 1.
[99] Quoted in Gregory Melleuish (2001), "Australian Liberalism", in Nethercote 2001, 34.

the policy and Deakin, was disappointed in the outcomes which often saw individual initiative stymied.[100]

A component of state paternalism was the implementation of what was labelled "Protection All Round" from the 1920s onward[101] and was initiated by the emergence of the Country Party (the forerunner of today's National Party).

The party's origins at the federal level began in the lead-up to the December 1919 election with a number of candidates running with the explicit backing of farming organisations. With the first sitting of the new parliament in February 1920, eleven members had formally become members of the new Country Party.[102] It initially supported a platform of free trade, seeking to reverse the protectionist consensus that had built up since Federation, noting that manufacturing protection simply raised the costs of inputs to farming operations thus damaging the interests of rural industries. However, as Harrigan notes "Protection all Round" was a direct result of the Country Party acquiescing to the Australian Settlement's core protectionist philosophy and seeking its extension to their constituency in the form of not only tariffs but also, crucially, statutory marketing authorities and other competition-restricting regulations.[103] It was a clear case of, "if you can't beat them then join them".

State paternalism was to remain a key feature of Australian economic policy for the better part of the next 90 years.

---

[100] Eggleston 1932.
[101] Shann 1930, 427-447.
[102] Earle Page (1963), *Truant Surgeon: The Inside Story of Forty Years of Australian Political Life*, Angus and Robertson, Sydney, 53.
[103] Nicholas Harrigan (2004) "The Australian Settlement in the Countryside: Small Farmers and the Rise of Statutory Marketing in Australia", paper presented to the Australasian Political Studies Association Conference, University of Adelaide, 29 September-1 October 2004.

Imperial benevolence

Kelly says very little about imperial benevolence, except to note that Australia, as part of the British Empire, relied overwhelming through the first half of the 20th century on the Empire for its defence and trading markets. As he noted "the Royal Navy was the guarantor of White Australia. British finance and trade preference underwrote Australian growth".[104]

These facts are undeniable, although the power of Empire receded very rapidly after World War II and the significance of a British stamp was breaking down culturally from the instigation of the massive increase in non-British immigration from that time onward, albeit slowly at first. By the 1970s and 1980s there was further questioning of links with Britain by a significant minority of the population. This culminated in the debate on the icon issue of whether Australia should remain a constitutional monarchy, owing allegiance to the British Crown, or a republic. Although there was strong support for a change it did not receive the necessary majority in the 1999 Constitutional referendum on a republic.

In summary, this framework or "settlement" was obviously social as well as economic. It had as its core the goal of securing a decent, stable and civilised society. It was also about securing a homogenous and unified Australia that provided a lifestyle for the ordinary (white) citizen that could be described as one that would provide modest comfort and the opportunities for a decent life.[105] Deakin's New Protectionism was according to Hancock[106] seen as anchoring "the distinctive ethics of Australian democracy".

Indeed, Melleuish also adds to the interpretation of the Australian Settlement his view that it nourished the "thymotic aspirations"

---
[104] Kelly 1992, 11.
[105] Gregory Melleuish, (1998), *The Packaging of Australia: Politics and Culture Wars*, University of New South Wales Press, Sydney, 25.
[106] Hancock 1961, 66.

of ordinary Australians in their pursuit of both security and the hope for a better future. He takes his lead here from work done by Francis Fukuyama in his work *The End of History and the Last Man*, where "thymos" is described as meaning those values that allow individuals to create for themselves a sense of their own self-worth and dignity.[107] Melleuish sees thymos as closely related to "identity" and believes that one of the reasons for the longevity of the Australian Settlement, even after it began to be criticised from as early as the 1930s[108] and certainly with a barrage of opposition from both the left (from a social and cultural perspective) and the right (in principally economic terms) from the 1960s onwards in particular, was its role in helping Australians identify to themselves who they were.[109]

The validity of the Australian Settlement concept

There has been a debate in the Australian academic community about the validity of the Australian Settlement concept.

As noted above a number of academics[110] have argued against Kelly's analysis as they are concerned that it is in effect a straw-man construct, used to legitimise the implementation of economic rationalist theories.

They argue that Kelly has manipulated a narrative of an

---

[107] Melleuish, Gregory (1996), "The Contradictory Democratic Culture of Modern Australia", *Quadrant*, September, 48-49; Melleuish 1998, 128-129; and Francis Fukuyama, (1992), *The End of History and the Last Man*, Hamish Hamilton, London, 162-165.

[108] e.g., Hancock 1930.

[109] Melleuish 1998, 128-129; and Gregory Melleuish (2004), "From the 'social laboratory' to the 'Australian Settlement'", in Paul Boreham, Geoffrey Stokes and Richard Hall (eds)(2004), *The Politics of Australian Society*, 2nd edition, Pearson Education Australia, French's Forest, 85-87.

[110] Roe 1998; Maddox 1998; Smyth 1998; Battin 1998; Sawer 2000; 2002; and 2004; MacIntyre 1999 and 2004b.

Australian Settlement simply as a way to point to a series of policies that he believes have failed and that in so doing he glosses over a great deal of legitimate, successful policy-making that, if it had been continued, would have saved Australia from suffering the high unemployment rates of the early 1990s. (For a very different interpretation on the reasons for high unemployment see writings by former Treasury officers Des Moore and John Stone.)[111]

Maddox[112] is particularly critical of how Kelly's account stresses a monolithic character of the Australian Settlement that overlooks or reduces the significance of contesting traditions and political alternatives. However, Stokes[113] while sympathetic to this critique, notes that this may be the price of any attempt to give a general account of an historical period (see more on Stokes alternative interpretation of the Settlement below).

Roe[114] offers up an alternative nomenclature, styling the so-called Australian Settlement instead as the "Australian Way". Her emphasis is to show how social policy developed in Australia gained a certain distinctiveness that characterises its difference (and superiority) to policies implemented in other Western countries. The Australian Way is seen as a "middle way" typified by the mixed-economy compromises of post-World War II industrialised nations.[115] It is less a set of particular substantive policies and "more a way of doing policy, of 'exercising democracy': hence the Australian Way".[116]

---

[111] Moore 1993 and John Stone (1993), "The critics of economic rationalism", in Chris James, Chris Jones and Andrew Norton (1993), *A Defence of Economic Rationalism*, Allen & Unwin, St Leonards, 95-103.
[112] Maddox 1998, 64.
[113] Stokes 2004, 6.
[114] Roe 1998.
[115] Smyth and Cass 1998, 12.
[116] Paul Smyth (2004), "Comment: Australian Settlement or Australian Way?", *Australian Journal of Political Science*, Vol 39, No 1, March, 40.

Melleuish notes that a similar, positive labelling of Australian development was the use of the term "social laboratory" in earlier decades, suggesting "these initiatives were progressive".[117]

Smyth[118] and Battin[119] present a slightly different critique, while adopting Roe's Australian Way nomenclature. They emphasise the overwhelming importance of the post-World War II implementation in Australia of Keynesian macroeconomic policy, which they characterise as the big spending, welfare state economic model. For them the Australian Way was actually the Keynesian Way or Keynesian Settlement that was agreed upon in Australia following the 1945 White Paper, *Full Employment in Australia,* which was then implemented by the Chifley and then Menzies Governments. However, Frank Castles[120] noted in an earlier work that during the Menzies era it was clear that it was "the older pattern of response, rather than the newer Keynesian welfarism, which was the dominant influence shaping public policy".

To return to Roe and others principal attacks on Kelly's motivations, Kelly[121] admits in a 2004 article that his exposition in *The End of Certainty* had as its principal proposition that the Hawke-Keating Government reforms represented a dismantling of a set of core policies implemented in the post-Federation era. Nonetheless the motivation and ideological world view of the originator of the term does not invalidate the concept itself. Indeed as noted above, Kelly has simply renamed (and popularised) an otherwise accepted historical interpretation, which the originators, using the term New Protection, believed was a nation-building, forward agenda.

---

[117] Melleuish 2004, 80.
[118] Smyth 1998.
[119] Battin 1998.
[120] Castles 1988, 143.
[121] Paul Kelly (2004), "Comment: The Australian Settlement", *Australian Journal of Political Science*, Vol 39, No 1, March, 23.

In a different approach, Geoffrey Stokes[122] has made a comprehensive critique of Kelly's five criteria that make up the Australian Settlement. While accepting the explanatory power of Kelly's proposition he reformulates the criteria and expands them into what he regards as a more comprehensive list of key factors.

Stokes[123] agrees that the Settlement has gained "wide currency", and believes that it provides an explanation of "a more or less enduring resolution of conflict" between competing groups in a whole range of areas. However, his principal problem with Kelly's analysis is that it did not adequately cover a wider range of key conflicts or "cleavages" that existed in Australia during this historical period. Indeed he concludes that "because of its neglect of key ideas and issues, and the way it frames the political options available, Kelly's framework is 'ideological' [in favour of neo-liberalism] in this sense". Stokes therefore proposes a critique that in his words "directs attention primarily to the wider traditions of political thought that comprised an Australian Settlement".[124]

Stokes notes that White Australia, industry protection and wage arbitration are "relatively uncontentious candidates" for inclusion in an Australian Settlement. However, he states that Kelly's use of the terms "state paternalism" and "imperial benevolence", gives them "a particular pejorative interpretation" that he believes is unwarranted.[125] Although, it should be noted that Kelly is not alone in this view. For example, Melleuish echoes the views of many commentators[126] when he states that the early Commonwealth was

---

[122] Stokes 2004.
[123] Ibid., 4, 5.
[124] Ibid., 7.
[125] Ibid., 8.
[126] e.g., see contributors to Chris James, Chris Jones and Andrew Norton (1993), *A Defence of Economic Rationalism*, Allen & Unwin, St Leonards; and Brennan and Castles 2002.

perhaps "the greatest paradox of Australian political history" in that it was founded on the basis of a "liberal Constitution being used by politicians to pursue illiberal and selfish policies", viz White Australia, protection and industrial arbitration.[127]

For his part, Stokes believes that Kelly's analysis ignores *Terra Nullius*; State secularism; Masculinism; and fails to adequately deal with Australia's brand of democracy. He therefore proposes nine features of the Australian Settlement to replace Kelly's five. The nine are:

- White Australia;
- *Terra Nullius*;
- State Secularism;
- Masculinism;
- Australian Democracy;
- State Developmentalism;
- Arbitration;
- Welfare Minimalism; and
- Imperial Nationalism.

I spend time on this analysis to give a comprehensive critique of the central focus of this book, which is the Australian Settlement. I hasten to note that I do not necessarily accept this critique. In summary, Stokes commentary on Kelly's analysis was the following:

- **White Australia**: Stokes agreed with Kelly's inclusion of the White Australia Policy, but criticised him for not clearly enunciating its corollary that saw the "exclusion and subordination of the Indigenous inhabitants of Australia".[128]
- ***Terra Nullius***: The above apparent fault then led Stokes to

[127] Melleuish 2001, 33-34.
[128] Stokes 2004, 8-9.

add *Terra Nullius* as an additional Settlement verity. The term *Terra Nullius* refers to the legal interpretation that the land of Australia was unoccupied at the time of White settlement, therefore leading to the Crown's practice of refusing to recognise prior indigenous rights. Stokes notes that *Terra Nullius* became a "foundation myth of Australia" that underpinned the legal regimes that marginalised indigenous people.[129] He argues that its exclusion leaves out an adequate account of attempts by various political movements from the 1960s through to the 1990s to reverse the discriminatory policies that grew out of *Terra Nullius*. These culminated in the two High Court of Australia cases: *Mabo* (1992) and *Wik* (1996).[130]

- **State Secularism**: Stokes notes that a critical aspect of the Settlement was the dominance of State secularism as a means to resolve ongoing religious tensions between Protestants and Roman Catholics. He noted that State secularism embodied "the major principles of Enlightenment rationalism and liberalism" and had its biggest influence in the education system where by 1893 all colonial governments had retreated from funding religious schools. The result was that, for all its flaws, the resulting liberal education prepared citizens for democratic participation and overcame sectarian conflicts. Finally he notes that not even the return of State funding of religious schools in the 1960s and 1970s constituted a significant retreat from ongoing secularism.[131]

- **Masculinism**: Stokes notes that Masculinism is the ideology that expresses the set of values, identities and practices in favour of men that became dominant before and after

---
[129] Stokes 2004, 9.
[130] Ibid., 10 and see *Mabo* 1992 and *Wik* 1996.
[131] Ibid., 10-12.

Federation. One of the peculiarly Australian versions of this was the wage arbitration system where the *Harvester* judgement established the "ideal" model of a male "breadwinner" and a female "housewife" and child-minder. He concludes that without the inclusion of Masculinism, "we cannot understand the early direction of arbitration and the later second-wave struggles for women's rights from the late 1960s".[132]

- **Australian Democracy**: Stokes disagrees with Kelly's[133] assessment that the Australian Settlement was "an achievement second only to the creation of Australian democracy". He argues instead that if we are examining the Settlement as a feature of nationhood then democracy should be included in its list. As he states, if anything defined national character in the eyes of many 19th century observers, it was the Australian capacity "for participating in a liberal democracy that was more radical and inclusive than nearly any other country in the world". And he concludes, that "to appreciate the dynamics of the 'end of certainty', one needs to understand that the process is not just one of the decline of economic traditions, but also one in which more opportunities for participation are created for key segments of the community".[134]

- **State Developmentalism**: Stokes combines and repackages both Kelly's "industry protection" and "state paternalism" categories to propose an alternative "state developmentalism". He disagrees with the overwhelmingly economic (and negative) interpretation that Kelly assigns to his original two categories. Instead Stokes notes that state

[132] Ibid., 12-13.
[133] Kelly 1992, 1.
[134] Stokes 2004, 12-13.

developmentalism had as its goals not just economic but also social and national advancement of the people, and was based on a need for state intervention "through sheer necessity in the context of high risk". He refers approvingly to Donald Horne's description of this as the "secular faith of development"[135] or "the cult of national development".[136] He further emphasises that through implementing a wide range of social and economic policies (he lists: borrowing overseas capital; attracting labour through immigration; providing education; promoting public works; creating public enterprises as monopolies or competitors with business; regulating labour and industry; and imposing tariffs) the role of the state was to ensure that all citizens were given the opportunity to develop their full potential.[137]

- **Arbitration**: Stokes does not dissent from Kelly's inclusion of wage arbitration. He emphasises its importance as one of the "central experiments in the Australian 'social laboratory'" and notes that when considering the erosion of the Australian Settlement it is essential to see how the decline of wage arbitration affects the social security system.[138]

- **Welfare Minimalism**: Stokes[139] adds "welfare minimalism" to highlight that Australia's particular form of social security was heavily focussed on the wage arbitration system constituting part of the social welfare policy. He notes Castles work which points out that wages policy in the

---

[135] Donald Horne (1977), *Money Made Us*, Penguin, Ringwood, 133.
[136] Donald Horne (1982),"Resources and the Cult of National Development in Australia", in S. Harris and G. Taylor (1982), *Resource Development and the Future of Australian Society*, CRES Monograph 7, Canberra.
[137] Stokes 2004, 14-15.
[138] Ibid., 16.
[139] Ibid., 17-18.

form of a "wage-earner's welfare state" was a substitute for welfare policy and a factor which inhibited the emergence of a social welfare state.[140]

- **Imperial Nationalism**: Finally, Stokes criticises Kelly's manipulation of foreign affairs, defence and trade issues under the category of Imperial Benevolence to bring them into the latter's narrative on Australia's identity and "spiritual emptiness" under the Australian Settlement. He points out that what Kelly calls benevolence implies dependence and acts of kindness from the British, while what occurred in reality was more a relationship of "mutual benefit" including the trade system of imperial preference. As a result Stokes believes a better term is "imperial nationalism" in that it also helps encapsulate the "nationalist aspirations set both within and in tension with the British Empire" that occurred throughout the years of the Settlement.[141]

Stokes' alternative interpretation was the subject of a symposium published in the March 2004 issue of the *Australian Journal of Political Science*.

In response Kelly[142] states that, while not disagreeing with a number of his observations such as that on imperial nationalism, he thinks Stokes' analysis "over-loads" the Settlement framework and effectively destroys its analytical power to explain what happened in Australia in the 1980s.

Judith Brett,[143] while generally accepting Kelly's analysis, nonetheless argued that both he and Stokes need to increase their lists. In her case she has sought to add what she calls "the settlement

---

[140] Castles 1994, 124.
[141] Stokes 2004, 18-19.
[142] Kelly 2004, 25.
[143] Brett 2004, 27.

between the city and the country", where the state compensated people living in the country for the costs of remoteness and sparse settlement. According to Brett this new category not only relates to policies like statutory marketing authorities, but also to cross subsidisation of postal and communication services, and fiscal equalisation through the Commonwealth Grants Commission.[144]

Stuart MacIntyre[145] believes, as noted above, that Kelly confuses the effects of the Australian Settlement with its purpose. He considers that the makers of the settlement were not "flinching from challenge" but were implementing "an affirmative and dynamic" project. He notes that Stokes' "extended inventory is less chronologically precise". He questions the inclusion of *Terra Nullius*, but thinks that Stokes is on more solid ground with masculinism and democracy. Nonetheless, he argues that from his historian's perspective, as opposed to that of a political scientist, the Settlement should be seen more as a series of "shaky foundations", which was a "fragile alignment of circumstances".[146]

Paul Smyth[147] notes that Stokes' analysis "does not share the ideological weakness" of Kelly's original Australian Settlement. However he wonders whether, with such a radical revision of Kelly's work, he should have sought a new name for his version of Australian political thought. Smyth continues his criticism of the Australian Settlement concept preferring his concept of the Australian Way based on the Keynesian economics, as described above. As he states, "when I consider the histories of the Great Depression/Second World War Keynesian regime and the Affluent

---

[144] See also Judith Brett (2007), "The Country, the City and the State in the Australian Settlement", *Australian Journal of Political Science*, Vol 42, No 1, March, 1.
[145] MacIntyre 2004, 32.
[146] MacIntyre 2004b, 32-33.
[147] Smyth 2004, 41.

Society-Welfare state, I cannot see how these later ideological agreements and policy solutions could be meaningfully said to be contained within the policy regime of the early 1900s".[148] In a rejoinder Stokes does not concede this point and notes that there is no reason not to recognise Keynes as providing a "further technical rationale" to the state developmentalism part of the Australian Settlement as, after all, he was a social liberal.[149]

Finally, and directly relevant to this last point about social liberalism, Marian Sawer's critique turns to the wider issue of value systems and is described in the next section.

Social Liberalism shaped Australia

In criticising the focus on the Australian Settlement, Professor Marian Sawer[150] of the Australian National University takes a somewhat different, but very legitimate, approach of arguing that the historical emphasis should not be on a package of specific policies, but instead the underlying set of values or philosophies that underpinned the strategic approach of governments over the period that is being examined. She argues that the emphasis should be on the fact that what she terms "social liberalism" (as opposed to neoliberal) was the basis of a bipartisan policy approach implemented over the period 1901 to the early 1980s.

Dr Ian Marsh also of the Australian National University (ANU) likewise characterises Deakin's program as social liberalism and describes it as "one of the enduring, and certainly the most generous, currents in the Australian liberal tradition".[151] He further notes that the broad principles of the Settlement "gave political expression to those aspirations for fairness and individualism

---

[148] Ibid., 40.
[149] Stokes 2004a, 46.
[150] Sawer 2004, also see Sawer 2000 and Sawer 2002.
[151] Marsh 2001, 69.

that then characterised, and perhaps continue to mark, Australian political culture". This is in contrast to otherwise similar countries like Great Britain and the United States.[152]

More specifically they define social liberalism as being "agnostic about the role of the state", "less sanguine about the beneficent effects of markets", "recognise that life chances can be diminished by social forces beyond individual control", and that "properly framed, action by the state can ameliorate or correct at least some unwanted effects".[153] This contrasts with "classical liberalism" or laissez-faire liberalism that places greater if not exclusive faith in markets.

Alternatively Hugh Collins[154] argues that the underlying values of post-Federation Australia were instead those espoused by the 19th century English philosopher Jeremy Bentham who characterised them as utilitarianism, legalism and positivism.

Utilitarianism was based on Bentham's political program that sought legislation and administration that would secure "that public good which maximises private interest". Legalism was seen in the approach to governance that saw legislation at the heart of government, and positivism is seen in a "practical" or even "pragmatic" approach to problem-solving.[155] Collins saw English Chartism as the real-world exposition of this suite of attributes and he refers to Sir Keith Hancock's view that Chartism played a significant role in influencing many of the policies of the new Federation. As he noted: "within ten years of the discovery of gold, practically the whole political programme of the Chartists is

---

[152] Ibid., 69-70.
[153] Ibid., 69.
[154] H. Collins (1985), "Political Ideology in Australia: The Distinctiveness of a Benthamite Society", in S.R. Graubard (ed)(1985), *Australia: The Daedalus Symposium*, Angus & Robertson, Sydney.
[155] Collins 1985, 148-149.

realised in the Australian colonies".[156] This includes the Deakinite program to implement land legislation; compulsory and secular education; payment of members of parliament; factory acts; early closing of public houses; and anti-sweating legislation.

Indeed Hancock and Collins saw individualism as a primary factor in the Australian Settlement, with Hancock noting that "to the Australian, the state means collective power at the service of individualistic rights. Therefore he sees no opposition between his individualism and his reliance upon Government".[157]

Collins conclusion is that so all-pervading was this philosophical approach in Australia, that "the sporadic appearance of different ideas, whether of the left or of the right, is better understood as a reaction against this hegemony than as the motion of independent forces".[158]

A number of authors dispute this analysis varying from the downright hostile[159] to the somewhat sympathetic.[160]

Graham Maddox states that while having insights, Collins' "eccentric" analysis places too much emphasis on individualism and discounts the significance of the major influence of the collectivist labour movement in Australian politics.[161] Melleuish notes that the Collins thesis is "a very materialist view" but agrees that it is arguable that in Australia "the crucial divide is between those who believe in the value of individual self-advancement and those who place more emphasis on achieving a society marked by greater equality".[162]

---

[156] Hancock 1961, 54.
[157] Ibid., 55; and also see Collins 1985, 153.
[158] Collins 1985, 152.
[159] Maddox 1998.
[160] Melleuish 2004.
[161] Maddox 1998, 59-60.
[162] Melleuish 2004, 79.

Sawer herself agrees that the Benthamite belief in the efficient aggregation of individual preferences as the best measure of policy was indeed an important factor in electoral innovation in the colonies in the mid-1800s. However, she argues that by the late 19th century a new form of (social) liberalism, which rejected the classical idea of contract and the utilitarian emphasis on private happiness rather than self-development, had begun to be implemented.[163]

It would appear that the consensus of opinion lies with the view that the policies implemented as part of the Australian Settlement formed part of a social liberal movement. And that the demise of the settlement indicates a swing to neo-liberal policies.[164] However, Catley[165] notes that while previous policy implementation can be described as social liberalism, in more recent years "Australian liberalism's intellectual core is found ... in Jeremy Bentham and his advocacy of the 'greatest happiness for the greatest number'", which it would appear that Catley equates with neo-liberalism.[166]

Importantly, the debate over whether the underlying philosophy of the Australian Settlement is social liberalism or Benthamite utilitarianism does not in itself detract from the validity of the concept itself. In a positive way it provides some insights into the motivations for the implementation of the policy framework.

---

[163] Sawer 2004, 35-36; also see Sawer 2000 and Sawer 2003.
[164] e.g. see Horne 1997; Howe 2001; Craven, Greg (2001), "A Liberal Federation and a Liberal Constitution", in Nethercote 2001, 53-68; Andrew Norton (2001), "Towards a New Australian Settlement? The Progress of Australian Liberalism", in Nethercote 2001, 230-242; Melleuish 2004; Stokes 2004; Warhurst 2004; Catley 2005.
[165] Catley 2005, 325.
[166] See also J.J. Pincus (2001), "Liberalism and Australia's Economic and Industrial Development", in Nethercote 2001, 266.

The demise of the Australian Settlement

In this section I will give an overview of the demise of the Australian Settlement. I will present a more detailed historical analysis in the next chapter.

Kelly[167] noted that the Settlement created a paradox, "a young nation with geriatric arteries". Over the course of a hundred years Australia's relative standing in the world league tables for standard of living fell steadily[168] and each time a recession hit the country from the 1960s onwards unemployment ratcheted up another notch, never falling to pre-recession lows.[169]

Based on the general acceptance that the Australian Settlement or New Protection was in fact a settled set of policies that were implemented over the bulk of the 20th century, the next question to explore is when did the Settlement meet its demise?

Richard DeAngelis interestingly parallels Australia's Settlement with a similar policy framework implemented by France from the late 19th century through to World War II. He notes that the French found the model unsustainable following the Great Depression and the War and a new consensus emerged for "globalising, post-imperial modernisation".[170] However, in the case of Australia the demise of the Settlement occurred a lot later.

In 1992, Paul Kelly stated that Australia "is in transition – in the 1980s, the Settlement ideas underwent a process of creative

---

[167] Kelly 1992, 13.
[168] F.H. Gruen (1985), "How Bad is Australia's Economic Performance and Why?", Paper No 127, Centre for Economic Policy Research, Australian National University, Canberra.
[169] Rodney Tiffen and Ross Gittins (2004), *How Australia Compares*, Cambridge University Press, Cambridge, 74-75; see also Peter Hendy (2002), "Don't Sell Australia Short", Telstra Address, National Press Club, Canberra, 4 December 2002.
[170] DeAngelis 2004, 658.

destruction from which there is no return".[171] Or, as he later put it: "this framework – introspective, defensive, dependent – is undergoing an irresistible demolition".[172] The result of these changes would allow Australia to "stand on its own ability". As he went on to add: "Australia, in fact, had waited longer than most nations to address the true definition of nationhood – the acceptance of responsibility for their own fate".[173]

As noted above, Kelly[174] admits that his exposition in *The End of Certainty* had as its principal proposition that the Hawke-Keating Government reforms represented a dismantling of the set of core policies implemented in the post-Federation era.

Indeed, it is a fact that, while the Settlement was bi-partisan its main steward was the Liberal and National Parties who governed Australia for the majority of the 20th century.[175] As Kelly[176] notes "the Liberal-National Parties administered the Australian Settlement. They governed with caution, dedication, lack of inspiration, a pacification of sectional interests, and an appreciation of Australia's national insecurity complex".

Nonetheless, depending on which authors are consulted the end of the Settlement began either as early as the Menzies Government, or at the other end of the spectrum did not begin until the latter half of the Hawke-Keating Government of 1983-1996; or indeed even the beginning of the Howard Government in 1996.

For example Kelly's analysis completely glosses over the historical timing of the demise of the White Australia Policy, which to

---

[171] Kelly 1992, 1.
[172] Ibid., 2.
[173] Ibid., 13.
[174] Kelly 2004, 23.
[175] Galligan 2007, 320.
[176] Kelly 1992, 12.

note again he nominated as "the foundation idea" of the Australian Settlement.[177]

In fact the White Australia Policy began to be dismantled in the 1950s and by the time that the Whitlam Government rhetorically "ended" the policy in 1972 it had ceased as a program for a number of years. The dismantling (tentatively) began during the Menzies Government which abolished the "Dictation Test" in the *Migration Act* of 1958 and the further announcement allowing the admission as permanent residents of "distinguished and highly qualified Asians" in 1959. This saw Asian immigration of around 700 to 1000 people a year around 1965 (the year before Sir Robert Menzies retirement). Further relaxation of restrictions on Asian immigration, allowing "well qualified" migrants and liberalisation of family reunions, came with the Minister for Immigration, Hubert Opperman's statement in March 1966.[178] This change in 1966 therefore ended the White Australia Policy. As Borrie notes: "under these more relaxed conditions, an average of 6500 Asians a year migrated to Australia between 1966 and 1970".[179]

Further, as discussed above, relatively high immigration levels (compared to other industrialised countries) is possibly a more relevant part of the Australian Settlement. These have continued in Australia throughout the 1980s, 1990s and into the 21st century. For example, by the year 2000 one in four of Australia's population was an immigrant, which is a higher proportion than for any other comparable country, and globally was second only to Israel.

---
[177] Kelly 1992, 2.
[178] A.T. Yarwood (1988), "The White Australia Policy", in Jupp, James (1988), *The Australian People: An Encyclopedia of the Nation, Its People and Their Origins*, Angus & Robertson Publishers, Sydney, 83.
[179] W.D. Borrie (1988), "Changes in Immigration Patterns Since 1972", in Jupp 1988, 111.

Importantly for this discussion this proportion had been steadily climbing in the last two decades.[180]

Kelly is definitely on more solid ground with respect to tariff protection.

There was some reduction of tariffs during the Menzies years (followed by the Governments of Holt, Gorton and McMahon). However, by 1970 Australia had the highest manufacturing tariffs amongst industrial nations bar New Zealand.[181] Whitlam slashed tariffs by a one-off overnight 25 percent reduction in 1974 (although at the time this was presented as an anti-inflation measure, not a change in the approach to tariffs). The Fraser Government rhetorically talked of reducing protection. On the one hand it actually increased it, especially in the areas of motor vehicles and textile, clothing and footwear. On the other hand it negotiated the Australia-New Zealand Closer Economic Relations (CER) free-trade agreement, which according to John Stone,[182] the former secretary of the Australian Treasury, "was a significant step in bringing down protectionism". Indeed, it was Australia's first free trade agreement.

It was not until a bipartisan consensus emerged between the Labor Party and the Liberal Party (courageously led by economic Drys like John Howard and John Hewson) around 1990 that the Hawke-Keating Government moved to implement an historic long-term reduction in tariffs. This reduction schedule was then further implemented by the Howard Government that came to power in 1996.[183]

---

[180] Tiffen and Gittins 2004, 11.
[181] Kym Anderson and Ross Garnaut (1987), *Australian Protectionism*, Allen & Unwin, Sydney, 6.
[182] Stone, John (former Assistant Secretary Federal Treasury; former Secretary Federal Treasury; former Senator and Shadow Minister) Interview with author on 18 June 2009.
[183] Reitsma 1960, 11-26; Brennan and Pincus 2002, 72; and Pincus 2001, 258-265.

Kelly's neat timeline is also not helped by the fact that the most significant changes to the wage arbitration system only began in 1996 under the Howard Government, although some minor changes had begun with legislation formally introducing enterprise bargaining under the Keating Government in 1993.[184]

In terms of state paternalism, views vary as to when the most significant acts of economic deregulation began.

For example MacIntyre[185] regards the Fraser Government as akin to Thatcherite Britain and the first implementers of economic rationalist theories. However, in some degree of revisionism a consensus has appeared to emerge that sees the Fraser Government as simply an extension of the Menzies era governments that continued to maintain a strong belief in the Settlement framework of state paternalism.[186]

Further, most commentators have seen the period of the Hawke-Keating Government from the late 1980s as the onset of economic rationalist sentiment in Canberra, which saw the end of the previous consensus on the Settlement.[187] The Hawke-Keating Government embarked on a policy of tariff reduction; fiscal consolidation (initially, i.e., before the 1990-1991 recession); industrial relations reform; floating the exchange rate; privatisation; and other significant economic reform. It was the pursuit of these policies

---

[184] Roy Green (1998), "The Accord and Industrial Relations: Lessons for Political Strategy", in Smyth and Cass 1998, 180-194.

[185] MacIntyre 1999, 242-243.

[186] John Carroll (1992), "Economic Rationalism and its Consequences", in John Carroll and Robert Manne (eds) (1992), *Shutdown: The Failure of Economic Rationalism and How to Rescue Australia*, The Text Publishing Company, Melbourne, 11; Paul Kelly (2000), "John Malcolm Fraser", in Grattan, Michelle (ed) (2000), *Australian Prime Ministers*, New Holland, Sydney, 357; and David McKnight (2005), *Beyond Right and Left: New Politics and the Culture Wars*, Allen & Unwin, Sydney, 1.

[187] e.g. Smyth and Cass 1998, 12.

that saw the end of state paternalism in Australia.[188] Although Cliff Walsh[189] has argued that the Labor Government accidentally came upon economic reform rather than deliberately started with an agenda to implement it. And Pincus[190] notes the importance played by (mostly) Liberal state governments in driving reform at the sub-national level.

However, Stokes[191] makes the point that not only neo-liberals criticised State developmentalism (or state paternalism and industry protection) and that one can date protests by the environmental movement and aborigines against many of these policies, back to the 1970s.

Finally, with respect to imperial benevolence it is apparent that the beginning of the end began with World War II as the British Empire began to disintegrate. The watershed was the entry of Great Britain into the European Economic Community (now the European Union) in 1971. Alternatively, Kelly[192] refers to the importance of the republican debate as an icon issue on the road to a separate Australian identity. If this is taken as the key turning point it has yet to occur and failed at a referendum in 1999.

In summary, the beginning of the end for the Australian Settlement may have actually started in the 1950s and spread through the last five decades of the 20th century. For the purpose of this book it is not necessary to accept the convenient chronological

---

[188] Michael Keating (2001), "Public Governance and Growth", in John Nieuwenhuysen, Peter Lloyd and Margaret Mead (2001), *Reshaping Australia's Economy: Growth with Equity and Sustainability*, Cambridge University Press, Cambridge, 183.
[189] C. Walsh (1991), "The National Economy and Management Strategies", in B. Galligan and G. Singleton (eds) (1991), *Business and Government under Labor*, Longman Cheshire, Melbourne.
[190] Pincus 2001, 264.
[191] Stokes 2004, 15.
[192] Kelly 1992, 12.

presentation by Kelly. The overall concept has greater strength than his attempts to shoehorn it into an overwhelmingly, pro-Hawke-Keating Government thesis. Although it does need to be acknowledged that a core pillar of the Australian Settlement in the form of the tariff component of New Protection, did indeed end with the Hawke-Keating Governments. The White Australia Policy was already dead by this stage, but this Government sealed the fate on industry protectionism and state paternalism and allowed the Howard Government the ability to break the back of the wage arbitration system – if only by admitting that enterprise bargaining was a legitimate reform of the award system.

The Australian Settlement 2.0: "The neo-liberal consensus"?

There has also been a debate whether in fact there is a new Australian Settlement or what I call an Australian Settlement 2.0.

Melleuish argues that nothing has replaced the Australian Settlement and believes that it will take some time for a new order to settle into place.[193] In an earlier work he set out a historical analysis that mapped three phases of Australian history: Colonial Australia; Modern Australia; and Contemporary Australia.[194] Modern Australia was the period of the Australian Settlement and Contemporary Australia is post-Australian Settlement. Melleuish believes that this latter period has been dominated by what he calls a period of "packages", which have attempted (unsuccessfully in his view) to replace the Settlement. He regards the *Fightback!* package of the Liberal and National Parties during the 1991-93 period as an example.

Earlier, Painter put the view that the structural economic reforms "did not boldly affirm a new order so much as seek to remedy the particular defects of an old one". He called it the "doctrine of

---
[193] Melleuish 2004, 88-90.
[194] Melleuish 1998, 8-15.

problem solving and management".[195] McAuley also thinks that there is no updated Settlement and that "into this policy void has come a set of disjointed, unconnected ideas".[196] However this interpretation would appear to deny that the Australian Settlement did not just fall apart by itself. Indeed its demise was a deliberate act in the face of mostly bitter political and community opposition, which saw the old verities of policy taken down one by one. And more importantly, in relation to this discussion, were replaced with other policies that, as we saw above, have been variously described as economic rationalism and neo-liberal.

Kelly noted that the 1980s campaign to dismantle the Settlement had as its goal the aim of securing smaller, less interventionist government and a more competitive Australia.[197] This was typified by the following outcomes:

- A public sector surplus.
- An attack on government regulations.
- Privatisation of public enterprise.
- Needs-based welfare.
- Deregulation of the labour market.
- Micro-economic reform to achieve better results in energy, communications and transport.[198]

In fact, many of the opponents of this policy direction themselves readily acknowledge this outcome and tend to use what they regard as a value-laden, negative term "economic rationalism" to describe

---

[195] Martin Painter (1996), "Economic Policy, Market Liberalism and the 'End of Australian Politics'", *Australian Journal of Political Science*, Vol 31, No 3, 293.
[196] Ian McAuley (2005), "Updating the Australian Settlement", Centre for Policy Development, published on-line www.cpd.org.au
[197] Kelly 1992, 11.
[198] Ibid.

it.[199] Economic rationalism is a term that is used to describe the philosophical approach that argues for market-based solutions for the allocation of resources and for minimal regulation of markets for goods, services, labour and finance. I have no problem in calling myself an economic rationalist.

As I noted in chapter 2, probably a more commonly used label across the world is neo-liberal. Tim Rowse also speaks of the end of the Australian Settlement and the consequent implementation of neo-liberal policies,[200] as do Boris Frankel[201] and David McKnight[202] to name a few amongst many.

Although it is not central to this thesis to come up with new nomenclature, alternatives to "the Australian Settlement 2.0" could be "The Great Australian Consensus"; "The Great Australian Compromise"; or "The Neo-Liberal Consensus". The latter is the most descriptive and accurate. But in the end I personally like the Australian Settlement 2.0.

Many commentators have not been pleased with the development of this neo-liberal consensus. We have already seen that some[203] have called for an alternative framework that they

---

[199] e.g., Michael Pusey (1991), *Economic Rationalism in Canberra: A Nation Building State Changes its Mind*, Cambridge University Press, Cambridge, Michael Pusey (1992), "Canberra Changes its Mind – The New Mandarins", in John Carroll and Robert Manne (eds)(1992), *Shutdown: The Failure of Economic Rationalism and How to Rescue Australia*, The Text Publishing Company, Melbourne, 38-48, Michael Pusey (2003), *The Experience of Middle Australia: The Dark Side of Economic Reform*, Cambridge University Press, Cambridge; Smyth and Cass 1998; Roe 1998, Carroll and Manne 1992.

[200] Rowse 2002, 357.

[201] Boris Frankel (2001), *When the Boat Comes In: Transforming Australia in the Age of Globalisation*, Pluto Press Australia, Annandale; Boris Frankel (2002), "Towards the New Australian Settlement", *Arena*, Vol 58, April-May, 28-35.

[202] David McKnight 2005, 1-2 and 246-248.

[203] Roe 1998; Smyth 1998, Battin 1998 and Maddox 1998.

label the Australian Way to be revived and expanded. McKnight argues that the neo-liberalism framework should be replaced with a "New Humanism", which incorporates a new moral framework that puts "human values at the centre of a new political vision rather than theories of rights or class or cultural or gender identity".[204] Frankel believes that a new "social-industrial complex" should be created that would build upon the existing neo-liberal framework, using private superannuation savings for national priorities and the creation of additional government controlled investment funds to finance various social policy initiatives.[205] And, Duncan, Leigh, Madden, and Tynan[206] and McAuley[207] argue for an update and restoration of the Australian Settlement model which "invests in its physical, human, institutional and social capital so as to reduce the need for welfare dependence".

For his part, Paul Kelly[208] defines the ideological fight that occurred during the 1980s and 1990s as being between the "international rationalists" and the "sentimentalist traditionalists". The first group believe in the power of markets and the internationalisation of the Australian economy. He describes the sentimentalist traditionalists as those who dismiss the views of the former group and placed continued faith in a "new triumph" of government regulation.

As a final observation it is noted that the longevity of the Australian Settlement 2.0 or the neo-liberal consensus will depend upon whether the original settlement was a superstructure on top

---

[204] McKnight 2005, 254.
[205] Frankel 2001, 214-230; and Frankel 2002, 58-59.
[206] Macgregor Duncan, Andrew Leigh, David Madden and Peter Tynan (2004), *Imagining Australia: Ideas for our Future*, Allen &Unwin, Crows Nest.
[207] McAuley 2005.
[208] Kelly 1992, 2.

of either a Benthamite/neo-liberal or alternatively a social liberal values system that existed at the heart of the national consciousness, and whether one of these value systems remains the core Australian mindset of the majority of citizens. If it is the Benthamite/neo-liberal value set, as suspected by Catley[209], then we may see the current consensus remaining for potentially decades yet. However, if it actually is the social liberal values system then we may see yet another, "newer" consensus emerge during the years to come. In my view that is another way of surrendering to the sentimentalist traditionalists that Paul Kelly has talked of. It will lead us back to the sleepwalking of a zombie nation.

Conclusion

This chapter has examined the 19th century path to the Australian Federation and the drafting of the Commonwealth Constitution, and the subsequent related implementation in the 20th century of the Australian Settlement or New Protection.

While there is no doubt that Federation itself is the watershed event in the modern history of Australia there have been arguments about the historical significance of the Australian Settlement. This chapter has explored the literature on the issue and comes to the conclusion that whatever descriptive title you give to the set of policies that were principally introduced by Alfred Deakin (subsequently forming the basis of bipartisan political policy consensus for the best part of eighty years) they are also a watershed development in modern Australian history.[210]

The consensus view that there has over the last two decades been a subsequent demise of the Australian Settlement to be replaced by a neo-liberal consensus or as I call it the Australian Settlement 2.0, becomes a candidate for the third watershed event of our history.

---

[209] Catley 2005.
[210] See the similar conclusions of Stokes 2004, 5; and Brett 2007, 2.

In the next chapter I explain the rise of the Australian Settlement 2.0 in detail and note the long and tortuous path that eventually led to it being established. I go through this detail to help people understand the critical role that the business community played in its development. It was not simply a policy change thought up by politicians. It was essentially a set of policies developed by the wider community.

In my view if we do not sustain this new Australian Settlement 2.0, as I have said above, it will lead us back to the sleepwalking of a zombie nation. And that will be the discussion in chapters 4 to 12.

3
WHAT LED TO THE AUSTRALIAN SETTLEMENT 2.0?

Introduction

Where did the intellectual case for pulling down the Australian Settlement come from?

This chapter examines the development of the policies that saw the end of the Australian Settlement and its replacement by a new consensus, which I have named the Australian Settlement 2.0.

It is worth noting how a bipartisan, mainstream position between government officials, the business community and academic economists emerged, particularly during the 1980s, which led to the victory of a neo-liberal consensus. Ironically, the business community had in the past been the champions of the Australian Settlement. Now a critical mass of the business community were to swing around to being its biggest critics.

I should note that in this chapter when I discuss the attitudes of the "business community" I am referring to the most important business associations of the day, which were initially the Associated Chambers of Manufactures of Australia (ACMA), the Australian Council of Employers Federation (ACEF) and the Australian Chamber of Commerce (ACC). The first two merged to form the Confederation of Australian Industry (CAI) in 1977 before it merged with the ACC in 1992 to form today's Australian Chamber of Commerce and Industry (ACCI). This of course was the body that I was honoured to be the chief executive of for six years in the earlier 2000s. The other dominant business group during this period was the Business Council of Australia (BCA), which was created in 1983. However, I readily acknowledge that there were many other influences on policy development and they are referred to in detail throughout the chapter.

Again this chapter is a bit dry and academic. For those who want to skip to the policy issues of today please feel free to by-pass this chapter and head straight to chapter 4.

The economic and political context

The original Australian Settlement was not simply put in place and then not thought about for another 80 years. It was the subject of review and discussion over the decades, although for the most part it was overwhelmingly supported by the Australian community.

Indeed as early as the 1920s the Brigden Committee's *Economic Inquiry on the Australian Tariff* was established to examine these questions. Even though the Brigden Committee found in favour of retaining the protectionist tariff system on the basis that "the advantage of the tariff is in the maintenance of a larger population than could have been expected at the same standard of living without the protective tariff"[1], it argued that "the burden of the tariff has probably reached the economic limits, and an increase ... might threaten the standard of living".[2] Nonetheless, in the short term at least, the recommendations of the Brigden Committee were swept off the policy table by external factors caused by the economic catastrophe that was the Great Depression.[3]

Also particularly noteworthy was the 1965 Vernon "Committee

---

[1] J. Brigden (1929), *The Australian Tariff: An Economic Enquiry*, Melbourne University Press, Melbourne, 140.
[2] Ibid., 6.
[3] F.G. Davidson (1977), "Brigden, Vernon, Rattigan, Jackson", in J.P. Nieuwenhuysen and P.J. Drake (eds)(1977), *Australian Economic Policy*, Melbourne University Press, Melbourne, 147.

of Economic Inquiry" (The Vernon Report), which concluded that "infant industries" had to at some stage "grow up" and that there should not be "indiscriminate protection regardless of circumstances".[4]

Public debate began to turn in the 1960s. The political climate slowly moved in favour of reduced protection, assisted by the fact that Alf Rattigan, appointed by the Menzies Government as chairman of the Tariff Board in 1962, was a major advocate for tariff reductions.[5] There were many other advocates in favour of reduced protection. Their number included Bert Kelly, Liberal Party Federal Member for Wakefield, who from around 1961 began a sustained public campaign for tariff reform[6], Professor Max Corden of the ANU who began articulating a more rigorous academic case for change in the 1960s[7], academic Professor Heinz Arndt (also of ANU), and a number of journalists foremost of who was probably Max Newton of the *Australian Financial Review*.[8] Parts of the business community, in this case in the guise of the ACC, also called for tariff reform.[9]

---

[4] ACCA (1965), *Canberra Comments*, Vol 19, No 10, 15 October.
[5] W.T. Dobson (1979) "The Associated Chambers of Manufactures of Australia", MA Thesis, Melbourne University, Melbourne, 99; Stephen Bell (1993), *Australian Manufacturing and the State: The politics of industry policy in the post-war era*, Cambridge University Press, Cambridge, 30; Kosmas Tsokhas (1984), *A Class Apart? Businessmen and Australian Politics 1960-1980*, Oxford University Press, Melbourne, 19.
[6] See C.R. Kelly (1978), *One More Nail*, Brolga Books, Adelaide.
[7] See Peter Groenewegen and Bruce McFarlane (1990), *A History of Australian Economic Thought*, Routledge, London, 173-204; W.M. Corden (1971) *The Theory of Protection*, Oxford University Press, Oxford; and W.M. Corden (1974), *Trade Policy and Economic Welfare*, Oxford University Press, Oxford.
[8] Kelly 1978, 75.
[9] ACCA (1967a), 63rd Annual Conference, Perth, 22-25 May; ACCA (1968a), Council of Management, Minutes, 6 February, ACCA (1969b), Council of Management, Minutes, 7 October & ACCA (1970a), Council of Management,

As for the centralised wage fixing, the business community were unhappy with the actual operation of the system from the earliest days. Some businesses maintained a position of complete opposition to the system[10] while the majority maintained support for the system because they believed that it was the best way to reduce violence and thuggery on worksites.

Famously, there was an attempt in the 1920s to reform the system that was plagued by major problems due to the overlapping of the federal and state systems of arbitration. At the 1923 Premiers' Conference Nationalist Party (a forerunner of the Liberal Party) Prime Minister Stanley Bruce unsuccessfully proposed to Premiers amending the Constitution to resolve the overlapping jurisdiction problems.[11] This proposal would have been an extension of federal reach and was also opposed by many in the business community.[12] He again tried at the 1925 Premiers' Conference, but made little headway in negotiating a cooperative deal with Premiers (with five of the six being Labor Governments). As a result in May 1926

Minutes, 3 February; ACCA (1967b), *Canberra Comments*, Vol 21, No 10, October, 2; ACCA (1968b), *Canberra Comments*, Vol 22, No 6, June, 2; also see ongoing strong vocal support for the Tariff Board in *Canberra Comments*: ACCA (1968c), *Canberra Comments*, Vol 22, No 10, October, 3-4; ACCA (1968d), *Canberra Comments*, Vol 22, No 12, December, 1; ACCA (1969a), *Canberra Comments*, Vol 23, No 9, September, 1; ACCA (1970b), *Canberra Comments*, Vol 24, No 9, September, 1-2; ACCA (1971a), *Canberra Comments*, Vol 25, No 1, January, 3 and ACCA (1971b), *Canberra Comments*, Vol 25, No 8, August, 3.

[10] CCEA continued to call for its abolition at its 1928 Conference (CCEA (1928), Annual Conference, Minutes) and in 1929 resolved that "compulsory arbitration has largely failed, and that it has not achieved the purpose for which it was introduced. Having this in view, we consider that it should be abolished" (CCEA (1929), Inter-State Conference of Employers' Federations, Sydney, 1-3 October).

[11] CCEA (1923b), Annual Conference, Minutes, 14 August and CCEA (1923a), Meeting, Minutes, Melbourne, 1 March.

[12] Ibid.

he proceeded with a Constitutional referendum that sought to radically increase federal industrial relations powers.[13] However, this Referendum was rejected by the electorate.

The year 1929 was one of the most momentous in the development of the Australian industrial relations system with a series of strikes, the most prominent being a ten month long timber workers' strike that began in January 1929,[14] and an economic recession. At the Premiers' Conference that year Bruce again (unsuccessfully) sought a referral of powers on industrial matters from the states to the Commonwealth.[15] On 22 August 1929 he used the *Maritime Industries Bill* to repeal the *Conciliation and Arbitration Act* and the *Industrial Peace Act* and substituted federal industrial relations jurisdiction only for stevedoring and maritime industries, by way of Round Table Conferences. As a result all residual matters would reside with state jurisdictions. When Bruce failed to get support for the Bill in the House of Representatives, the nation went to the polls on 12 October 1929. In an election dominated by the arbitration issue Bruce's Government was defeated and he lost his Parliamentary seat.[16] It would be wrong to accept the popular belief, but nonetheless ill-informed opinion, that Bruce was attempting to abolish arbitration.[17] He may have lost because many people were led to this conclusion but he was, ironically, actually trying to strengthen the system by solving the overlapping jurisdiction

---

[13] Aaron Wildavsky (1958), *The 1926 Referendum*, Cheshire, Melbourne, 11.
[14] R. Ward (1977), *A Nation for a Continent*, Heinemann, Melbourne, 167.
[15] *Commonwealth Parliamentary Papers* 1929, Vol 1, 1429.
[16] W.M. Hughes (1941), "The Tribute of a Contemporary" in J. Groom (ed) (1941), *Nation building in Australia: The Life and Work of Sire Littleton Groom*, Angus and Robertson, Sydney, 254-258; and Doug Aiton and Terry Lane (2002), *Digest of Australia's Federal Elections Since 1901*, Pennon Publishing, Essendon, 39-40.
[17] Dagmar Carboch (1958), *The Fall of the Bruce Page Government*, Studies in Australian Politics, F.W. Cheshire, Melbourne, 263-265.

problem. He had been supported by a large part of the business community in this agenda.

However, the onset of the Great Depression in October 1929 was to have a further impact on business attitudes. Initially the manufacturers maintained their longstanding position that "the best interests of Australia will be served if the federal government retires from the field of industrial legislation, except as it affects shipping and shearing".[18] However the deepening of the Depression caused a revision of this policy. For example it was decided "that manufacturers in all states be asked to give every assistance possible to the employers of other states desiring to come under a federal award".[19]

In summary, the 1930s saw a consolidation in the business community's support for the federal arbitration court. This was a pragmatic acknowledgement that the political failure of the Bruce Government on the issue had ruled out their primary call for a transfer of jurisdiction to the states and also the view that had been developing amongst employers over the previous decades that the tribunal was a bulwark against union demands and a reasonable alternative for dispute settlement. The Court decision in 1930 to cut the basic wage in light of the Great Depression and not fully restore this reduction until 1937 had convinced employers that the Court would not always be biased in favour of the labour movement. However, this was not a black and white *volte face* during the 1930s but a case of the majority within the business organisations switching from a states-rights agenda to a federal centred agenda (that had been argued by some participants since 1904).

After WWII the business community's dealings with the post-War Labor government were framed in the context of its concern

---

[18] ACMA (1930), 22nd Annual Meeting, Minutes, Melbourne, 27-29 October.
[19] ACMA (1931), 23rd Annual Meeting, Minutes, Sydney, 26-28 October.

about the party's adoption of a socialist political and economic agenda. ACEF's president Frederick A Johnston stated that: "The threat of socialism which is advancing without serious check in all countries, with the exception of the United States, impels us, as protagonists of free enterprise in Australia, to take stock of what we are doing to halt this dangerous retrogression".[20] However with the defeat of the Chifley Government at the Federal election on 10 December 1949 the employer groups collectively breathed a sigh of relief. During the next two decades Liberal Prime Minister Sir Robert Menzies dominated the political scene. He supported tariff protection as a means of building up secondary industry[21] and was also a very strong supporter of the federal wage fixing system.[22]

Nonetheless, through the late 1950s and 1960s there was growing dissatisfaction with the outcomes that the arbitration system was delivering and, as a result, "unions and employers in the context of a fully employed economy increasingly bypassed the Commonwealth Court of Conciliation and Arbitration and came to their own arrangements on wages and working conditions".[23]

Of course it is relevant that the 1950s and 1960s were comparatively speaking prosperous days. In contrast, the three decades of the 1970s, 1980s and the 1990s were turbulent times for the Australian economy.

---

[20] ACEF (1949), Executive Committee Meeting, Sydney, 2 August.
[21] Jenny Stewart (1995), "Trade and Industry Policies", in Scott Prasser, J.R. Nethercote and John Warhurst (1995), *The Menzies Era: A Reappraisal of Government, Politics and Policy*, Hale & Iremonger, Sydney, 185.
[22] Robert Menzies (1970), *The Measure of the Years*, Cassell Australia Ltd, Melbourne, 133-134; 1967, 31-37; and A.W. Martin (1993), *Robert Menzies*, (volume 1), Melbourne University Press, Melbourne, 48-49.
[23] Braham Dabscheck (1983), *Arbitrator at Work: Sir William Raymond Kelly and the Regulation of Australian Industrial Relations*, George Allen & Unwin, Sydney, 155.

During the roller-coaster ride of the Whitlam Government from 1972 to 1975, the economy experienced its worst problems since the end of World War II and the relationship between the business community and the government of the day reached a nadir. Later, the economy temporarily improved during the course of the Fraser Government. However, in 1981-82 the community again faced the ravages of deep recession.

Australian business in particular gradually came to the view that things had to change and to radically change. For example, the ACC underwent a major change of direction. During the early 1980s it became a leading proponent of 'radical' neo-liberal economic reform calling for major deregulation of Australia's sclerotic economy and a more pro-market economic policy. Its (co-) leadership of the so-called "New Right" was a crucial element in laying the groundwork for the change in attitudes to economic management in both the Liberal and Labor parties.

The decade of the 1990s began with the deepest recession for 60 years, which created a further stimulus to policy analysis and consideration of alternatives. That decade and the 2000s saw the eventual demise of the Australian Settlement and the implementation of the neo-liberal agenda.[24]

---

[24] For a general overview of developments over this period in Australian industry policy and industrial relations policy see references in footnotes 77 and 88 in chapter 2. In addition see: Stephen Bell (1997), *Ungoverning the Economy: The Political Economy of Australian Economic Policy*, Oxford University Press, Melbourne; Stephen Bell and Brian Head (eds) (1994), *State, Economy and Public Policy in Australia*, Oxford University Press, Melbourne; Tom Conley and Brendon O'Connor (2004), "Trade Policy: Moving Towards Freer Trade?", in van Acker and Curran 2004, 141-160; Braham Dabscheck (1994), "The arbitration system since 1967", in Stephen Bell and Brian Head (eds) (1994), *State, Economy and Public Policy in Australia*, Oxford University Press, Melbourne, 142-168; Braham Dabscheck (2001), "The Slow and Agonising Death of the Australian Experiment with Conciliation and Arbitration", *The Journal of Industrial Relations*, vol 43, no 3, September 2001, 277-293 & Braham Dabscheck (2004), "Arbitration and

The next few sections will cover these developments in more detail.

The Gorton and McMahon Governments (1967-1972)

It is not often acknowledged in economic histories but the first tentative steps to start the wind-back of the high tariff walls began at the end of the long run of Coalition governments as the corner was turned into the 1970s.

The pro-protectionist manufacturers were not happy. As a typical example of their growing anxiety, in 1970 ACMA's Federal director Bob Anderson wrote to Prime Minister John Gorton stating that "despite a number of private and public reassurances from government sources during the past two and a half years, our concern is deepened by the government's apparently ready acceptance of a number of Reports of the Tariff Board which have been released recently".[25]

In contrast to this concern, in January 1971, the Gorton Government made a watershed decision to agree to the Tariff Board's call for a general review, prompted by the resignation of the long-term

---

Relations Between the Parties", *The Journal of Industrial Relations*, vol 46, no 4, December 2004, 385-399; Doug McEachern (1991a), *Business Mates, The Power and Politics of the Hawke Era*, Prentice Hall, Melbourne; Doug McEachern (1991b), "Taking Care of Business: The Hawke Government and the Political Management of Business", in B. Galligan and G. Singleton (eds) (1991), *Business and Government under Labor*, Longman Cheshire, Melbourne, pp 134-145; Shaun Goldfinch (1999), "Remaking Australia's Economic Policy: Economic Policy Decision-Makers during the Hawke and Keating Labor Governments", *Australian Journal of Public Administration*, vol 58, no 2, June, pp3-20; Michael Barry and Nick Wailes (2004), "Contrasting Systems? 100 Years of Arbitration in Australia and New Zealand", *The Journal of Industrial Relations*, vol 46, no 4, December 2004, 430-447. Lastly the author can supply a more comprehensive bibliography upon request.

[25] ACMA (1970), letter from RWC Anderson to JG Gorton, 8 December.

Minister for Trade and Industry and Deputy Prime Minister John McEwen, a strong supporter of protection. His replacement, Doug Anthony, proceeded with a review schedule and on behalf of the new McMahon Government (William McMahon having deposed Gorton in a leadership spill) in April 1971 sent the formal terms of reference to the Tariff Board.[26] ACMA became increasingly alarmed and in a famous press release Bob Anderson of ACMA warned the McMahon Government that "manufacturers are getting sick and tired of being pushed around. ... It is not a threat but merely a statement of fact to suggest that the present Government would be out of power in quick time if it monkeyed about too much with tariff levels".[27]

The Liberal Party did lose the election but it would be wrong to sheet that home to changes to the tariff schedule.

The Whitlam Government (1972-1975)

The election of Whitlam Government on 2 December 1972 began a confronting time for the business community.

For example, by the end of 1974 a typical damning pronouncement of the Government was made by ACMA president Roy Nicholls in a press release titled "Government Policies Destroying Industry", which stated that "Australia is heading for the dubious distinction of becoming the world's first developed nation to regress into a feudal state of peasant farmers, miners and cottage industry workers".[28] The ACEF also found dealings with the Whitlam Government frustrating and perceived a strong anti-

---

[26] Snape, Gropp and Luttrell 1998, 56-57; and Rattigan 1986, 66-89 & 91-106.
[27] ACMA and Metal Trades Industry Association (1971),"ACMA and MTIA Join in Tariff Review", joint press release, Canberra, 2 August.
[28] ACMA (1974d), "Government Policies Destroying Industry – Retiring ACMA President", media release, Canberra, 29 November.

business bias.[29] They felt under siege and statements calling for "a guarantee from Government that national policies recognise the right of industry to exist and remain viable" were common.[30]

However, there were dramatic changes in tariff policy during this Government that have a bearing on the demise of the Australian Settlement. I will concentrate particularly on these developments in this chapter.

On 1 February 1973, two months after the election of the Whitlam Government, the ACMA released its Tariff Policy. It differed little from the past and emphasised support for "effective protection for economic and efficient Australian industry" and the importance of "the fullest possible reporting by the Tariff Board". Interestingly in an acknowledgement of increasing trends across the GATT membership to lower protection levels it noted that this should be done over "an adequate period to permit the adjustment" and the need for "adjustment assistance".[31]

However, in complete contrast to these views, on 18 July 1973 in a dramatic decision that involved basically no industry consultation the Whitlam Government implemented a 25 per cent tariff cut. It was justified not on the basis of reducing protection as an industry policy goal, but as an anti-inflation measure.[32] However, Prime Minister Whitlam did personally lean toward lower protection as he indicated in his famous statement while in Opposition that "I

---

[29] ACEF (1973), Annual Report and Presidential address to the 69th annual meeting; Canberra, 23 March; ACEF (1974), Annual Report and Presidential address to the 70th annual meeting; Wellington, NZ, 16 May; and ACEF (1975), Annual Report and Presidential address to the 71st annual meeting; Canberra, 14 May.
[30] ACEF 1975.
[31] ACMA (1973a), *Industry News*, Vol 1, No 1, 1 February.
[32] John Warhurst (1982), *Jobs or Dogma? The Industries Assistance Commission and Australian Politics*, University of Queensland Press, St Lucia, 36-37; and Snape, Gropp and Luttrell 1998, 58-59.

am a strong Rattigan man"[33] (recalling that Rattigan was a strong advocate for lower tariffs). Gough Whitlam was subsequently to startle an ACMA audience when he declared to them in the wake of the 25 per cent cut that his was "the first free enterprise government in 23 years".[34]

As would be expected ACMA's reaction was hostile. They stated that it "confirms the manufacturers worst fears that the Government is singling out the private sector to bear the brunt of its counter inflation measures" and that "the surgery for some will be far worse than the disease".[35] It warned that some 45,000 to 50,000 jobs would be lost[36]. One of the major concerns of ACMA was the secrecy and lack of consultation with the business community and affected manufacturing unions in the lead-up to the decision and it immediately sought a meeting with the Prime Minister, which was held the following Sunday afternoon.[37] The ACMA Executive Board seriously explored options to mount a legal challenge against the decision[38], but by March 1974, after a number of conflicting legal opinions, they decided to restrict their attention to lobbying activity.[39]

ACC also opposed the across the board cut. They observed that if the cut was an anti-inflationary measure it simply signalled

---

[33] Bell 1993, 56.
[34] Stephen Bell (1992a), "Business and Government Relations: The Ideological Context", Stephen Bell and John Wanna (1992) (eds) *Business-Government Relations in Australia*, Harcourt Brace Jovanovich, Publishers, Sydney, pp 37-45, 44.
[35] ACMA (1973b), "Statement by Mr W.J. Henderson, Director-General ACMA on Government's Tariff Cut Decision", media release, Canberra, 18 July.
[36] ACMA (1973e), *Industry News*, Vol 1, No 5, August.
[37] ACMA (1973c), "ACMA Wants Discussions with Government on Tariff Cut", media release, Canberra, 19 July and ACMA (1973d), "ACMA Asks Prime Minister for Tariff Cut Exemptions", media release, Canberra, 22 July.
[38] ACMA (1973f), Executive Board Meeting, Minutes, Canberra, 28 November.
[39] ACMA (1974a), Executive Board Meeting, Minutes, Canberra, 1 March.

that the Government was unprepared to deal with excessive public spending and excessive wage demands. It was described as a "precipitate" measure and they noted that ACC "strongly" supported "the review of the Tariff on an industry by industry basis where due regard is given to the degree of excess protection received by industries as well as economic effects on those industries of a lowering of tariff duties, but the present across the board tariff reduction takes none of these factors into consideration".[40]

The fact that former Treasury Secretary John Stone[41] has noted that the Australian Treasury also opposed the decision for much the same reasons, is an indication of the power of a Prime Minister to make decisions based on his own policy preferences.

To confirm Prime Minister Whitlam's proclivities for lower protection, the Government passed the *Industries Assistance Commission Act* which created the Industries Assistance Commission (IAC) out of the Tariff Board, effective from 1 January 1974. With Alf Rattigan still at the helm, the IAC pursued a vigorous agenda of tariff cuts.

ACMA were critical of the IAC's first annual report which they stated "sounds the death knell for thousands of small firms which are the very backbone of the nation's economy".[42]

Further in May 1974 the Harris Committee Report on "The Principles of Rural Policy in Australia" catalogued the cost to the rural sector of manufacturing protection and argued for tariff reductions and, as a second-best policy, the compensation of rural

---

[40] ACC (1973b), *Canberra Comments*, Vol 27, No 7, July.
[41] John Stone (former Assistant Secretary Federal Treasury; former Secretary Federal Treasury; former Senator and Shadow Minister) Interview with author on 18 June 2009.
[42] ACMA (1974c), "IAC Annual Report – Sounds Death Knell for Many Small Firms", media release, Canberra, 30 October.

industries.[43] Of even more significance, in October 1975, just prior to the dismissal of the Whitlam Government the Jackson Committee Green Paper on "Policies for Development of Manufacturing Industry" was released.[44] The majority view was for the retention of a low level protectionist policy. However the Green Paper is more famous for the dissenting report of Committee member Alf Rattigan who rejected the "corporatist" and sectoral approach to industry assistance of the Committee's majority in favour of a more general, non-discriminatory approach.[45]

Despite the important long-term role played by the Whitlam Government in initiating these reports, after the political backlash from the 25 per cent cut, it increased protection by expanding the use of import quotas, particularly for Textile Clothing and Footwear (TCF) and the Passenger Motor Vehicle (PMV) sectors.[46] It is not clear to what extent this turnaround was due to lobbying by business as opposed to union opposition or the impact of electoral politics.

*****

The Whitlam Labor Government, with its formal trade union affiliation, created a difficult political environment for the business community to influence industrial relations policy. Economic developments in the early 1970s saw employers and unions increasingly resort to collective bargaining as "over-award" payments, whereby centralised National Wage decisions fell from representing 52.6 percent of increases in male average minimum wages in 1967-1968 to only 19.1 per cent in 1973-1974.[47]

---

[43] See Snape, Gropp and Luttrell 1998, 26, 64-67.
[44] See Glezer 1982, 132-138; and Snape, Gropp and Luttrell 1998, 67-70.
[45] Snape, Gropp and Luttrell 1998, 26-27.
[46] Kym Anderson and Ross Garnaut (1987), *Australian Protectionism*, Allen & Unwin, Sydney, 53; and Conley and O'Connor 2004, 147.
[47] Dabscheck 1994, 147-148.

Like its predecessors the Whitlam Government fully supported the federal arbitration system. However it sought expanded union collective bargaining; increased union amalgamations; wanted to remove all penal provisions and the Commission's ability to ban strikes; change national standards; and introduce workers' councils.[48] However, these amendments were stopped by the Liberal-Country Party Coalition controlled Senate – because of their clear intent to favour the union movement – and a significantly watered down Act came into effect in November 1973.

The period of the Whitlam Government was a time of major industrial disputation[49] and Whitlam[50] noted his great difficulties in dealing with the unions. As an example, in 1974 the Whitlam Government concluded the "Kirribilli Accord" with the ACTU to reintroduce full wage indexation linked to the inflation rate and in 1975 they were successful in convincing the Australian Conciliation and Arbitration Commission to do just that. The argument in support was that it would reduce industrial unrest and contribute towards a reduction in the rate of inflation and thereby increase employment opportunities. Importantly it was also seen as a way for the Commission to regain control over the system. In contrast, the proposal was opposed by all three peak employer organisations noting that the system would only work efficiently if wage increases were linked to productivity.[51]

---

[48] Singleton 1990, 10 and David Plowman (1989a), *Holding the Line: Compulsory arbitration and national employer co-ordination in Australia*, Cambridge University Press, Sydney, 174-175.
[49] See Bill Harley (2004), "Managing Industrial Conflict", in Isaac and Macintyre 2004, 322-325.
[50] Gough Whitlam (1985), *The Whitlam Labor Government 1972-1975*, Viking, Ringwood, 201.
[51] ACMA (1974b), *Industry News*, Vol 2, No 2, 27 March; ACEF (1976), Annual Report and Presidential address to the 72nd annual meeting; Melbourne, 18 March; and ACC (1975), *Canberra Comments*, Vol 29, No 9, September.

As inflation accelerated during 1973-1974 it is clear that the new approach had failed to work. However, for those who wanted to strengthen the hand of the Commission, in one respect indexation was very successful as by the time indexation ended in 1981, 91 per cent of male average wage increases were due directly to National Wage Case decisions, up from only 19.1 percent in 1973-1974.[52]

The Fraser Government (1975-1983)

The Fraser Liberal-National Country Parties Government won the election of 13 December 1975, following the dismissal of the Whitlam Government on 11 November 1975 by the Governor-General.

Liberal Leader Malcolm Fraser's promise in the lead-up to the election was that: "We will give Australian industry the protection it needs. We would sooner have jobs than dogma".[53]

The most significant statement on industry policy during the Fraser Government was the release of the *White Paper on Manufacturing* by Minister for Business and Consumer Affairs, John Howard, on 24 May 1977[54] as the Government's formal statement of policy in response to the Jackson Committee Green Paper. It represented a significant development in that it acknowledged the argument for reduced protection and the need to encourage a trade-oriented manufacturing sector. It concluded that: "As a long-term objective in protection policy the Government will seek to establish a simpler and more stable tariff structure", but nonetheless it also explicitly stated that: "A time of lower economic activity, such as the present, is generally not an appropriate time for reducing protection".[55]

---

[52] Dabscheck 1994, 150-151.
[53] J. Warhurst and J. Stewart (1989), "Manufacturing Industry Policy", in B. Head and A. Patience (eds) (1989), *From Fraser to Hawke: Australia Public Policy in the 1980s*, Longman Cheshire, Melbourne, 164.
[54] See Snape, Gropp and Luttrell 1998, 73-76; and Glezer 1982, 138-140.
[55] Reprinted in Snape, Gropp and Luttrell 1998, 75.

Nevertheless, ACMA saw that it had to change its position on tariffs because governments were moving away from high protection. And indeed this fact eventually saw the merger of the ACMA with ACEF (which supported lower levels of protection) to form the Confederation of Australian Industry (CAI).

After the release of the *White Paper* the Fraser Government commissioned yet another review to focus on adjustment problems faced by industry. The Crawford Committee's *Report of the Study Group on Structural Adjustment* was released in March 1979.[56] It too supported tariff reductions and noted that "once a general program of gradual reductions of long-term protection has been commenced, it is critical that it be suspended only in the most exceptional circumstances".[57] However this recommendation was subject to a major caveat, namely that: "The general program of reducing protection not be implemented while unemployment remains above, say, 5 per cent".[58] (As an observation it is worth noting that unemployment was not to get to this level for 26 years, i.e., 2005.)[59]

In its submission to the Study Group inquiry Australia's then peak business group the CAI had argued, maybe as a "last-throw-of-the-dice", that the Government should focus on general economic growth policies rather than lowering tariffs and that "there can be justification for the continuation of high protection where above-average external economies, such as employment effects, defence and technological inter-relationships, are generated by an industry".[60] However, in what would appear to be a major about-

---

[56] See Snape, Gropp and Luttrell 1998, 76-79; and Glezer 1982, 140-144.
[57] Reprinted in Snape, Gropp and Luttrell 1998, 77.
[58] Reprinted in Snape, Gropp and Luttrell 1998, 78.
[59] Sue Richardson (2005), "Unemployment in Australia", paper for the Academy of Social Sciences in Australia, Canberra, 3.
[60] CAI (1978a), *CAI News*, Vol 1, No 4, April.

turn, it supported the final Report stating that: "when regarded as a total package" it provided "a realistic forward policy for the manufacturing sector". Thus importantly, it would appear that for the first time, this indicated CAI support for a general program of tariff reductions, although strictly subject to the 5 per cent unemployment threshold trigger.[61]

The Government's response to the Crawford Report was released by Minister for Industry and Commerce, Philip Lynch, on 23 August 1979.[62] In it the Government accepted the basic arguments of the Study Group to "hasten slowly", and in the short term deferred any reference to the IAC to conduct an inquiry into the general reduction in protection levels.

By 1981 Australia's new peak business body the CAI had a position that was moving quite a distance from ACMA's strident appeals of the past. In July CAI reversed 80 years of support for high protection when it stated: "CAI, like many industry organisations, is committed to gradual reductions in the levels of tariff protection". However, critically, the caveat (based on the Crawford Committee recommendations) was that: "this must be a gradual process, closely tuned to the prevailing economic conditions and the situation in the labour market and should realistically take into account the likely degree of reciprocity in relation to every significant alteration in domestic protection levels" and it argued that in the current economic circumstances "it is particularly inappropriate to initiate moves for rapid protection reductions".[63] This is a position that was

---

[61] CAI (1979), *CAI News*, Vol 2, No 2-3, March-April.
[62] See Snape, Gropp and Luttrell 1998, 79-81.
63 CAI (1981a), *CAI News*, Vol 4, No 4, June/July.

to be repeated.[64] Generally, Bell[65] summarises the reasons for the change of manufacturers' views as being a growing frustration with the failure of government industry policy, a hope for "simpler and clearer" industry support measures and the growth of neo-liberal sentiments within the business community.

For its part the other peak business group of the era of the 1970s, ACC, retained its protectionist policy from the 1950s and 1960s, albeit calling for a program of structural adjustment to reduce the levels of protection. For example, a typical pronouncement was made in 1976 when ACC called for a 12 month moratorium on IAC review enquiries.[66] Further at the 73rd Annual Conference in 1977 ACC still recognised "the need for protection to selected industries, consistent with efficiency, national security and external viability but expresses concern that a timetable does not exist to review a move from the short-term to the long-term policies outlined in the Government's White Paper on Manufacturing Industry".[67] However as we shall see below this position was to radically change from 1980 onwards.

---

[64] CAI (1981b), Chief Executive Officers of National Trade and Industry Council Meeting, Canberra, Minutes, 26 August; CAI (1981c), Chief Executive Officers of National Trade and Industry Council Meeting, Melbourne, Minutes, 10 November; CAI (1981d), National Export Committee Meeting, Minutes, 3 December; CAI (1982a), *CAI News*, Vol 5, No 2, May/June; CAI (1982c), CAI Trade Council, Meeting, Minutes, 8 September and CAI (1982b), Chief Executive Officers of the CAI Trade Council Meeting, Melbourne, Minutes, 6 August.
[65] Bell 1993, 94.
[66] ACC (1976c), "New Round of Economic Consultations Urged", press release, Canberra, 27 October; ACC (1976b), *Canberra Comments*, Vol 30, No 10, October.
[67] ACC (1977c), 73rd Annual Conference, Brisbane, 30 May-3 June; see also ACC (1973a), 69th Annual Conference, Adelaide, 30 April-2 May; ACC (1977e), *Canberra Comments*, Vol 31, No 10, October and ACC (1978c), 74th Annual Conference, Melbourne, 22-24 May.

For example, the ACC's 76th Annual Conference on 1-3 May 1980 passed a resolution stating: "The dilemma of the eighties is that whilst Australia can and will export massive volumes of raw materials earning substantial trade surpluses; the country will be required to import significant volumes of manufactured goods necessitating reduced tariffs and a total revision of manufacturing policies coupled with a recognition of these facts and problems by trade unions and the Australian people as a whole"; and very explicitly that "Where Government protection or assistance is considered appropriate, the cost to the community should be clearly measured and should include a clearly defined phasing-out provision".[68]

The most radical break with the past was its submission in late 1981 to the IAC *General Reductions in Protection* inquiry where ACC proposed a timetable to phase down all tariffs over 20 per cent to 20 per cent; all tariffs between 10 per cent and 20 per cent to 10 per cent and all tariffs under 10 per cent progressively reduced to zero on a 10-15 year timetable to 1995.[69] This is a much more ambitious programme than was to be announced in either of the Hawke Government's 1988 or 1991 tariff reduction statements, in that many rates would go to zero and, most importantly, because the PMV and TCF sectors would not be exempted from the general schedule (as they were to be in the Hawke, Keating and Howard Government schedules).

Thus one of the peak business groups, the ACC, was now arguing for an end to the protectionist policy of the past and the knocking down of one of the two key economic pillars of the Australian Settlement. Importantly, this did not go unnoticed within the government. John Howard, who was Federal Treasurer for much of this period, recalls that: "My experience was that the groups

---

[68] ACC (1980), 76th Annual Conference, Adelaide, 1-3 May.
[69] ACC (1982a), *Canberra Comments*, Vol 36, No 1, January.

that supported the freer approach were the farmers, the miners, to some degree the crowd that Ken Court was president of, the ACC and [Alexander] Downer was deputy to it, and also small business groups".[70]

*****

Despite the hopes of the business community, the Fraser years saw a continuation of the industrial relations turmoil experienced throughout the Whitlam Government.

During the term of the Fraser Government CAI continued to strongly support the wage fixing system because "the community would not support any attempt to bring about its abandonment", although it warned that the system was facing "serious challenges" from changing economic and social conditions.[71] The reason for the CAI's position was that: "In the Australian context, a system of conciliation and arbitration provides the best opportunities for the achievement of the basic [economic] objectives"; "there is general community support for a system of conciliation and arbitration, and little support for a change to a collective bargaining system"; and that "radical change ... is not practicable".[72] However, external economic factors overwhelmed the voice of CAI.

In 1982 an exasperated Fraser Government, facing a severe drought, a deep recession and wage and inflation rates that were out of control, wildly swung in the other policy direction and sought a highly centralised "Wages Pause". It obtained agreement at a Special Premiers' Conference held on 7 December 1982 for all governments to implement a wages pause for their

---

[70] John Howard (Member of the House of Representatives; Federal Minister; Federal Treasurer; Shadow Minister; Leader of the Federal Opposition; Prime Minister) Interview with author on 25 June 2009.
[71] CAI (1978b), *CAI News*, Vol 1, No 10, October-November.
[72] CAI (1981e), National Employers' Industrial Council meeting, Minutes, 3 December.

own employees and to support coordinated submissions to the Australian Conciliation and Arbitration Commission for a National Wage Case proposing the same (the Commonwealth proposed a 12 month freeze while some states only agreed to six months). CAI supported a 12 month freeze.[73] The Commission agreed to a 6 months pause on the basis that with Australia being in a recession it did not believe it could now afford another round of wage increases.[74]

Thus while the Fraser Government had flirted with moving to more enterprise based bargaining, in the end, with its last major economic policy initiative before losing office, it opted to continue to use the Commission as a central plank of its economic policy process. This is but one further example of how larger economic events can rapidly lead to major changes in policy irrespective of long held positions within the government and business groups.

Meanwhile ACC began its radical transformation on industrial relations a full decade earlier than CAI. Through the last half of the Fraser Government the ACC became increasingly alarmed about the inflation and wages problems and the apparent inability of the federal arbitration system to resolve issues.[75] As president

---

[73] CAI (1982d), CAI Industrial Council Meeting, Minutes, 12 December.
[74] CAI (1983i), Annual Report of the Industrial Council and the Trade Council 1982-1983, Canberra, 2 December, 7-8.
[75] ACC (1976a), "Private Enterprise Convention Succeeds", press release, Canberra,6 June; ACC (1976d), "Industrial Disputes", press release, Canberra, 16 November; ACC (1977a), "Press Statement by the President of the ACC, Mr SFN Hickson", press release, Canberra, 31 March; ACC (1977b), "Wage Price Pause: ACC Makes Public Appeal to Trade Union Movement", press release, Canberra, 17 April; ACC (1977d), "National Conference on Industrial Relations", press release, Canberra, 14 July; ACC (1978a), "Wage Threats", press release, Canberra, 21 March; ACC (1981a), "Industrial Relations Initiative", press release, Canberra, 27 July; ACC (1981b), "Chamber Consultations with Federal Government", press release, Canberra, 25 September; ACC (1981c), "Press Statement by the President of the ACC, Mr Bill Wills", press release,

Burrell noted in 26 April 1978 "Australia does not have limitless time in which to correct the evident deficiencies in her wage-fixing system"[76] although at this stage ACC had not formed a view as to a viable alternative. Through the very early 1980s it built a portfolio of policies in total opposition to the Australian Settlement and federal arbitration was directly in its sights. We will see that an alternative was formulated as a direct reaction to the election of the Hawke Government and the implementation of its Prices and Incomes Accord.

While the membership of ACC may have waned over the years it will be evident that its policy objectives did eventually have an impact on the policy direction that the Government took on this issue.

The Hawke and Keating Governments (1983-1996)

After the election of the Hawke Labor Government on 5 March 1983 it began with a policy of so-called 'consensus'. At least early on, this approach involved more structured consultation with business and community groups than had existed previously.

Initially the Hawke Labor Government did not threaten the continuation of the post-War consensus on the Australian Settlement. On the contrary, the new Government's key economic policy was based on a Prices and Incomes Accord with the ACTU. There was a focus on centralised wage fixing and, if anything, an increased role played by the federal arbitration system. The period 1983-1990 has been described as the "zenith" of the federal tribunal and by 1986 some 96 per cent of award wage increases resulted from National Wage Cases.[77]

Canberra, 11 December & ACC (1982b), "Appeal for Economic Sanity: Basic Principles Being Ignored", press release, Canberra, 16 November.

[76] ACC (1978b), "CPI Increase: More Decisive Role Needed for Commonwealth in Wages Policy", press release, Canberra, 26 April.

[77] Dabscheck 2001, 277, 281.

The Hawke Government's pre-election industry policy was decidedly protectionist stating that "although reductions in protection are proper long term objectives, such reductions are neither desirable nor necessary while a substantial rate of unemployment, and a significant level of under-utilisation of other resources, prevails in the economy".[78] The trigger unemployment rate for proceeding with tariff reductions was formally set at 5 per cent in the Accord.[79]

Prime Minister Hawke stated that one of his aims in government was to "get employers to match the trade union movement in reorganising themselves into a more unified and effective force for change".[80] However, this was not to be evident at the new Government's first set-piece event – the 1983 National Economic Summit, where the invited participants were predominantly representative of business and labour interests.

The Government's principal focus at the Summit was to get wide community support for its Prices and Incomes Accord with the ACTU.[81] Prior to the meeting CAI decided that: "It is not likely that the conference will effect any alterations in the Government/ACTU Accord but that it may be possible for the conference to moderate some of the Accord's proposals".[82] The status of CAI as a significant representative of business is evident in its allocation of 10 positions for the Summit[83] and its influence was also evident

---

[78] Quoted in CAI (1983b), *The Australian Economy – An Approach to Recovery*, submission for the National Economic Summit Conference, April, 27.

[79] John Button (1998), *John Button: As it Happened*, The Text Publishing Company, Melbourne, 247.

[80] Stephen Bell (1995a), "Between the Market and the State: The Role of Australian Business Associations in Public Policy", *Comparative Politics*, Vol 28, No 1, October, 32.

[81] Dabscheck 1994, 154.

[82] CAI (1983a), Joint Meeting of CAI Industrial Council and Trade Council, Minutes, 23 March.

[83] Ibid.

from the fact that its director, George Polites, played an important role in drafting the Summit's final communiqué.[84] And as a result of Polites' role "much of the employer agenda was adopted".[85] However the general view was that CAI had in fact failed in its attempts at presenting a unified employer position[86] and many of the membership internally criticised CAI based on the adverse media reports.[87] Prime Minister Hawke was not unhappy with this outcome and he saw the Summit as an opportunity to challenge the leadership of CAI amongst the business community[88] with his encouragement of the creation of the BCA as a rival business organisation, discussed below.

The creation of the Business Council of Australia

From a business community point of view one of the most important early events during the Hawke-Keating era was the creation of the BCA in 1983.[89] Its formation was the direct result of unhappiness

---

[84] CAI (1983c), Executive Officers of the CAI Industrial Council Meeting, Minutes, 18 April.
[85] Debora Campbell (1996) "The Evolution of Enterprise Bargaining Policy in Australian Employer Organisations: 1982 to 1992", PhD Thesis, Monash University, Melbourne, 139.
[86] Trevor Matthews (1994), "Employers' associations, corporatism and the Accord: The politics of industrial relations", in Bell and Head 1994, 204.
[87] CAI (1983d), Executive Officers of the CAI Industrial Council Meeting, 15 June.
[88] McEachern 1991a, 25; Shaun Carney (1988), *Australia in Accord: Politics and Industrial Relations under the Hawke Government*, Sun Books, South Melbourne, 67-70.
[89] See McEachern 1991a; P.A. McLaughlin (1991), "How Business Related to the Hawke Government", in B. Galligan and G. Singleton (eds) (1991), *Business and Government under Labor*, Longman Cheshire, Melbourne, 147-167; Campbell 1996; and Stephen Bell (2006a), "Institutional influences on business power: how 'privileged' is the Business Council of Australia", *Journal of Public Affairs*, Vol 6, May, 156-167, Stephen Bell (2006b), "A Victim of Its Own Success: Internationalization, Neoliberalism, and organizational Involution at the Business Council of Australia", *Politics & Society*,

with CAI of a number of chief executives of large corporations and their view that it was not satisfactorily representing their interests. It grew out of the disaffection of the "Big 50" companies from 1973.[90]

Sir Arvi Parbo, the inaugural BCA president, notes that a tentative approach for merger between the small manufacturing association the Australian Industries Development Association and the Business Roundtable (an offshoot of the Committee for Economic Development of Australia) was made by the former in 1980 but serious discussions did not begin until 1982. The CAI Board minutes of 2 May 1980 record that the president of the CAI, Sir Max Dillon, had been approached by Sir Rod Carnegie "regarding the proposed establishment of a Round Table, the membership of which would include the major companies in Australia" and the possibility of CAI involvement.[91] The subsequent CAI minutes are silent on any developments from these discussions, but it is clear that the approach must have been rejected. Indeed, former CAI/ACCI chief executive, Ian Spicer[92] notes that while CAI did internally debate at the time altering its membership model to one like that of the Confederation of British Industry, which had direct corporate membership, this was eventually rejected by the state-based chambers.

Parbo[93] notes "by the time of the change of federal government in March 1983 there was a commitment to merge". The intention was to prove the CAI/ACEF's Polites wrong when he had famously

---

Vol 34, No 4, December, 543-570; and Stephen Bell (2008), "Rethinking the Role of the State: Explaining Business Collective Action at the Business Council of Australia", *Polity*, Vol 40, No 4, 464-487.
[90] Arvi Parbo, (1993), *Address to the Tenth Anniversary Dinner of the Business Council of Australia*, Melbourne, 14 October.
[91] CAI (1980), Office Bearers, Meeting, Melbourne, 2 May.
[92] Ian Spicer (Chief Executive Officer VEF, Chief Executive Officer CAI; Chief Executive Officer ACCI) interview with author on 19 March 2007.
[93] Parbo 1993.

stated in early 1973 that "it won't work; no-one can corral these stallions at the head of big companies".[94]

The BCA launch occurred at Sydney's Regent Hotel in September 1983. Bob White, who was managing director of Westpac between 1977 and 1987 and was to be the second president of the BCA in the years 1984-85, has stated that the reason for the BCA's formation was to ensure that the business community "would never again appear so fragmented and disorganised" as it had at the Economic Summit.[95] The irony is that by creating a new business lobby in competition with the existing bodies to influence government, the outcome was more fragmentation and disorganisation than had occurred before.

It is evident from the detailed accounts given by Parbo and White that policy disputes with the pre-existing employer associations were not a significant factor in the split. To some degree this is reinforced by a review of the BCA's first 18 months by journalist Michael Stutchbury,[96] who noted that even though its industry assistance policies supported a "rejection of import replacement as an industrial strategy and support for greater 'self-reliance' for Australian industry", its manufacturing members "don't interpret the policy as espousing free trade, pointing to its emphasis on international competitiveness and the need for efficiency". He added that the BCA "steered clear of intra-industry issues, such as the car industry plan". With respect to industrial relations policy Stutchbury noted that while the BCA saw the need for "long term industrial relations change, it so far has relied on the CAI to present its national wage case submissions, has not put a formal submission

---

[94] Parbo 1993, also see Bob White and Cecelia Clarke (1995), *Cheques and Balances: Memoirs of a Banker*, Viking, Melbourne, 162-163.
[95] White and Clarke 1995, 162-163.
[96] Michael Stutchbury (1985), "Chief executive commitment to BCA faces test", *Australian Financial Review*, 9 January 1985.

to the Hancock Inquiry and is not expected to push for inclusion on the National Labour Consultative Council, which is dominated on the employers side by the CAI". However Bell[97] has a different interpretation and argues that the BCA was formed to pursue an alternative neo-liberal agenda. Whichever interpretation is correct (and I would disagree with Bell, while not denying that the BCA was to soon become a leader of neo-liberal advocacy) it does not detract from the significance of the split to the potential of the CAI to influence government.

At a special general meeting on 2 December 1983 CAI adopted a set of "Broad Policy Guidelines",[98] the most significant of which for the purpose of this study related to industrial relations and industry policy. This included "an industrial relations system which is based on an orderly process of conciliation and arbitration"[99] and an industry policy that believed "that Australian industry should be supported and its development encouraged by means of customs duties, bounties, quotas and other more broadly based measures – such measures should be increasingly be aimed at facilitating cost reduction and achieving adequate profitability for industry".[100] These remained the policies of CAI on these two critical issues until events discussed below caused a change during the period 1989-1991.

Difficult economic circumstances during the late 1980s, that also moved the Hawke Government towards a low tariff policy and deregulation, encouraged the business community to reassess its own approach to protection, otherwise its lobbying would have been increasingly irrelevant in the context of the government's changing policy agenda.

---

[97] Bell 2008, 471.
[98] CAI (1983j), Special General Meeting, Canberra, 2 December.
[99] Ibid.
[100] Ibid.

The CAI, as outlined above, had already moved some distance towards a policy of lower protection, although some resistance remained within the organisation's membership. This is evident from its submission to the 1983 National Economic Summit where it indicated that its membership was split on the issue of protection noting that some members argued: "that reductions in higher levels of tariff protection will provide a stimulus to growth in other industries which will offset the inevitable loss of jobs in the industries for which protection is reduced". However, it noted that there was "a majority view that assistance levels should be maintained during current economic conditions".[101] In fact CAI was beginning to slowly change its policy focus for the manufacturing industry away from tariffs (and non-tariff barriers) to more positive taxation and research and development (R&D) support programs and had initiated a project to produce a "Stronger Manufacturing" paper to promote these views.[102]

The New Right

The Australian Settlement was not dead yet, far from it.

Indeed, in a deliberate attempt to further strengthen the federal arbitration system, in mid-1983 the Hawke Government established a "Committee of Review into Australian Industrial Relations Law and Systems" chaired by Professor Keith Hancock. Its recommendations were incremental and

---

[101] CAI 1983b, 27.
[102] CAI (1986g), Officers of the CAI Manufacturing Council and the CAI Commerce and Industry Council Meeting, Adelaide, Minutes, 2 September; CAI (1986k), Officers of the CAI Manufacturing Council and the CAI Commerce and Industry Council Meeting, Canberra, Minutes, 26 November; CAI (1987a), Officers of the CAI Manufacturing Council and the CAI Commerce and Industry Council Meeting, Sydney, Minutes, 5 March & CAI (1987c), Officers of the CAI Manufacturing Council and the CAI Commerce and Industry Council Meeting, Melbourne, Minutes, 4 June.

evolutionary and did not question the long-term viability of federal arbitration.[103]

There was significant division within the business community on policy because, as we shall see below, the ACC were decidedly unhappy with the Hancock Committees' outcome in May 1985. In stark contrast the CAI noted with approval that it was broadly consistent with its submission and welcomed "the constructive contribution it made to the debate about reform".[104] However in retrospect this was the high water mark of the conciliation and arbitration era because from this point on CAI, academics, other employer groups, and key figures in the Labor movement started to join those advocating more radical changes to the system. For example, from 1985 CAI began to internally debate the concept of increased "labour market flexibility" that was being argued for by the OECD.[105]

CAI's movement away from a fully centralised system continued because of pressure from its members to expand its support for bargaining. This was provoked by the highly centralised proposals by the ACTU in its documents *Australia Reconstructed* (ACTU/TDC 1987) and *Future Strategies for the Trade Union Movement*.[106]

As we will see below, in 1988, in response to the Hawke Government's drafting of an Industrial Relations Bill to advance the ACTU

---

[103] CAI (1983f), Executive Officers of the CAI Industrial Council Meeting, Minutes, 17 October; CAI (1983h), CAI Industrial Council Meeting, Minutes, 1 December; CAI (1984b), CAI Industrial Council Meeting, Minutes, 16 March.

[104] CAI (1985a), Executive Officers of the CAI Industrial Council Meeting, Minutes, 11 June.

[105] OECD 1985; and CAI (1985c), CAI Industrial Council Meeting, Minutes, 28 November.

[106] ACTU 1987. See also CAI (1987d), National Employers Industrial Council meeting, minutes, 3-4 September.

agenda for larger industry based unions and provision for union dominated certified agreements, CAI began to develop a policy in favour of enterprise-based negotiation and enterprise-based unions.[107]

*****

In contrast to the slower moving CAI, radical changes in industrial relations policy started to accelerate at ACC during the early 1980s.

By the mid-1980s ACC was a principal member of a loose association or movement dubbed by the media the "New Right", of which ACC president Andrew Hay was considered a leader.[108]

We have already seen that ACC in the early 1980s had a high profile as a peak lobby group[109] despite its policy differences with government. It had opposed a consensus protectionist industry policy from 1981 onwards and shared with CAI concerns about developments in the industrial relations arena. However, unlike its sister organisation, from 1983 and the election of the Hawke Government ACC broke decisively from the consensus model of federal arbitration – almost a decade earlier than the other organisations. Not surprisingly, ACC opposed the Prices and Incomes Accord as soon as it was announced. They stated that "if implemented [it would] lead to business failures, increased unemployment and shortages of goods".[110]

---

[107] CAI (1988a), National Employers Industrial Council meeting, minutes, 18 March.

[108] See Damien Cahill (2004) "The Radical Neo-liberal Movement as a Hegemonic Force in Australia, 1976-1996", PhD thesis, University of Wollongong, Wollongong, 247 and Damien Cahill (2000) "Neo-liberal intellectuals as organic intellectuals? Some notes on the Australian context", paper presented to the Australian Political Studies Association Conference, Australian National University, Canberra, 5; McEachern 1991a, 50-51; *Sydney Morning Herald* 9 June 1987.

[109] John Stone interview 2009.

[110] ACC (1983a), "ALP's Prices and Incomes Policy", press release, Canberra, 2 March.

This opposition to the Accord was reaffirmed in November 1983 by ACC's newly appointed executive director (designate), Alexander Downer on the basis that "the centralised wage fixing system had performed poorly in the past, and the business community was by no means confident that it would work in the future". He argued that the emphasis on centralised wage fixing with "the principle of comparative wage justice being institutionalised through the Conciliation and Arbitration Commission" had "only acted to weaken Australia's overall economic performance".[111]

ACC's proposed solution, pre-dating similar developments in Liberal Party policy (to be later championed by John Howard), was that: "if individual enterprises or industries as a whole were given the opportunity to opt out of the centralised system they would have a greater opportunity of fixing wage levels at rates relevant to the employer's capacity to pay. Once they had opted out, they should be required to stay out for a minimum period".[112]

The clearest enunciation of its new policy direction came with ACC's submission to the Hancock inquiry. It noted that for the first time in 40 years ACC had decided to become involved in the mechanics of the system "because of the failure [of the system] to seek greater flexibility". It argued that "ultimately, wage rates should be determined by collective bargaining at the enterprise level", but accepted "that for political and industrial reasons this goal can only be achieved incrementally". Six major initiatives as interim steps were proposed (1) end full wage indexation; (2) alter the Act to assist the ACAC to make decisions on the basis of productivity; (3) use the Constitution's existing powers or hold a referendum to abolish state tribunals; and most radically (4) allow enterprises

---

[111] ACC (1983e), "Centralised Wage Fixing", press release, Canberra, 25 November.
[112] Ibid.

to opt for over or under-award agreements should they wish to do so, to be registered with the Commission; (5) strengthened legal penalties against breaching awards and agreements; and (6) the creation of "Industry Councils" to bring together employer and employee representative in specific industries.[113]

In the preparation of this policy ACC had consulted extensively with two leading neo-liberal economists Professors John Niland of the University of NSW and Richard Blandy of Flinders University.[114] With some differences this policy position was to be as radical a demand to end the existing federal arbitration system (because employers could "opt out" of compulsory arbitration) as the groundbreaking changes that first CAI in 1991 and then the BCA in 1992 were to later argue for.

Unsurprisingly, upon its release in 1985 ACC labelled the Hancock Report, with its strong support of the existing federal wage fixing system, "a dismal failure".[115]

As Bell[116] notes the system was sustained by "a relatively closed policy network (featuring unions, employer associations, governments, and state and federal tribunals)". Gerard Henderson[117] was to famously name the network the "Industrial Relations Club". George Polites has denied that there was really a club. He stated to the author that "No, there was no such thing, It was a figment of the

---

[113] ACC (1984), "Industrial Relations – The Hancock Inquiry", press release, Canberra, 9 January.
[114] ACC (1983b), Council of Management, Melbourne, Minutes, 10 June; ACC (1983c), Executive, Minutes, 7 July and ACC (1983d), Council of Management, Canberra, Minutes, 5-6 October.
[115] ACC (1985b), "Hancock Report a Dismal Failure", press release, Canberra, 20 May and ACC (1985c), "ACC Comment: Hancock Report a Dismal Failure", press release, Canberra, 1 June.
[116] Bell 1997, 196.
[117] Gerard Henderson (1985), "The Industrial Relations Club", in J. Hyde and J. Nurick (eds) (1985), *The Wages Wasteland*, Hale and Iremonger, Sydney.

imagination of the people who never quite made it".[118] Although in a separate interview he noted that if there had been one he would have been a member.[119]

ACC distanced itself from the insider "Industrial Relations Club"[120] which included at the time the CAI, the ACTU and all those who benefited from the highly regulated industrial relations system. ACC officers used it as a term of derision and clearly regarded themselves as neither being Club members, nor wishing to be.[121] Its support for the end to the Club and the essential dismantling of the federal wage fixing system was repeated often in the ensuing years.[122] ACC deputy president Andrew Hay stated: "I would like to see the Conciliation and Arbitration system abolished. I don't believe we have time on our side which will allow us to take an evolutionary route over a 10 year period".[123] ACC commenting on amendments to the *Industrial Relations Act* in 1987, argued the maintenance of the existing system was simply "tunnel vision"[124] and in response to the ACTU's *Australia Reconstructed* document in September 1988 it stated that it "categorically rejects any contention that the Conciliation and Arbitration Commission

---

[118] George Polites (Executive Director ACEF; Director General CAI) Interview with author 19 March 2007.

[119] Interview with Steve Kates reprinted in Isaac and Macintyre 2004, 261.

[120] Gerard Henderson (1983), "The Industrial Relations Club", *Quadrant*, Sydney, September 1983 & 1985.

[121] e.g., ACC (1985a), "Active Year Ahead in Industrial Relations", press release, Canberra, 6 February; ACC (1987h), *Australian Commerce Review*, Vol 2, No 7, Canberra, July and ACC (1988d), *The ACTU's Game Plan: 'Australia Reconstructed'/'Future Strategies'*, An ACC Research Paper, Canberra, September, 35.

[122] e.g., ACC (1987f), *Australian Commerce Review*, Vol 2, No 6, Canberra, June & ACC 1987h.

[123] *The Bulletin*, 22 August 1986.

[124] ACC (1987i), *The Industrial Relations Bill 1987 – Agenda for Reform*, Canberra, July.

is unassailable in the public policy processes. This is no more evident than in the Chamber's continued work in developing and promoting less centralised and less regulated alternatives to the award/Commission based processes under the hegemony of the 'Industrial Relations Club'".[125]

Because ACC policy was not supported by the Government at the time, it pursued direct action through the legal system and the arbitration process to pursue its objectives. This included Melbourne Chamber of Commerce's involvement in bankrolling (with a fundraising effort from other Chambers) the famous Dollar Sweets case[126] and ACC's direct participation in the industrial relations system by employing advocates to represent them in the 1986 National Wage Cases and other "test cases" to argue for increased recourse to enterprise-based bargaining and greater links between wages and productivity.[127] This prompted a request from CAI to stop intervening in cases, which was rejected.[128] For the 1987 National Wage Case they employed future Howard Government Treasurer Peter Costello as their advocate.[129] ACC continued to be actively involved in the ACAC until it decided that it had become too expensive (eg in the vicinity of $100,000 to comprehensively participate in a National Wage Case) for it to maintain the momentum.[130] However, a joint submission with

---

[125] ACC 1988d, 35.
[126] ACC (1986b), Council, Canberra, Minutes, 20-21 March.
[127] ACC (1985d), 81st Annual Conference, Canberra, 11-12 June; ACC (1985e), Council, Canberra, Minutes, 10-11 October; ACC 1986b; ACC (1986c), Executive, Minutes, 2 May & ACC (1986g), Council, Canberra, Minutes, 30 October.
[128] ACC (1986d), Executive, Minutes, 1 June.
[129] ACC (1987j), Executive, Minutes, 21 August and ACC (1987L), Annual General Meeting, Canberra, 30 November.
[130] ACC (1987c), Council, Canberra, Minutes, 27 March; ACC (1987e), Council, Scarborough WA, Minutes, 30 May; ACC (1987k), Executive, Minutes, 30 November; ACC (1988a), Executive, Minutes, 11 March & ACC (1988b), Council, Canberra, Minutes, 29-30 March.

the National Farmers' Federation (NFF) was prepared for the 1988 National Wage Case.[131] Indeed the lack of resources was an increasing problem for ACC and it was a crucial factor that would lead just four years later to its merger with the more financially robust CAI. As we will see throughout this chapter, these activities together had an influence on policy change at the political level.

In contrast CAI's senior industrial relations specialist Bryan Noakes publicly opposed the policies being proposed by ACC and the New Right saying "the notion that industrial relations should be a matter for the individual employer and individual employee is ... so far removed from reality that it is a dangerous distraction"[132] and his CAI colleague David Nolan thought decentralisation would only "make matters here worse".[133] CAI described the policy positions as "escapist fantasies"[134] and "zealots on a crusade".[135] Famously Australian Chamber of Manufactures' (the renamed Victorian Chamber of Manufactures) executive director Brian Powell stated that the New Right were showing "truly fascist tendencies that make it harder and harder for us to negotiate change".[136] This prompted an angry trading of insults between Powell and Hay on ABC radio.[137] For its efforts CAI was to receive praise from the Government for their "professionalism" in contrast to groups like

---

[131] ACC (1988c), Council, Canberra, Minutes, 29 July and ACC (1988f), *National Wage Case*, ACC Submission Papers No 1: 1988-1989, Canberra, October.

[132] *The Bulletin*, 8 October 1985.

[133] Ibid.

[134] Milton Cockburn (1986b), "CAI Attacks 'Escapist Fantasies' of New Right", *Sydney Morning Herald*, 21 November.

[135] Ross Gittins (1986), "CAI is Getting Back on Top", *Sydney Morning Herald*, 22 December.

[136] Ibid; *Sydney Morning Herald* (1986), 2 October.

[137] Matthew Moore (1986b), "New Right Hits Back After 'Fascist' Claim", *Sydney Morning Herald*, 3 October; John Stone (1986b), "Why Small Business is Leaving the Club", *Sydney Morning Herald*, 8 October.

What Led to the Australian Settlement 2.0?

the ACC and NFF,[138] a distinct 'reward' for being part of the insider group working closely with government.

The ACC sought cooperation with NFF to establish the Australian Federation of Employers (AFE) in 1986. The ACC Executive resolved that: "The development of a coalition of employer interests in support of Chamber policy is not only highly desirable, but extremely urgent".[139] The resultant AFE was the brainchild of ACC deputy president and Victorian Employers' Chamber of Commerce and Industry president Hay[140] and was a deliberate attempt to promote radical neo-liberal reforms at the expense of the CAI's steady-as-you-go approach. Certainly, CAI saw the AFE as a genuine threat and recognised that it was a reaction to member dissatisfaction with its policies and performance.[141] There was substance to this view because, according to Hay, the organisation's goal was to "establish a campaign for change and to tackle the Confederation of Australian Industry head on".[142] Cheekily, Hay wrote to CAI asking whether they would join,[143] but this was declined.[144]

The AFE's interim committee consisted of the NFF; the Melbourne Chamber of Commerce; Housing Industry Association; Australian Small Business Association; Victorian Automobile Chamber of Commerce; Real Estate Institute of Australia; Australian Chamber of Fruit and Vegetable Industries; and the Australian Society of Orthopaedic Surgeons and first met in Melbourne on 11 April 1986.[145] By 25 June membership had expanded to also

---

[138] McEachern 1991b, 138.
[139] ACC (1986a), Executive, Minutes, 19 March.
[140] ACC 1986b.
[141] CAI (1986a), Executive Committee, Meeting, Sydney, 5 March; CAI (1986c), CAI Industrial Council Meeting, Minutes, 21 March.
[142] Cahill 2004, 172.
[143] CAI (1986d), Letter from AO Hay to KD Williams, 14 April.
[144] CAI (1986e), Letter from KD Williams to AO Hay, 24 April.
[145] CAI 1986d.

include Australian Bus & Coach Association; Australian Courier & Taxi Truck Operators Association; Australian Tourism Industry Association; First National Group of Independent Real Estate Agents Ltd; Life Underwriters Association of Australia; Qld Retail Traders and Shopkeepers Association.[146]

While it was initially focussed on tax reform issues,[147] AFE quickly branched out to examine wider economic issues including, importantly, industrial relations. An AFE conference on 4 June 1986 included prominent neo-liberal economists Ted Sieper of the Australian National University; Cliff Walsh of the University of Adelaide; Michael Porter of Monash University; and Geoff Carmody of ACIL.[148] In 1986 it also made a National Wage Case submission to the Australian Conciliation and Arbitration Commission stating that "It is time to formally abandon the objective of comparative wage justice" and "Enterprise negotiations with different settlements on a company by company basis are the only way in which to allow true flexibility in wage outcomes".[149] While only lasting for around three years AFE made a mark principally by adding to the pressure on CAI to change its policy positions.

*****

The New Right industrial relations agenda also gained traction within the Liberal Party. ACC's industrial relations policy released in May 1986 strongly pushed for enterprise bargaining and a break with the old system of federal arbitration.[150] At the

---

[146] CAI (1986m), 9th Annual General Meeting, Canberra, 28 November.
[147] CAI 1986d.
[148] CAI (1986b), Executive Officers of the CAI Manufacturing Council and the CAI Commerce and Industry Council Meeting, Sydney, Minutes, 5 March.
[149] Australian Federation of Employers (1986), National Wage Case submission to Australian Conciliation and Arbitration Commission, monograph, December 1986, 7.
[150] Wayne Errington and Peter van Onselen (2007), *John Winston Howard*, Melbourne University Press, Melbourne, 135.

same time a favourable attitude towards ACC was indicated in a leaked internal memo titled "Industrial Relations Policy Marketing" from Liberal Party secretariat policy coordinator David Trebeck. In contrast it was noted that there was "some serious disquiet" about CAI because of Noakes' opposition to reform. There was also a list of six prominent businessmen who it was argued needed to be "neutralised".[151] Errington and van Onselen[152] conclude that by and large Liberal Leader Howard was ahead of the business groups on industrial relations, however "The success of [the New Right's] tactics against the unions was pivotal to Howard's ability to make the case for change within the Opposition". In contrast the CAI publicly criticised the Liberal Party policy after its release.[153]

The influence of ACC in Liberal Party policy is confirmed by Leader of the Opposition at the time John Howard who informed me that "We really had quite a radical policy in '87. We led the debate. Absolutely." However, he further stated that "[ACC] certainly argued the case. The farmers argued it and it was around this time that the HR Nicholls [Society] was created. There was those cases, Mudginberri, and there was the state power dispute in Queensland. ... Were these people helpful? Yeah they were helpful. ... My recollection is that the CAI, well it changed its policy in 1991 and that was a recognition that time for change had come. They certainly lagged the debate".[154] So while the Liberals led the debate it can be claimed that the closeness of ACC to them indicated an influential insider status with the party and the distance of the CAI on this particular policy issue. In a domino effect former senior economics adviser to Prime Minister Keating, John Edwards, acknowledged

---

[151] Shaun Carney 1988, 123.
[152] Errington and van Onselen 2007, 108.
[153] Matthew Moore (1987a), "Bosses Warn Over Voluntary Pay Deals", *Sydney Morning Herald*, 2 February 1987.
[154] John Howard interview 2009.

the importance of the support of the Liberal Opposition for tariff cuts and industrial relations reform.[155]

*****

As we have seen, the economic problems of the 1970s and 1980s, operating as an external stimulus to policy development, led to a sea-change in the way many in the business community viewed the way that the Australian nation should be governed. Through its involvement in the wider New Right movement ACC became a driving force in leading this changed sentiment. Despite the limitations of its slim resources ACC was single-minded in advancing a deregulatory agenda in the public arena, including academic publications and an association with a new-liberal think tank.

The changing attitudes in the business community were crucial to the dismantling of the Australian Settlement. Without this it would not have happened. However, it is worth spending a bit of time explaining these wider linkages.

An early marker, only indirectly involving ACC with a contribution from Andrew Hay, was a manifesto *Australia at the Crossroads* published in 1980 proposing comprehensive, top-to-bottom reform. The document was prepared by a group of leading neo-liberal economic and international relations experts, viz, Wolfgang Kasper (University of NSW), Richard Blandy (Flinders University), John Freebairn (La Trobe University), Douglas Hocking (Shell Australia Limited) and Robert O'Neil (Australian National University).[156]

It was argued in *Australia at the Crossroads* that "The longer Australia postpones the necessary reforms, the greater is the prospect

---

[155] John Edwards (1996), *Keating: The Inside Story*, Penguin Books, Melbourne, 168, 177.

[156] W. Kasper, R. Blandy, J. Freebairn, D. Hocking and R. O'Neil (1980), *Australia at the Crossroads: Our choices to the year 2000*, Harcourt Brace Jovanovich Group, Sydney.

of yet another decade of depressed economic conditions".[157] It compared the difference between what was described as "the mercantilist trend" which Australia had followed for its federal history and the "libertarian alternative".[158] In summary the book argued that: "If Australia follows the Mercantilist Trend, we will not only see a continuing inability to cope with some aspects of economic welfare – such as high unemployment, particularly of the young, continued inflation, slow growth in living standards, and a more unequal distribution of income – but also serious failures in meeting the non-economic objectives to which Western societies aspire ... ".[159]

Think tanks such as the Institute of Public Affairs (IPA),[160] the Centre for Independent Studies (CIS), and the Australian Institute for Public Policy (AIPP) became influential players in the ongoing policy debates.[161] ACC had a longstanding relationship with the IPA in advancing pro-business policies. In the mid-1980s this was to switch to the AIPP which was founded in 1983 by John Hyde, an economic 'dry', and was initially funded by Harold Clough from Clough Engineering.[162] (Clough was to be president of ACCI in 1994-95). Subsequently, AIPP merged with IPA in 1991.[163]

ACC took direct action using its publications to take the policy

---

[157] Kasper et al 1980, 93.

[158] Ibid., 93.

[159] Ibid., 211-212.

[160] The IPA was created by the various employer organisations (principally the Chambers of Manufactures) in 1942 as a propaganda arm of the business community to extol the virtues of free enterprise. Robert Menzies was also personally involved in a number of meetings that led to its establishment (Martin 1996, 404-405 & Martin A.W. (1999), *Robert Menzies*, (volume 2), Melbourne University Press, Melbourne, 4-5).

[161] Cahill 2004.

[162] Kelly 1992, 46-47.

[163] John Hyde (2002), *Dry: In Defence of Economic Freedom*, Institute of Public Affairs, Melbourne, 112.

debate into the public arena. In partnership with the AIPP, the ACC continued the effort for reform in another major manifesto released in 1987: *Mandate to Govern: A handbook for the next Australian Government*, edited by John Nurick, editorial director of AIPP.[164] Most of the text was written by Nurick and John Hyde, with acknowledged assistance from Wolfgang Kasper, Brian Buckley, and Steven Carr. Although not acknowledged in the text, the ACC's chief economist Dr Brent Davis also provided research support.

The AIPP began to work on Mandate to Govern in 1985 and was joined by the ACC in 1986.[165] The project was inspired by the work of the Heritage Foundation in Washington which had produced *Mandate for Leadership* and *Mandate II* to successfully lobby for economic reform by the US Administration after Ronald Reagan's 1980 and 1984 election wins.[166] Its neo-liberal agenda is apparent. It argued inter alia to "unleash innovative and productive forces by removing rigidity in labour market and product markets".[167] On industrial relations a key recommendation was to: "Legislate to end compulsory arbitration in the Commonwealth industrial relations jurisdiction, and provide for legally-enforceable contracts of employment negotiated between employers and workers or workers' representatives".[168] And on trade and industry key recommendations include: "The Government should make the popularisation of free trade a major, immediate goal";[169] "Phase out all protection in ten equal steps over five years, starting six months

---

[164] John Nurick (1987) (editor), *Mandate to Govern: A handbook for the next Australian Government*, The Australian Chamber of Commerce and the Australian Institute for Public Policy, Perth.

[165] ACC (1985f), Executive, Minutes, 5 December and ACC 1986b; see also ACC (1986f), Executive, Minutes, 29 October; ACC (1987a), Executive, Minutes, 12 February; ACC (1987b), Executive, Minutes, 26 March & ACC 1987c.

[166] Nurick 1987, xv and Hyde 2002, 118.

[167] Nurick 1987, 5.

[168] Ibid., 48.

[169] Ibid., 134.

from the announcement";[170] "Any deviation from the free trade programme will be a breach of faith with all people who have based their career and investment plans on the programme";[171] "The free trade programme should be accompanied by modest adjustment assistance measures"[172]; and "The Government should identify major non-tariff barriers against imports to Australia, undertake cost-benefit analyses of the most important ones and abolish those that are not justified".[173] It was launched on 16 February 1987.[174] Hyde was to later claim that many of its recommendations were taken up by the Keating Government.[175]

Further evidence of the development of the neo-liberal policy agenda is evident from another manifesto for reform supported by ACC – the *National Economic Priorities 1987, Spending and Taxing: Australian Reform Options* publication. A large proportion of the membership of the CAI also put their names to the document, but ACC was a key member and had a seat on the Board of Trustees.[176] The Board of Trustees was chaired by then chairman of the ANZ Banking Group, Sir William Vines, and a research management group, including Professors John Freebairn, Michael Porter and Cliff Walsh (all of the Centre of Policy Studies, Monash University) and chief economist at the ACC, Brent Davis, which guided the project.[177] There were 25 sponsoring organisations including the ACC, the Australian Mining Industry Council and the

---

[170] Ibid., 136.
[171] Ibid., 137.
[172] Ibid., 138.
[173] Ibid., 139.
[174] ACC 1987b.
[175] Hyde 2002, 228.
[176] ACC (1986e), Executive, Minutes, 1 August; ACC 1986f; ACC 1987a; ACC 1987b; ACC 1987c & ACC (1987d), Executive, Minutes, 6 May.
[177] John Freebairn, Michael Porter and Cliff Walsh (1987) (editors), *National Economic Priorities 1987, Spending and Taxing: Australian Reform Options*, Allen and Unwin, Sydney, 1-3.

BCA. The inaugural meeting including CAI and ACC was held in July 1986.[178]

The CAI, one of the initiators of the project, was concerned about the lack of editorial control and did not lend its name to the final publication.[179] In fact Plowman[180] notes that the Victorian Employers Federation, the Australian Chamber of Manufactures and Metal Trades Industry Association (the latter two merged to create the Australian Industry Group in 1998) threatened to resign their memberships unless the CAI withdrew from the project. Nonetheless six CAI members did sign on, viz: Australian Bankers' Association; the Australian Bus and Coach Association; Australian Chemical Industry Association; the Housing Industry Association; Pharmacy Guild of Australia; and the Victorian Automotive Chamber of Commerce.[181]

The document proposed a number of policies and was presented as "a logical 'next step' beyond the current path to greater competition in financial and product markets. Indeed, there is a sense in which these other liberalisations have placed pressure in two areas in which Australia is highly exposed: – our relatively rigid and restrictive labour markets; and our overexpanded and relatively inefficient public sector".[182]

The National Priorities project followed-up with other publications. ACC again participated in *National Priorities 1988,*

---

[178] ACC 1986e.
[179] CAI (1986f), Executive Committee, Meeting, Melbourne, 14 August; CAI (1986h), CAI Commerce and Industry Council meeting, Minutes, 3 September; CAI (1986i), CAI Manufacturing Council, Minutes, 3 September; CAI 1986k; CAI (1986j), Executive Committee, Meeting, Canberra, 26 November & CAI (1986L), Special General Meeting, Canberra, 28 November.
[180] David Plowman (1987a) "Economic Forces and the New Right: Employer Matters in 1986", *The Journal of Industrial Relations*, Vol 29, No 1, 87.
[181] Freebairn et al 1987, 283.
[182] Ibid., 5.

Spending and Taxing II: Taking Stock, as did CAI members noted above (except for the Australian Bus and Coach Association).[183] This volume revisited the same themes as the earlier work. It also focussed on proposals to reform tertiary education and improving the performance of public enterprises.[184]

Lastly a third book in the series was published in 1989 entitled, *National Priorities 1989, Savings and Productivity: Incentives for the 1990s*. By this time ACC, like the CAI before, had dropped out over concerns about editorial control.[185] However, CAI members Australian Chemical Industry Association; Pharmacy Guild of Australia; and the Victorian Automobile Chamber of Commerce continued to participate. Again similar themes were explored and expanded on. In this edition the *National Priorities* project looks more closely at industrial relations reforms and suggests greater use of contracting and enterprise level bargaining.[186]

Other key groups were also involved in the New Right movement of 1986-1988. The NFF led by then president Ian McLachlan was a principal participant and the HR Nicholls Society was particularly important in bringing together a number of like-minded individuals such as founding members John Stone, Peter Costello and Andrew Hay. Behind the scenes there was also significant support from substantial business figures such as Hugh Morgan at Western Mining. For example Hay is reported as noting that Morgan was "strongly supportive of the Chamber of Commerce and the things

---

[183] John Freebairn, Michael Porter and Cliff Walsh (1988) (editors), *National Priorities 1988, Spending and Taxing II: Taking Stock*, Allen and Unwin, Sydney, 205; see also ACC 1987e; ACC (1987g), Executive, Minutes, 25 June and ACC 1987j.
[184] Freebairn et al 1988, 2-3.
[185] ACC 1988a.
[186] John Freebairn, Michael Porter and Cliff Walsh (1989) (editors), *National Priorities 1989, Savings and Productivity: Incentives for the 1990s*, Allen and Unwin, Sydney, 73.

it was doing".[187] Other participants in the New Right movement were Charles Copeman, Padriac McGuiness, Greg Sheridan, Des Keegan, John Leard, Gerard Henderson, and Geoffrey Blainey.[188]

As Ian McLachlan[189], then NFF president and later Howard Government minister, noted for this study: "So this group, with Hay and Cullen – I didn't know Cullen so well, but I knew of him – and don't forget Ken Court, he was important, he was from a mining company, and so we [the NFF] were absolutely in lock step with them on protectionism. ... Then Andrew Hay became their leader, he was also maniacal. He was on our side. But I suppose we were all maniacal." Gerard Henderson[190] also noted at the time "the vitally important role that would be played in the industrial relations debate by the National Farmers' Federation, the Australian Chamber of Commerce, and the various small business organisations".

Business argues for tariff reform

Difficult economic circumstances during the first half of the 1980s had an impact on government tariff policy. Economic indicators such as the rates of unemployment and inflation remained stubbornly high. For example after inflation fell to a low of just over 5 per cent in December 1984 it had climbed back to nearly 10 per cent by mid-1987; and in the same period the unemployment rate had only shaved off 2 percentage points from the depths of the recent Recession and was stuck at around 8 percent. The household savings ratio was on a relentless long term decline; as was the terms of trade; foreign debt was rapidly rising; interest rates were consistently above 10 percent with some indexes above 20 percent; and industrial dis-

---
[187] Cahill 2004, 174.
[188] McEachern 1991a, 50-51.
[189] Ian McLachlan, (president NFF; Member of the House of Representatives; Shadow Minister; Cabinet Minister) Interview with author on 24 June 2009.
[190] Gerard Henderson (1986), "Trade Union Chaos: Blame the Fridge Dwellers", *Sydney Morning Herald*, 30 September 1986.

putation remained at historically high levels.[191] In a search for solutions the Government was increasingly swayed by the arguments for a radical change in direction that would rely on a comprehensive program of de-regulation, privatisation and increased resort to "market-based" solutions (ie the neo-liberal agenda).

A watershed event for the Government was Treasurer Paul Keating's warnings on 14 May 1986 that if Australia did not confront these issues head-on it risked becoming a "Banana Republic". The solution, according to the Treasurer, was "an internal economic adjustment" to "get manufacturing going again and keep moderate wage outcomes".[192]

As part of the solution ACC argued "against industry protectionism".[193] Similar statements and related anti-protectionist arguments were repeated often including two detailed papers: *International Trade Policy*[194] and *Protection: An Economic Millstone.*[195]

And they were getting a sympathetic ear. Prime Minister Hawke had, as ACTU president, been a member of both the Jackson and Crawford Committees and had subscribed to reductions in protection.[196] He and Treasurer Keating were to "grasp the nettle" on this issue and in two bold moves essentially ended the previous policy of tariff protection as the mainstay of national industry policy.

The May 1988 *Economic Statement* released by Treasurer Keating announced general reductions in tariffs to levels of assistance of around 10-15 per cent by July 1992. PMV and TCF were not

---

[191] David Clark (1995), *AFR & Commonwealth Bank Economic Update* 9th Edition, Financial Review Library, Sydney, 10, 11, 13, 20, 26, 35.

[192] Reprinted in Snape, Gropp and Luttrell 1998, 84.

[193] ACC 1987a.

[194] ACC (1986h), *International Trade Policy*, Occasional Papers in Commerce, Vol 1, Canberra.

[195] ACC (1988e), *Protection: An Economic Millstone*, Agenda for Reform No 1, Canberra, October.

[196] Snape, Gropp and Luttrell 1998, 28-33.

included[197] (see Snape, Gropp and Luttrell 1998, 85-87). In 1991 Prime Minister Hawke released the Government's second policy document, *Building a Competitive Australia* in 1991(see below).

The still protectionist CAI opposed the May 1988 cuts.[198] However, this was to change. For example, by 1990 the ACC's "Industry Policy" no longer made any references to protection but instead stated that "interventionist and deterministic industry policy stances have been and remain an impediment, not an answer, to structural adjustment".[199]

The Hawke Government intensified its push for lower tariffs after the 1988 May Economic Statement. In 1989 a report commissioned by the Government and written by Prime Minister Hawke's former economic advisor, Professor Ross Garnaut, titled *Australia and the Northeast Asian Ascendancy* argued for the removal of all protection by the year 2000.[200] In the same year the Government passed the *Industry Commission Act* and the IAC became the Industry Commission (IC) with expanded scope for conducting inquiries.

The case for lower protection had also won adherents in the Opposition. In a dramatic gesture on 15 August 1990 the John Hewson-led Liberal-National Party Coalition called for the implementation of "negligible" (i.e., 0-5 per cent) tariffs for all sectors. Like Labor, the Liberals had abandoned protectionism and indeed "argued for a faster and more comprehensive shift to freer trade".[201]

The various influences on the Opposition at the time explain

---

[197] See Snape, Gropp and Luttrell 1998, 85-87.
[198] CAI (1988b), National Manufacturing and Commerce Council, Minutes, 18 March & CAI (1988c), National Manufacturing and Commerce Council, Minutes, 9 June.
[199] ACC (1990), Council, Perth, Minutes, 9 July.
[200] Reprinted in Snape, Gropp and Luttrell 1998, 90.
[201] Conley and O'Connor 2004, 140.

this decision and indicate the effectiveness of the pro-free trade lobby within the business community. Lisa Gropp,[202] who was at the time senior policy advisor to Ian McLachlan, the then Shadow Minister for Industry, noted that: "Over the years, the main body [influencing the Coalition views on tariffs] I remember was the NFF [National Farmers' Federation] with David Trebeck and Andrew Robb, being influential on industrial relations and also when they turned around on tariffs that became a real force for change. ... The turning of the agricultural lobby was very important. ... I remember Andrew Hay and more indirectly the ACC. We used to always cite them. There was that document *Mandate to Govern*. They were important as being out there arguing the case for reduced protection. But specifically on the zero tariffs, it was principally Hewson acting alone. In fact my memory is that we might have been a bit surprised about it. It was Hewson and [shadow Treasurer Peter] Reith who were pushing for zero tariffs rather than it necessarily being initiated by us. Not that we opposed it".

Ian Grigg,[203] chief executive of the Federal Chamber of Automotive Industries during this period also recollects that the NFF were more effective than other groups in arguing against tariff protection and noted that "ACC was more careful on tariffs". Greg Evans, a former senior policy adviser to John Moore, another Shadow Minister for Industry during the 1990s, agreed that: "In fact in those days the National Farmers' Federation actually took a lead on a lot of policy reform which were not necessarily agricultural specific in terms of economic reform, like industrial relations, broader issues

---

[202] Lisa Gropp (Federal Opposition staffer; Senior Executive Productivity Commission) Interview with author on 23 June 2009.
[203] Ian Grigg (Senior Advisor to Treasurer Harold Holt; Principal Private Secretary to Prime Minister William McMahon; First Assistant Secretary Department of Prime Minister & Cabinet; CEO Federal Chamber of Automotive Industries)Interview with author on 22 June 2009.

in terms of tax reform and free trade".[204] Although former Cabinet Minister John Kerin believes that as a general observation "I think [the NFF] were just noisier. They were not as polite as the BCAs or the other manufacturing industry groups".[205]

The formal end of the 90 year bipartisan policy of protectionism came when Prime Minister Hawke released *Building a Competitive Australia* on 12 March 1991. It detailed the second phase of tariff cuts from general level of assistance of 10-15 per cent to 5 per cent by 1996, although PMV and TCF remained at substantially higher tariff levels.[206] In his memoirs former Minister for Industry John Button[207] noted that "I and the government were fortunate that the reborn opposition did not, between 1983 and 1993, oppose reductions in protection. If they had, in the climate of the time, we would have been hard pressed to remain in government".

The Prime Minister's view on this policy and a range of other influences, including competing business interests represented by ACC and BCA, made it very difficult for the CAI to maintain its support for continued protection if it was to remain a major player. Hawke recounts that he had formed his anti-protectionist views during his participation in the Jackson and Crawford Committee reviews and that "I aimed to do something about it from the very beginning".[208] Other factors also had an impact. As well as the domestic debate and the work of the Industries Assistance Commission,

---

[204] Greg Evans (Staffer for Federal Opposition; Treasury Officer; Chief of Staff for Federal Minister; Policy Director ACCI) Interview with author on 24 June 2009.

[205] John Kerin (Member of the House of Representatives; Cabinet Minister; Federal Treasurer) Interview with author on 29 June 2009.

[206] Reprinted in Snape, Gropp, and Luttrell 1998, 94-96.

[207] John Button (1998), *John Button: As it Happened*, The Text Publishing Company, Melbourne, 264.

[208] Bob Hawke (1994), *The Hawke Memoirs*, William Heinemann Australia, Melbourne, 166.

"increasingly overseas ministers and industrialists visiting Australia came to have an impact on government thinking" on protection.[209] Button's ministerial colleague at the time, John Kerin, noted for this study "The work of the Industry Assistance Commission or the Industry Commission was clearly showing us [protection] was just not working. ... The whole intellectual community, intellectual environment had changed about this thing".[210]

At the margins the business groups also played their role in influencing the Government. According to my correspondence with Dennis Richardson, who was Prime Minister Hawke's chief of staff in 1991, the freer-trade positions of ACC and BCA were helpful in deciding on the watershed March 1991 long-term tariff reduction schedule.[211] And John Edwards, economic adviser to then Treasurer Paul Keating, notes that "Paul's views were very much changed by his time in mining, as shadow mining and then briefly as mining minister in the Whitlam Government, and the mining industry always wanted zero tariffs and Paul absorbed that".[212]

In the lead-up to the Government statement and as a "last gasp" of its protectionist past, CAI prepared a submission seeking a "postponement of further Tariff protection reductions beyond 1992 at the 10 and 15% levels pending progress in correcting major impediments to Australian competitiveness".[213] They were concerned about "a danger of adjustment 'burnout'".[214] However, in the end

---

[209] Button 1998, 264.
[210] John Kerin interview 2009.
[211] Dennis Richardson (Chief of Staff for Prime Minister Hawke; Ambassador to the United States; Secretary Department of Foreign Affairs and Trade) Correspondence with author on 27 June 2009.
[212] John Edwards (financial journalist; economics advisor to Prime Minister Paul Keating; Chief Economist HSBC) Interview with author on 3 June 2010.
[213] CAI (1991a), General Council, Agenda and Background Notes, Sydney, 21-22 March, 361.
[214] CAI 1991a, 375.

they welcomed the statement noting a package of accompanying microeconomic reforms, but thought more needed to be done on reforming transport, the waterfront and industrial relations in particular "if tariff reductions are not to lead to deepening recession".[215] The realistic view that the protectionist cause had been lost is evident from a statement the following March by (future ACCI president 1993-1995) Harold Clough, who noted that "the day of tariff protection was basically over, and that support for one sector of industry meant that other sectors were penalised". It was his view that "CAI should oppose Government assistance as much as possible".[216]

The Government's support for a low tariff regime expressed in the context of its external trade relations also had an impact on CAI policy. For example, the Hawke-Keating Governments strongly supported the GATT Uruguay Round of trade protection reductions and the establishment of the World Trade Organisation (WTO) in 1994. In the early 1980s CAI remained sceptical about GATT negotiations but gradually participated more enthusiastically in negotiations.[217] By 1987 the fact that they had moved a considerable way from their past policies facilitated its consultative relationship with the Government. For example, at its meeting on 6 March 1987 the CAI Manufacturing Council discussed the latest round of multilateral tariff negotiations and it was noted that CAI had been in close consultation with Government ministers on the subject. The Council agreed that "CAI policy towards the negotiations

---

[215] CAI (1991b), General Council, Agenda and Background Notes, Adelaide, 18-19 July, 13-14.

[216] CAI (1992), General Council, Agenda and Background Notes, Brisbane, 16-17 July, 6.

[217] CAI (1983e), Chief Executive Officers of the CAI Trade Council Meeting, Sydney, Minutes, 7 September; CAI (1983g), Chief Executive Officers of the CAI Trade Council Meeting, Canberra, Minutes, 30 November; CAI (1984a), Chief Executive Officers of the CAI Trade Council Meeting, Sydney, Minutes, 7 March & CAI (1985b), Officers of the CAI Manufacturing Council and the CAI Commerce and Industry Council Meeting, Sydney, Minutes, 10 September.

should incorporate the following elements: – acceptance of gradual tariff reform – comprehensive consultation with affected industries before decisions are taken, and – maximum credit is obtained for the significant tariff reductions which have taken place in recent years".[218] By the time of the creation of ACCI this was to change to more enthusiastic support.

Business changes industrial relations policy

However, reform was moving a lot slower in the area of industrial relations.

The Government's principle point of negotiation on industrial relations remained its Accord with the trade union movement, where the original agreement on a fully centralised wage-fixing system was gradually amended to include a form of enterprise-based bargaining. The impact can be seen on CAI's response, which by January 1990 had reached a half-way-house to more radical reform of the industrial relations system. This is evident in a public statement by CAI Chief Executive, Ian Spicer, that: "CAI supports increased flexibility through collectively bargained agreements provided that it is in a form which ensures some control by the Industrial Relations Commission over aggregate labour cost outcomes".[219]

Developments in the nature of the membership of the peak business associations and probably more importantly the impact of external economic factors now came to the fore in influencing the CAI's policy on industrial relations. As we will see below, the subsequent decision by the CAI to change its policy on centralised wage-fixing, and its subsequent lobbying of the Opposition, federal parliamentarians, key public servants and academics, as well as discussions with the BCA, NFF, Metal Trades Industries Association and the Australian Chamber of Manufactures created

---

[218] CAI (1987b), CAI Manufacturing Council, Minutes, 6 March.
[219] CAI (1990a), Executive Committee, Minutes, Melbourne, 6 February.

a broad-based business policy community that was influential in persuading the AIRC to change its mind.

Through the course of 1990 CAI debated at its General Council meetings the prospect of a new industrial relations policy and at the August 1990 meeting a new draft policy formed the basis of discussions which overturned decades of policy support for conciliation and arbitration.[220] The paper argued for enterprise bargaining; the ability to also negotiate at the individual level; freedom of choice for employers and employees to negotiate the way they wanted, including as an alternative to the award system; and a dramatic minimisation of the role of third party tribunals.[221] It was debated thoroughly over the course of the next 11 months before it was finally agreed, but the substantive proposals did not change.

Indeed the year 1991 was a seminal year for the wider employer movement in terms of industrial relations policy. At the General Council meeting on 18-19 July 1991 CAI[222] turned on its head its long-held views on a centralised system with its adoption of a major new direction that was "designed to take Australia into the 21st century". The principal elements of the policy were:

- A rationalisation of the federal and state systems of industrial relations so as to produce one set of legislative obligations and one statutory tribunal.

- An abandonment of compulsory conciliation and arbitration except in certain defined circumstances (eg essential services and individual grievances).

- A greater emphasis on enterprise level industrial relations.

---
[220] CAI (1990b), General Council, Agenda and Background Notes, Perth, 9-10 August.
[221] Ibid.
[222] CAI 1991b.

- A greater freedom for employers and employees to make their own agreements.
- Freedom of choice for employees in respect of representation arrangements.

Spicer[223] has said that the impetus for the change came from Western Australia, principally the Confederation of Western Australian Industry. This reflected a strong influence from the mining company community (a similar observation can be made about the BCA debates on industrial relations policy).[224]

CAI declared that it "now [had] the most advanced policy of any employer group or political party, and will be able to exert a strong influence on the direction of change". CAI chief executive Spicer[225] recalled this was a "thunderclap" through the organisation and he then went to see the then Shadow Minister for Industrial Relations, John Howard, to inform him of this very significant change. Henderson[226] said the CAI decision "is akin to, say, the Roman Catholic Archbishop of Sydney announcing that he would no longer follow the directives of the Vatican".

As CAI's Bryan Noakes has said: "Perhaps surprisingly, this change did not meet with significant opposition within the CAI membership. We had done a pretty good job over the years in educating the members, especially at executive officers' meetings".[227]

During the same period the ACTU had adopted the "enterprise bargaining" rhetoric of the employer groups and the Liberal Party. However, while they appreciated the need for greater flexibility in agreement making they were concerned to restrict any increase in

---

[223] Ian Spicer interview with author 2004.
[224] Bell 2006b, 554.
[225] Ian Spicer interview with author 6 September 2004.
[226] Gerard Henderson (1991b), "Our Economic Past Imperfect Needs More than Hindsight", *Sydney Morning Herald*, 30 July.
[227] Campbell 1996, 198.

bargaining between employers and individuals and they wanted to heavily bias any new system to union dominated collective agreements. This was negotiated with the Government in the form of Accord Mark VI.

The influence of the commission on Government policy was evident when in April 1991, in worsening economic conditions and in opposition to the Accord partners (i.e., the Hawke Government and the ACTU), the Australian Industrial Relations Commission (AIRC) rejected Accord Mark VI and deferred a decision on the future scope for "enterprise bargaining". The AIRC was not yet prepared to surrender its central role in wage setting.[228] The ACTU described the decision as "unjust, flawed and unworkable" and verbally abused and denigrated the AIRC with the ACTU secretary, Bill Kelty, variously calling the decision "a rotten egg" and "vomit" and compared AIRC president Mr Justice Barry Maddern to Fidel Castro, while the CAI described it as "a victory for employers and a defeat for the ACTU and the government" as it had stopped what they considered a flawed model of enterprise bargaining.[229] Noakes has previously acknowledged that "this decision and the ACTU and government's rejection of it were the catalysts which allowed CAI to get the policy change through our organisation".[230]

Subsequently in a decision on 30 October 1991 the AIRC very reluctantly agreed to endorse enterprise bargaining given the array of interests of the various industrial parties.[231]

Business groups consolidate their voice for reform
In 1991, the economic situation and the pre-eminence of the Accord partnership in defining industrial relations policy encouraged

---
[228] Dabscheck 1994, 158 & 2004, 396-397; Singleton 1997a, 65.
[229] CAI 1991b.
[230] Campbell 1996, 203.
[231] Dabscheck 2001, 282.

the merger of CAI and ACC. According to Spicer[232] the parlous economic conditions of the day demanded that "we needed to do better in terms of presenting views from the business community" and after many years of the Accord between the Government and the ACTU "to some extent the business community found itself dealt out of that environment in which they could have as much influence as they thought was appropriate. So it's the circumstances, the pressures, the concerns, that we are not really getting our message across and not being able to influence policy makers to the extent we should – it is those circumstances that bring people together to say 'how can we do it better'?"

Importantly, policy issues figured in the merger negotiations. While it is clear from the foregoing discussion in this study that the two organisations had met on industrial relations policy, the more neo-liberal ACC could have possibly made industry policy (and tariff protection) a stumbling block. Nonetheless in a policy audit undertaken by the ACC chief economist, Brent Davis, it was concluded that "there are few, if any, real differences in the general substance of the policies of the two organisations" and that "a straightforward way of describing any policy differences would be to say they are 'slight shades of grey', most of which would disappear quite easily in any robust program of policy integration" (ACC 1992c). As to the specific policies of interest in this study, it was concluded that: "Finally, it should be pointed out the differences on industrial relations and industry policy which have existed in the past have largely disappeared, with the remaining differences being largely confined to questions of sequencing and timing rather than fundamental objective. As a general statement, one could reasonably say there are few, if any, policy differences which would impede any merger of the two bodies, with development of any

---

[232] Ian Spicer, Interviewed by Peter Anderson at *Captains of Industry* book launch on 4 December 2008 and found at www.acci.asn.au

comprehensive and integrated policy compendium for any new body being much easier to achieve than many may well think".[233]

CAI had the same view. Spicer notes:

> ... by the time of the merger the issue of free-trade versus tariff policy was possibly talked about, but it was not an area of significant debate between the organisations at all. This was a reflection of the lessening of the importance of the manufacturing sector within [CAI]. That debate was not pushed within the organisation. In fact it had really just run into the sand.[234]

*****

The inaugural General Council meeting of the new ACCI on 19-20 November 1992[235] immediately turned to synthesising the key policies. Firstly, the tariff policy was clarified in the general *Economic Policy*, and the *Industry and Trade Policy*. After vigorous discussion (with the South Australian Employers' Chamber of Commerce & Industry typically urging caution) the Council adopted a relatively free-trade position evident from the *Economic Policy* which stated that: "Protectionist measures must be removed at a pace and in an environment in which these lower protection levels produce positive benefits to the Australian economy"[236] and, more specifically, a statement in the *Industry and Trade Policy* that: "ACCI does not accept the premise of the Garnaut Report that tariffs should automatically wind down to zero by the year 2000. However, ACCI supports a continued and phased wind back of tariff assistance

---

[233] ACCI (1992a), Executive Committee meeting, minutes, Canberra, 18 November.
[234] Ian Spicer interview with author 18 June 2009.
[235] ACCI (1992b), 1st General Council, Background Notes, Canberra, 19-20 November.
[236] ACCI 1992b, 106-115 & ACCI (1993), 2nd General Council, Background Notes, Sydney, 18-19 March, 16.

but within a time frame consistent with the necessary economic management parameters, micro-economic reforms, and efficient and competitive regulatory and taxation environment referred to in other parts of this policy". Also it stated that "ACCI's support for continuing tariff reductions is also contingent on: – phase out of inappropriate elements of developing country preference scheme and anti-dumping arrangements in Australia; – clear and decisive steps being taken to remove other forms of international protection (particularly non-tariff barriers)".[237]

External policy debates in favour of freer-trade continued in this period with the Bogor Declaration in November 1994 which committed Asia Pacific Economic Cooperation (APEC) nations to a future free-trade area with developed countries committing to removing all trade barriers by 2010 and developing countries by 2020. This was heavily pushed by Prime Minister Keating who lorded it as "an absolute triumph".[238] Although expressing scepticism that it would be implemented ACCI supported the comprehensive nature of the agreement and argued that cuts in protection should be "front-loaded" (ie implemented earlier than the agreed timetable).[239] This is the clearest indication that the new entity, ACCI, was firmly against the protectionist policy that was

---

[237] ACCI 1992b, 134-135 and ACCI 1993, 17-18; also see further support for lower protection during the 1990s referred to in ACCI (1992c), *The Employer*, No 45, Melbourne, December; ACCI (1994a), *A Competitive Industry Strategy for Australia*, submission presented to the Minister for Industry, Technology and Regional Development, Melbourne, March; ACCI (1994d), *ACCI Review*, No 8, Melbourne, December 1994/January 1995, 6-9; ACCI (1996), *ACCI Review*, No 26, Melbourne, December, 10-12; ACCI (1997a), *ACCI Review*, No 27, Melbourne, February, 6-7; ACCI (1997b), *ACCI Review*, No 28, Melbourne, March, 1-3 and 9-12; ACCI (1997c), *ACCI Review*, No 33, Melbourne, September, 1-3; ACCI (1998), *ACCI Review*, No 44, Melbourne, September, 1-3 and ACCI (1999), *ACCI Review*, No 50, Melbourne, April, 1-2.
[238] Conley and O'Connor 2004, 148.
[239] ACCI (1995d), *ACCI Review*, No 16, Melbourne, October, 1-3.

the basis of the Australian Settlement. In the event, the 2010 Bogor deadline was not reached by signatories and there is little prospect that the 2020 deadline will be reached either.

*****

As to industrial relations, the almost identical pro-deregulation policies of both ACC and CAI made the synthesis quite straightforward and the comprehensive July 1991 CAI policy was adopted by the new organisation.[240] This has subsequently remained the policy of ACCI.

ACCI maintained its contacts with the Opposition on the industrial relations policy discussed above. In October 1992 the Liberal and National Parties released the most radical industrial relations policy ever produced by a main political party in Australia – the *JobsBack* policy. ACCI claimed that it had a major influence in its drafting,[241] which substituted the previously proposed "opt out" from federal arbitration with a proposal requiring employers and employees to mutually agree to "opt in" to federal arbitration. There is some support for this view of history from John Howard who told me that: "My strong recollection is that the people who shared our world view about IR were the farmers and the miners and to some extent the Chamber of Commerce and small business. The MTIA remained very agnostic on the whole thing and the CAI until 1991. They did have a big change in policy in '91, there is no doubt about that".[242]

Direct action was also undertaken by the ACCI to push for a watering down of the powers of the AIRC in favour of a substantial move toward enterprise bargaining.[243]

---

[240] ACCI 1992b, 220-227 & ACCI 1993, 19-20.
[241] ACCI 1993.
[242] John Howard interview 2009.
[243] ACCI (1994c), *ACCI Review*, No 5, Melbourne, September, 1-4; ACCI

It is evident that the business community, despite its distance from the Government on industrial relations issues, did have an indirect influence on policy because of concerns by the union movement and the Labor Government about what the Coalition would do in terms of the business community's deregulatory policies, if it won government. Paul Keating replaced Bob Hawke as Prime Minister on 19 December 1991 and in his first term he changed little of the industrial relations environment. However, according to his economic advisor of the time, John Edwards, after his unexpected win in 1993 election, the Government knew that they needed to tackle industrial relations reform.[244] Edwards' comments are illuminating because while stating that the direct influence of employer groups was virtually nil on enterprise bargaining – "I don't think we were interested in what they had to say" – he does concede that in other ways that the New Right push was critical. He notes that the Government's motivation "was the realisation that we might have won in 1993 but we were unlikely to win next time and if we didn't win the Libs, influenced by this change in view on the arbitration system, then the Libs would destroy the trade union movement. So the idea was to bring in a system that would bring in sustainable survival on our terms or lose the lot. That was [the ACTU's] Kelty's point of view and that was [the ACTU's] Iain Ross's point of view. And that was how we were able to do things like enterprise bargaining". An indirect influence of business on this decision is evident from his comment that, "employer federations had zero influence except we knew that they were out there and if we didn't get it straightened out when they got in they would do it their way. It is a very powerful influence. It is quite possible that in the Department of Industrial

---

1994d, 5-6; ACCI (1995a), *ACCI Review*, No 9, Melbourne, February, 1-2 & ACCI (1995b), *ACCI Review*, No 10, Melbourne, March, 4-6.
[244] John Edwards interview 2010.

Relations they were talking to the employers and no doubt they were."[245]

The policy outcome implemented by the Government, however, did not meet the full expectations of the business community. Although ACCI welcomed a landmark speech that Prime Minister Keating gave on 19 April 1993 as essentially a restatement of ACCI policy[246], they were very disappointed with the Government's subsequent amendments to the *Industrial Relations Act*, publicly stating that "while very little of what ACCI asked for was achieved, a number of significant steps were taken which ACCI strongly opposed"[247] such as the substantial weakening of the secondary boycott provisions. However ACCI did acknowledge that there were some changes in the direction of more enterprise bargaining[248] and they were pleased with the Government's announcement in June 1995 that it would ease the regulatory burden of the unfair dismissals regime.[249] It would also be true to say that while the changes implemented by the Keating Government were a long way short of what business groups sought, they were nevertheless a fundamental acknowledgement that enterprise bargaining was a legitimate and mainstream alternative to centralised wage fixing and removed the AIRC from the "apex" of the system.[250]

But it was not the end of the Australian Settlement, as the Keating Government – despite its rhetoric – did not dismantle a key plank, namely the centralised wage fixing system. That final hurdle occurred with the Howard Government.

---

[245] Ibid.
[246] ACCI 1994c, 1; see also Willox, Innes; and Gettler, Leon (1993), "PM to Push Work Reforms", *The Age*, 21 April.
[247] ACCI 1994c, 2.
[248] ACCI (1994b), *ACCI Review*, Vol 1, No 1, Melbourne, May, 7-8 and 10-11 and ACCI 1994c, 2.
[249] ACCI (1995c), *ACCI Review*, No 13, Melbourne, June, 1-2.
[250] Dabscheck 2001, 282-284; see also Barry and Wailes 2004, 438.

So in conclusion, the business community's close links with the Liberal Party continued to be an impediment to its relationship with the Hawke-Keating Governments because during that whole period CAI was considered "close" to the Party.[251] Spicer[252] verified the links between CAI/ACCI and the Liberal Party during 1990-1993:

> We established at the officer level, my level, regular meetings with the Opposition parties, with the Coalition. With John Hewson and some of his senior shadow cabinet ministers. We met with them and talked about a whole range of policy issues, the same way we talked to the Government on a whole range of policy issues. It was quite a good relationship with him and the others. *Fightback!* [the Coalition election manifesto] was not shown to me officially in the drafting but one might have seen some of the issues we had raised in it.

The business group obviously considered its insider status with the Liberals was of higher long term value than trying to become a close insider with the Labor Government.

Indeed, I should note in passing that I was personally heavily involved in writing the *Fightback!* manifesto. It was a magnificent policy document. Unfortunately as a political document it was a disaster that helped John Hewson lose the unloseable election in 1993. Nevertheless, Hewson deserves an enormous amount of credit for producing it. It is a fantastic legacy not least because it formed the blueprint for reform over the next 20 years as it was gradually implemented by the Keating and Howard Governments.

Finally, in summary, a survey of the key influential stakeholders on economic policy during the Hawke-Keating Government

---

[251] John Wanna (1992c), "Furthering Business Interests: Business Associations and Political Representation", in Bell and Wanna 1992, 74.
[252] Ian Spicer interview 2007.

era Goldfinch[253] found that the key personal influencers were overwhelmingly bureaucrats themselves plus a small number of politicians, in particular Prime Ministers Hawke and Keating, and ACTU officials, with no businessmen or lobby groups officials on the list. At 7th place the BCA was the only business group mentioned in a more narrowly defined list of the "top ten institutions" that had influence.[254] However, the value of this analysis may be limited for the purposes of this study as Goldfinch himself questions his findings regarding the lack of direct business input into the policies examined and notes that this "does not mean that business, or at least certain sections of business, did not exert a considerable indirect influence on the direction of economic policy-making".[255]

The Howard Government (1996-2007)

By the time of the election of the Howard Government on 2 March 1996 the Australian Settlement and the 90 year plus implementation of New Protection was dying, but not yet dead. The federal centralised wage fixing system was still strong and there were still some lingering tariff protection measures that had to be finally dealt with. Importantly, the principle of enterprise bargaining (if not implemented) had been accepted as a bipartisan policy. However, the Howard Government was crucial in "locking-in" the demise of the Australian Settlement. It comprehensively implemented enterprise bargaining[256] and went a long way in dismantling the centralised wage fixing system.

In one of its first acts the Howard Government established a National Commission of Audit to set the parameters of a reform

---

[253] Goldfinch 1999.
[254] Ibid., 5.
[255] Ibid., 16.
[256] Sheldon, Peter and Thornthwaite, Louise (1999c) (eds) *Employer Associations and Industrial Change, Catalysts or Captives?*, Allen & Unwin, Sydney, 2.

agenda. As would be expected, the Commission's 1996 Report recommended a strongly neo-liberal approach to further reduce any industry assistance and promote the full implementation of competition policy.[257]

There was now a relatively new bipartisan policy of the two major political parties viz a pragmatic support for freer trade – acknowledging the political and structural concerns about the pace of change on the wider manufacturing sector; and the PMV and TCF industries in particular. However, the Howard Government was far from perfect in the eyes of free traders. Early in the term the Industry Commission released its report *Review of Passenger Motor Vehicle Assistance* in 1996-1997 which recommended reductions in assistance. In reply to the Commission the Howard Government announced in 1997 a five year freeze on the tariff reductions schedule for PMV and TCF until 2005.[258]

Nonetheless to suggest that the Howard Government was some kind of throwback to the protectionist past as suggested by Kelly[259] is wide of the mark. As Conley and O'Connor[260] note: "The Coalition Government has consolidated the shift to freer trade. There has been no policy reversal, despite the growing anti-globalisation sentiment". For example, the Howard Government passed the *Productivity Commission Act* and the Industry Commission became the Productivity Commission in April 1998. It also supported the WTO Doha Development Round of trade negotiations and between 2000 and 2007 the Government signed free-trade agreements with Singapore; Thailand; United States and began negotiations with

---

[257] Commonwealth of Australia (1996), *National Commission of Audit*, monograph, Canberra.
[258] Conley and O'Connor 2004, 149.
[259] Paul Kelly (2009), *The March of Patriots, the struggle for modern Australia*, Melbourne University Press, Melbourne, 405-407.
[260] Conley and O'Connor 2004, 141.

China; Japan; Malaysia; ASEAN; the Gulf Cooperation Council; Chile; India; Indonesia and South Korea.

On industrial relations the Howard years resulted in an acceleration of change.[261] It is interesting to note that in the lead-up to the 1996 election Shadow Minister for Industrial Relations (and subsequent Minister), Peter Reith, who drafted the Coalition's industrial relations policy, recalls that neither ACCI nor any other business group (including the BCA) had any direct input into this process.[262] John Howard[263] recalls that the policy in 1996 was principally a variation of the "opt out" policy that had been formulated in 1986 and taken to the 1987 and 1990 elections (the *JobsBack* policy of 1993 having been shelved as too radical).

In 1996-1997 the Howard Government introduced the *Workplace Relations Act* severely weakening the power of the AIRC to arbitrate and creating alternative bargaining options such as Australian Workplace Agreements between employers and individual workers which were regulated by a new (rival) institution, the Office of the Employment Advocate.

In doing so, one commentator[264] observed that the new industrial environment was one dominated by a new "Workplace Relations Club" in lieu of the old "Club". This was made up of ACCI, the BCA, other employer groups, the Howard Government and its appointees to the AIRC, who sought out the "systematic individualisation" of the system and an approach of "employer adversarialism",[265] effectively a neo-liberal agenda. As another

---

[261] Dabscheck 2001, 278.
[262] Peter Reith, (Member of the House of Representatives; Shadow Minister; Deputy Leader of the Federal Opposition; Cabinet Minister) Correspondence with author on 18 June 2009.
[263] John Howard interview 2009.
[264] Peter Sheldon and Louise Thornthwaite (2001), "Employer Matters in 2000", *The Journal of Industrial Relations*, Vol 43, No 2, June 2001, 219.
[265] Ibid., 221.

commentator[266] has noted "by any yardstick one cares to apply, employer organisations were enormously successful in 2005 in getting the federal government to adopt the reforms to industrial relations they had long advocated".[267]

The industrial relations system changes were dramatic. In 1990 approximately 80 percent of employees were covered by federal awards. By 2000 awards only accounted for 23.2 per cent and that after adding registered collective agreements (35.2 percent) this left more than 40 per cent of employees covered by individual agreements, mostly in the form of common law contracts outside the award system.[268] In 2005 Howard Government introduced the *WorkChoices Act* which further substantially weakened the power of the AIRC.[269]

Of course there are many other policies implemented by the Howard Government that formed part of the neo-liberal agenda. They included a long list of privatisations of government business enterprises, culminating in the sale of Telstra towards the end of the government. Importantly the introduction of a new tax system with the creation of the goods and services tax (GST) was monumentally important. This was announced prior to the 1998 Federal election. Howard was able to win that (just) and the GST started in the year 2000. This permitted wholesale changes to the taxation system including substantial cut in the income tax levels.

---

[266] Bruce Hearn Mackinnon (2006), "Employer Matters in 2005", *The Journal of Industrial Relations*, Vol 48, No 3, 2006, 397.

[267] Also see Michael Barry (2009), "'The Combination of Masters': The Role of Employer Organisations in Shaping the Queensland Industrial Relations System", in Bradley Bowden, Simon Blackwood, Cath Rafferty and Cameron Allan (eds) *Work and Strife in Paradise: The History of Labour Relations in Queensland 1859-2009*, The Federation Press, Annandale, 2009; 24 for the same conclusion.

[268] Barry and Wailes 2004, 438-439.

[269] Australian Government (2005), *WorkChoices: A New Workplace Relations System*, monograph, Canberra.

An assessment: who fathered the Australian Settlement 2.0?

As we saw in the previous chapter, Alfred Deakin lays claim to being the father of the Australian Settlement. Is there a father or mother of the Australian Settlement 2.0?

The neo-liberal agenda had been comprehensively implemented. The Australian Settlement 2.0 has arrived. I can't tell you the exact birth date. It probably will have been 1998 when the Howard Government's initial industrial relations reforms. However, I can tell you for sure that it was delivered sometime before 2007.

As we have seen from the foregoing discussion, the success of these changes can claim many fathers.

Clearly beyond any acknowledged role of the business groups, the wider "intellectual environment", as former Labor Minister John Kerin[270] has described it, was critical in the demise of the original Australian Settlement in relation to protection and industrial relations. Many commentators either believe that the key explanatory variable in these seismic shifts in policy were the result of a top-down determination of key political players,[271] or alternatively simply necessitated by economic forces.[272]

There is little doubt that these two elements are the key factors in explaining governmental policy change. However, obviously the changing attitudes of the business community had a crucial impact on and involvement in the radical change in policy direction in the 1980s and 1990s.[273]

---

[270] John Kerin (Member of the House of Representatives; Cabinet Minister; Federal Treasurer) Interview with author on 29 June 2009.
[271] Capling and Galligan 1992, 263.
[272] Peter Gahan and Bruce Hearn-MacKinnon (2005), "A *New Province for Law and Order*, Assessing One Hundred Years of Industrial Arbitration in Australia" Review, *Australian Bulletin of Labour*, Vol 31, No 2, 130.
[273] See C. Wright (1995), *The Management of Labour: A History of Australian Employers*, Oxford University Press, Melbourne, 3 and Singleton 1997a, 66.

There is no doubt that the ACMA and ACEF had immense influence over government policy in the early to mid-1970s. Certainly at the beginning of the period discussed in this chapter, when the Australian Settlement remained embedded as economic policy, the role of ACMA remained important in both the protectionist and industrial relations debates.[274] However, the manufacturers had mixed success in the 1970s as their authority declined and they failed to stem the growing arguments for lower levels of protection.[275] Initially, and ironically, as the economic conditions failed to improve or indeed worsened, their "leverage" increased in parallel with the rise in unemployment.[276] Nonetheless, from the 1980s on these groups had been subsumed into the CAI that increasingly sought a change of direction. The newly formed BCA also added a strong voice for change.[277]

As an aside I note that, while the BCA gets much of the credit[278] for advancing on behalf of business the arguments in favour of enterprise bargaining a detailed comparison between CAI and BCA reveals that CAI was the first to formally change its policy for a wholesale move away from the federal arbitration system.[279] It is undoubtedly true that the BCA argued the benefits for enterprise bargaining from the late 1980s but this (like CAI's position during this period) was essentially about incremental change within

---

[274] Glezer 1982, 218.
[275] Ibid., 250-251.
[276] Ibid.
[277] Trevor Matthews (1997), "Interest Groups", in Rodney Smith (ed) (1997), *Politics in Australia*, 3rd edition, Allen & Unwin, Sydney, 273.
[278] e.g., Kelly 1992, 262-265, 276, 280, 545 & 680 and 2009, 136; Bell 2008, 472-473; Cahill 2000, 5-6; John O'Brien (1994), "McKinsey, Hilmer and the BCA: The 'New Management' Model of Labour Market Reform", *Journal of Industrial Relations*, Vol 36, December 1994, 468-490; Matthews 1994, 210-216 or Barry and Wailes 2004, 438.
[279] Campbell 1996, 34-36, 207.

the existing federal arbitration system.[280] Thus, while the CAI decisively changed policy in July 1991, it was only in August 1991 that the BCA began to formally and seriously question the existing system when it released its second in a series of three reports on the industrial relations system entitled *Avoiding Industrial Action: A Better Way of Working*.[281] And it was not until 1992 that the BCA decided to call for "the creation of a completely new system".[282]

However, the field of lobbying is crowded and there is also little doubt that during the mid-1980s the so-called New Right played a major role in the development (albeit indirectly) of Government policy and (more directly) of Opposition policy. While we saw above that the New Right was a loose collection of many individuals and groups it is clear that the organisational backbone of two industry associations, the ACC (with its offshoot the AFE) and the NFF, gave crucial institutional support and credibility to those advocating change. And the conversion of these two organisations in the very early 1980s to policies of freer-trade and industrial relations deregulation predated the policy development of the BCA and the CAI by nearly a decade.

Plowman[283] has also stated that "there is little doubt that the New Right has been a powerful force in the deregulation debate". Indeed he noted that: "The Coalition industrial relations policy, which was released in May [1987], very much reflects the AFE-

---

[280] See former BCA executive director, Peter McLaughlin, in P.A. McLaughlin (1991), "How Business Related to the Hawke Government", in Galligan and Singleton 1991, 164-165.

[281] Business Council of Australia (1991), *Avoiding Industrial Action – A Better Way of Working*, Report to the Business Council of Australia by the Industrial Relations Study Commission, Vol 2, Melbourne.

[282] Campbell 1996, 36, 100-105 and Business Council of Australia (1993a), *Working Relations*, Report to the Business Council of Australia by the Industrial Relations Study Commission, volume 3, Melbourne; Matthews 1994, 212-213 corroborates in respect of this timing.

[283] Plowman 1987a, 89.

BCA dichotomy on 'opting out'". However, overall he[284] concluded that for the business community the support for reforms to the system were principally pushed by "economic deterioration" and that "in short, the New Right has been a catalyst rather than the immediate cause of the increased preference for deregulation and decentralisation".[285]

The conversion of the BCA to enterprise bargaining is also attributed to the intellectual climate contributed by the New Right,[286] through the arguments of their think tanks and lobby groups which were publicised in the media.[287] The New Right were also influential in promoting neo-liberal views within the Australian public service.[288] There is no doubt that given the New Right's close links with the Liberals, it was "not surprising that the radical neo-liberal movement had its greatest impact upon this party".[289]

When it comes to the Hawke-Keating Governments it is obvious that the change in the views of the Government's Accord partner, the ACTU, were much more important to policy shifts during the 13 years of Labor governments than those of business groups.

It has been argued that the Hawke Government's industry policy during the early 1980s was more a reflection of the influence of

---

[284] Ibid., 91.
[285] Matthews 1994, 211-212 puts the same argument.
[286] Kelly 1992, 255.
[287] Peter Sheldon and Louise Thornthwaite (1999e), "The Business Council of Australia", in Peter Sheldon and Louise Thornthwaite (eds) *Employer Associations and Industrial Change, Catalysts or Captives?*, Allen & Unwin, Sydney, 56.
[288] Pusey, Michael (1991), *Economic Rationalism in Canberra: A Nation Building State Changes its Mind*, Cambridge University Press, Cambridge, 64 & Pusey, Michael (1992), "Canberra Changes its Mind – The New Mandarins", in Carroll, John; and Manne, Robert (eds)(1992), *Shutdown: The Failure of Economic Rationalism and How to Rescue Australia*, The Text Publishing Company, Melbourne, 46.
[289] Cahill 2004, 316.

the trade union movement rather than the lobbying of business and academics.[290] The same has been argued in relation to industrial relations policy. Former secretary of the Department of Prime Minister and Cabinet during the early 1990s, Michael Keating, has stated that "the government didn't embrace enterprise bargaining because the Business Council was in favour of it. It embraced it because senior members of the government were in favour of it ... also the ACTU was in favour of it".[291] John Edwards[292] also supports this view with his statement that "The truth was that by that point, 1993 when we got back into office, we knew what we wanted to do [on industrial relations] and we knew it was what we wanted to do because the ACTU knew that it had to happen." Although I personally think it is a stretch to argue that the ACTU supported a neo-liberal agenda, as opposed to simply wanting to guide the implementation of policies forced on it by a changing world.

Finally, it is clear that while the business community did not have any great success in directly lobbying the Hawke-Keating Government it did have a powerful indirect impact on the outcomes. They did this by proselytising the neo-liberal intellectual case to a wider audience and, in a domino effect, by directly influencing the Liberal Party (first in Opposition and then in Government) and therefore bringing their views to the forefront of the national political agenda.

Indeed, the importance of the changes in the Liberal Party position and the triumph of the "Drys" (like John Howard and John Hewson) in the party was crucial. Further it cannot be denied that at a personal level the leadership of John Howard, both in Opposition

---

[290] Stephen Bell (1992b), "Structural Power in the Manufacturing Sector: The Political Economy of Competitiveness and Investment", in Bell and Wanna 1992, 193.
[291] Stephen Bell 2006b, 550.
[292] John Edwards interview 2010.

and Government, in supporting the implementation of a neo-liberal agenda was paramount. If one single person could be singled out for being *the* key player in the changes throughout the 1980s and 1990s it would be him.

So, in conclusion, there was a general realisation across the community – business, academic, public servant and politician – that the Australian Settlement was no longer working for the nation. There was a wholesale move to a neo-liberal consensus. As I will catalogue below this had positive economic impacts.

What has happened 2007 and beyond?

For this section I do not intend to give a blow by blow account of recent Australian political and economic history. Instead I am going to give an overall assessment of the deterioration of the Australian economy that has occurred since the fall of the Howard Government in 2007.

I think it is undeniable that the Howard Government followed what could be described as a neo-liberal agenda. I believe it has proved to be the apex of the Australian Settlement 2.0 and for many Australians, looking back to 2007, it was a high water mark in economic prosperity.

The Budget was in surplus and had been for years. Indeed billions of dollars were being stashed away in a newly established Future Fund. Further, a series of personal income tax cuts seemed to have become a permanent feature of Government Budgets.

When John Howard left office the unemployment rate was 4.0 per cent and very soon after the 2007 election it fell slightly further to 3.9 per cent. That was a magnificent effort that Prime Minister Howard and his team was able to deliver after inheriting from the Keating Government an unemployment rate of over 8.0 per cent in 1996. And it is very instructive how many years it took – that is

12 years – to get to that 3.9 per cent figure. Unemployment is an incredibly hard social problem to deal with, it takes years of effort. It is clearly apparent to me that it was the implementation of the Australian Settlement 2.0 that led to these outcomes.

But the advent of the Rudd Government seemed to have started a change that is battering at the walls of the Australian Settlement 2.0.

After declaring himself to be a "fiscal conservative"[293] in the 2007 election campaign the new Prime Minister Kevin Rudd (2007-2010 & 2013) quickly changed his approach. With the advent of the Global Financial Crisis he appeared to have reverted to the position he held before becoming the Labor Party leader, calling himself a "Christian socialist"[294] and an avowed enemy of neo-liberalism.[295]

Together with his Labor successor, Prime Minister Julia Gillard (2010-2013), he massively increased federal government spending and started a process that ended budget surpluses. Not one surplus has been seen since the 2007-2008 fiscal year – 10 years ago.

There was a massive spending increase in the areas of welfare, education and health – with even greater increases promised for the future. Ironically, with all this largesse and despite rhetoric to the contrary, defence spending was actually reduced to the lowest levels since the 1930s. This was particularly dangerous in light of the precarious international environment,

The Howard era's progress on signing free trade agreements was almost slowed to a complete halt during these years. In a sense they therefore ended 20 years of systematic reduction in tariff barriers that had previously been championed by Prime

---

[293] Chris Uhlmann (2007), *Rudd mouthing fiscal conservatism: PM*, The World Today, ABC Radio, transcript, 11 May 2007.
[294] Kevin Rudd (2006), "Faith in Politics", *The Monthly*, October 2006.
[295] Kevin Rudd (2009), "The Global Financial Crisis", *The Monthly*, February 2009.

Ministers Hawke and Keating. Most egregiously the 20 years of steady increases in the flexibility of the industrial relations system was also thrown into screeching reverse. Ignoring the reforms even of their own Keating Government the introduction of the Fair Work legislation, which astoundingly abolished the old AIRC and replaced it with a heavily centralised, red-taped bound alternative and the abolition of the Australian Building and Construction Commission massively changed the industrial relations environment.

Another way to look at this period is the measurement of productivity.

Simply put we need productivity growth if we are to remain a high-wage, generous social welfare net, first world economy. It is directly related to the ability to generate jobs.

Australia's multifactor productivity has seen a long-term growth rate over 40 years of 0.8 per cent – it doesn't sound much, but it's big enough. It has helped make us one of the wealthiest countries on the planet.

That growth rate dipped dramatically in the period 2007 to 2013 to -0.1 per cent.

I am not the only observer to make these observations. Even Labor Party supporters have made similar comments, although some apportion blame differently to me.

The first is Professor Ross Garnaut who is currently a professorial research fellow at the University of Melbourne, and has had a distinguished career as an economist.

In his book *Dog Days: Australia after the boom*[296] he basically follows a neo-liberal agenda and if anything argues that the Howard Government failed to meet up to his expectations of good policy. He

---

[296] Ross Garnaut (2013), *Dog Days: Australia After the Boom*, Redback, Collingwood.

too is concerned about the increase in public debt, but sheets home much of the blame on the Howard Government. For example, he criticises the Howard Government for mishandling the resources boom because they gave a lot of the revenue back to the people in the form of tax cuts. According to him this was wasted savings and created the setting for the public debt problems that emerged during the Rudd Gillard years.

The second is Dr John Edwards, who is an adjunct professor with the John Curtin Institute of Public Policy at Curtin University. He has also recently been a member of the Reserve Bank of Australia board. He is also a friend of mine, as we worked together in Bahrain in the Middle East at that country's Economic Development Board.

In his book *Beyond the Boom*[297] published by the Lowy Institute for International Policy, Edwards also praises the neo-liberal agenda and notes many of the important reforms implemented by the Howard Government while not being uncritical on a number of matters. Interestingly he counters Garnaut's criticism on the Howard Government and debt, pointing out that the bulk of those Howard tax cuts resulted in a significant rise in the household savings rate.

I note that neither man would resile from being described as Labor Party fellow travellers. Both had strong involvement in the Hawke and Keating Governments and the recent Rudd-Gillard-Rudd Labor Government in Canberra. You will particularly recognise Garnaut's name in relation to the Climate Change debate.

Nonetheless both are avowed opponents of the original Australian Settlement. Indeed Garnaut and Edwards both played significant roles as advisors in the Hawke-Keating Governments in going a long way to establishing its replacement by the Australian Settlement 2.0.

---

[297] John Edwards (2014), *Beyond the Boom*, A Lowy Institute Paper, Penguin Books, Melbourne.

Another recent monograph is that by Professor Tony Makin – professor of economics and director of the APEC Study Centre at Griffith University. Titled *Australia's competitiveness: Reversing the slide*[298] it was published by the Minerals Council of Australia.

Makin notes that between 2000 and 2008, when commodity prices started to surge, Australia's average annual GDP growth rate was 3.3 per cent. That was below the long run average of 3.6 percent.

Makin's conclusion is that the mining boom did not compensate for the lower levels of productivity across the total economy and we need to look at the reform task to boost productivity and the long term wealth-creating potential of the economy. Makin also argues that the massive stimulus package of the last Government is having long term adverse consequences for the Australian economy. Simply put, this is because it has resulted in higher levels of interest rates due to the massive acceleration in public debt.

The bottom line for him is that these higher interest rates have contributed to the higher value of the Australian dollar and therefore the consequent damage to manufacturing and other import competing industries.

Over the whole 45 years of budget data published in Budget Paper No. 1 – going back to 1970-71 – the longest the budget has previously stayed in deficit is seven years in a row, through the extremely severe early-1990s recession. Extraordinarily, the first six budgets of the 2000s saw a *faster* increase in net debt even than during that episode, both in dollar terms and as a percentage of GDP.

And as we noted earlier, this debt disaster problem occurred despite the benefit of a onceinacentury mining boom and commodity prices that reached record high levels

---

[298] Tony Makin (2014), *Australia's competitiveness: Reversing the slide*, Minerals Council of Australia, Canberra.

Of the three, the analysis of Edwards and Makin are the more convincing.

Economics texts can be inherently boring, but theirs are not and I would urge you to read them. The saving grace is that they are both short – one is 86 pages and one is 163 pages long.

Conclusion

As I wrote in concluding the previous chapter, the consensus view is that the Australian Settlement has been replaced by a neo-liberal consensus or as I call it the Australian Settlement 2.0.

This chapter picked up the baton from there and has provided greater detail on the intellectual arguments that led to that outcome – the reason the neo-liberal agenda actually triumphed. It has also explained the successful economic results that emanated from this agenda.

The last chapter detailed how the business community was critical in developing and sustaining the Australian Settlement. In this chapter we saw how the business community equally played a critical role in substituting it with the Australian Settlement 2.0.

However, the relatively new Australian Settlement 2.0 is in great danger and the agenda was put into sharp reverse by the Rudd-Gillard Governments. Continue on this route and it will lead us back to the sleepwalking of a zombie nation.

Ostensibly the Abbott-Turnbull Governments have advanced policy prescriptions to reverse the dismantling of the Australian Settlement 2.0. Those prescriptions have in many cases suffered either complete rejection or major compromises due to a hostile Senate. In the next series of chapters I turn to the economic and parliamentary reforms that I consider are necessary to save Australia.

4
HOW DO WE SUSTAIN THE AUSTRALIAN SETTLEMENT 2.0?

Introduction

How do we sustain the Australian Settlement 2.0? What is the framework in which to formulate policy?

There is a famous saying that "those who do not learn from past errors are condemned to repeat them". Why do I quote that? It's simple. We are in great danger of repeating the errors of the past. I do not mean the most recent past – that being for example the 1980s and 1990s. I mean those many long decades "when Australia slept".

Australians cannot ignore the wider international events on their economic well-being.

I won't say, as people often do, that this is more so the case today than ever before. I won't say it because it is patently untrue. Australia, since that defining moment in the nation's history when the First Fleet landed at Botany Bay, has been the subject of continual buffeting from international events.

Whether it be continual concerns about commodity prices like that for wool and wheat; and later iron ore and coal; or the big picture geo-political concerns about potential "enemies" – first, the French in the early days of settlement; to the Germans and Japanese; to international communism – international events have always shaped Australia.

In this chapter we discuss the overview to sustaining the Australian Settlement 2.0. It gives the context that leads to the discussions in chapters 6 to 12 on issues like raising the GST to allow major personal income tax reform; potentially radically changing our company tax system; the introduction of a state income tax; much overdue industrial relations reform; the further pursuit of free trade agreements; and some quite radical policies in the defence area such as nuclear options.

Where to start?

As I previously noted I have had a wide-ranging career. It started with the Federal Treasury in Canberra. Treasury gave me a great grounding in economics after the quite schizophrenic course I undertook at the University of Queensland in the late 1970s and early 1980s, which fluctuated between equally strong Monetarist and Keynesian teachers. These were the two prominent disciplines being taught in the economics profession at the time. In contrast, Treasury essentially synthesised the most creditable parts of the two views and retaught me the fundamentals of economics in the time I was there.

The Treasury synthesis then represented the consensus or "orthodox" view on economics for the bulk of the last 30 years until the recent fracturing of opinion that has occurred with the Global Financial Crisis (as we mainly call it here in Australia) or the Great Recession (as they call it overseas).

That long term consensus was pro-market economics, light touch regulation where possible, and strict budget management to prevent large increases in debt. If anything it leaned more towards the Monetarist view. However that is rather a crude generalisation and it would be better to see the synthesis as the neo-liberal consensus that I spoke of at the beginning of chapter 2. It is the explosion of debt and the intellectualising to support this, provided by born-again Keynesians, that has jeopardised the consensus.[1]

---

[1] See Justyn Walsh (2007), *The Keynes Mutiny*, Random House Australia, Sydney; and Wapshott, Nicholas (2011), *Keynes Hayek: The Clash that Defined Modern Economics*, WW Norton, New York.

However, the ever expanding debt fueled spending that has been condoned by many new Keynesians is simply not the way to go. I firmly believe that the orthodoxy of a synthesis between monetarism and Keynesianism remains correct.

Going back to the analysis of Professor Tony Makin[2] referred to at the end of the previous chapter, in my view as an economist, the number one priority for the Australian economy is to get the Budget into a sustainable surplus in the short term.

This reflects the opinion of world renowned economists such as former US Federal Reserve Chairman Alan Greenspan and former Governor of the Bank of England Mervyn King. Greenspan has said that "The bias toward unconstrained deficit spending is our top domestic problem."[3] And King has similarly said that globally speaking: "Debt has now reached a level where it is a drag on the willingness to spend and likely to be the trigger for a future crisis."[4]

One of the big economic reforms of the Howard years was Peter Costello's magnificent job in rapidly getting the Budget back into surplus and keeping it there (aided by Finance Ministers John Fahey and Nick Minchin). That was crucial to that Governments political success and it gave them the ability for the best part of 12 years to "buy" other reforms with electoral "sweeteners".

Australia can't go on borrowing $1 billion every single month just to pay the interest on the previous government borrowings. This is wasted money that could otherwise be building roads, schools and hospitals, or paying for tax cuts for long suffering taxpayers.

---

[2] Tony Makin (2014), *Australia's competitiveness: Reversing the slide*, Minerals Council of Australia, Canberra.
[3] Alan Greenspan (2014), *The Map and the Territory 2.0: Risk, Human Nature, and the Future of Forecasting*, Penguin Books, New York, 303.
[4] Mervyn King (2017), *The End of Alchemy: Money Banking and the Future of the Global Economy*, Abacus, 337.

Australia has just run 10 straight years of record budget deficits with gross debt projected to rise to $583 billion by 2021. A further $46.7 billion in projected deficits is expected. This compares to gross debt forecast to hit $667 billion when the Rudd-Gillard Government left office in 2013. The 2017 Mid-Year Economic and Fiscal Outlook shows that, even with the Government's efforts to repair the budget, we will not reach Budget surplus until 2021.[5] That would make 13 deficits in a row and would be unprecedented in our post-war history.

However there is an important point to make about spending cuts. Over the years an increasingly smaller proportion of spending has occurred through what is called the annual Appropriation Bills, or the Supply Bills, or sometimes called the Budget Bills.

During the Gillard Government, in particular, almost all the massive increase in spending was legislated through the special appropriation Bills for say health, welfare or education. Although I should add that this was spurred on by a Constitutional decision of the High Court in the *School Chaplaincy Case* of 2012.

The crucial point here is that previous Treasurers were able to actually cut spending much easier because both major parties have hesitated to block the annual Appropriation or Budget Bills, particularly since the 1975 Constitutional crisis. So that means that past Treasurers did not have as great a problem with the Senate that the Abbott and Turnbull Governments have had in cutting spending. In the last 20 years alone the Parliamentary Library has estimated that the proportion of expenditure coming through the annual appropriation Budget bills may have fallen from around 30 per cent to less than 20 per cent of total federal spending.

However, the Budget is a "short-term" priority. It is vitally

---

[5] Scott Morrison and Mathias Cormann (2017), *Mid-Year Economic and Fiscal Outlook 2017-18*, Commonwealth of Australia, Canberra, December.

important but there are even longer term structural issues that Australia needs to deal with.

One of the key ways to get the budget back into balance or surplus is to grow the economy and therefore grow tax revenues for the government without raising tax levels, particularly as a share of GDP. The principal way to do that is to boost productivity and therefore the economy.

You don't need to be a rocket scientist to generally know what you should do to run the country and boost the economy. The Productivity Commission has a long "shopping list" of what can and should be done.[6] I will come to that later in the chapter.

However, I think it is worth spending a little bit of time discussing what productivity is. As a former Assistant Minister for Productivity it's something I'm particularly interested in.

There is little that determines a country's standard of living more than its rate of productivity growth. I'm reminded of a quote from Nobel Laureate, Paul Krugman – it's an oldie but a goodie. He said: "Productivity isn't everything, but in the long run, it's almost everything. A country's ability to improve its standard of living over time depends almost entirely on its ability to raise its output per worker."[7]

As the Productivity Commission has stated: "productivity is not, as some would have it, about extracting more sweat from the brow of an already hard-working Australian. It is most of all about: not standing in the way of better investment in workplaces; not opposing the research and trialling of new ideas; not defending outmoded regulation that prevents consumers and businesses

---
[6] Productivity Commission (2017b), *Shifting the Dial – 5 year productivity review*, Inquiry Report No 84, Melbourne, 3 August.
[7] Paul Krugman (1994), *The Age of Diminished Expectations*, MIT Press, Cambridge, 13.

obtaining access to better services. We can make significant gains just by recognising the case for change and embracing it."[8]

Productivity performance has been the main source of Australia's long-term economic growth, business competitiveness, and real per capita income growth. There are essentially two ways of increasing the per capita income of our society – by producing more per person or by getting higher world prices for what we produce. The first we control. The second we don't.

Currently, Australian labour productivity is in line with our long-term trend and multi-factor productivity (MFP) is on the low side. That labour productivity performance is directly related to capital investment in the Australian economy over recent years. On multifactor productivity we have seen a long-term growth rate of 0.8 per cent – it doesn't sound much, but it's big – between 1973-74 and 2013-14.

That growth rate dipped dramatically in the period 2007-08 to 2013-14 to -0.1 per cent. You might recognise that six-year period.

I am happy to say that the multifactor productivity growth rate has improved and in 2013-14, the MFP growth rate has increased to 0.4 per cent. This is still below the long-term trend, but it is an improvement on the years 2007-2013. In 2013-14, the MFP growth and underlying proximate causes differ between the 12 industries that the Productivity Commission looks at. This data all comes from the Productivity Commission's report of July 2015.[9]

For example, the MFP rate in Agriculture, forestry, and fishing was -0.1 per cent. Whilst in Arts and recreation services, the MFP growth rate was 5.4 per cent. In Mining, it was -0.1 per cent. In Financial and insurance services, it was 3.3 per cent. In transport,

---

[8] Productivity Commission 2017b, 7.
[9] Productivity Commission (2015), *Productivity Update 2015*, Melbourne, 20 July.

postal, and warehousing, it was -3.1 per cent, whilst in wholesale trade, it was 3.1 per cent.

The latest *National Accounts* from the Australian Bureau of Statistics before the publication of this book shows that the story hasn't changed. GDP per hour worked, a common measure of labour productivity, fell by -0.1 per cent in 2017. This is the first time in seven years.[10]

Over the past decade, Australia's ability to produce more per person has been masked by the rise in our terms of trade. As we adjust to new terms of trade – a down-turn in commodity prices and mining investment – we must focus like a laser on productivity. Australia will need a big lift in productivity growth if our living standards are going to continue to grow.

The key to achieving this is through competing in world markets and substantive reform.

We refer to the maximum level of output as an economies productive potential. Economies that are well below their productive potential can experience rapid and dramatic productivity growth by being exposed to international competition. And we saw a very good example of this with the Asian Tigers of Hong Kong, South Korea, Taiwan and Singapore – who all experienced rapid growth between the 1960s and 1990s. Australia too, experienced strong productivity growth in the 1990s as a result of competition and trade reforms that created incentives for firms to reach their potential.

You can think of this like the top Formula One racing car team extracting those critical increases in horsepower performance at the margins. Increased performance at the lower end can be made with blunt measures that are easily – and relatively cheaply – achieved. The difficult – and expensive – work, is to produce that extra horse-

---

[10] Geoff Winestock (2018), "Productivity falls for the first time in 7 years", *Australian Financial Review*, 8 March.

power at the margin – where every increment can give a team a competitive advantage. This is true of Formula One motor racing, and it is true of our $1.7 trillion economy.

Reform that leads to even modest productivity gains is worth doing.

Former Chairman of the Productivity Commission, Gary Banks,[11] made this very point. He compared the projected rate of economy-wide labour productivity growth between the first Howard Government Inter-Generational Report in 2002 with that of ten years later in 2012. He noted that it fell from 1.75 to 1.6 per cent. He found that this 0.15 percentage point difference translated to a reduction in per capita GDP of nearly $7,000 per person by 2050.

The status quo should be entirely unacceptable.

The world appears to be changing at an ever increasing rate. This is typified by the latest observation of a "disrupted economy". Many authors have catalogued the monumental changes occurring across the world and how they have "disrupted" what has previously been considered normal practices.

A group of McKinsey analysts[12] have concluded that the four great disruptive forces are: (1) "the shifting locus of economic activity and dynamism – to emerging markets like China and to cities within those markets";[13] (2) "the acceleration in the scope, scale and economic impact of technology";[14] (3) "demographics. Simply put the human population is getting older";[15] and (4) "the degree to which the world is much more connected through trade

---

[11] Banks, Gary (2012), "Advancing the Reform Agenda: Selected Speeches", Productivity Commission, Melbourne, 7-8.

[12] Richard Dobbs, James Manyika and Jonathan Woetzel (2015), *No Ordinary Disruption: The Four Global Forces Breaking All the Trends*, Public Affairs, New York.

[13] Ibid., 4.

[14] Ibid., 5.

[15] Ibid.

and through movements in capital, people, and information – what we call flows".[16]

However, abstracting from the new buzzword, what is being seen here is a continuation, although at accelerated speeds, of what economist Joseph Schumpeter famously called capitalism's "creative destruction".[17] For example, as *The Economist*'s regular columnist, Adrian Wooldridge, says "Schumpeter once celebrated capitalism's ability to turn silk stockings from a rarity reserved for queens into an everyday luxury available to factory girls in a mere three centuries. Mobile phones went from being toys of the rich to tools of three-quarters of the earth's population in two decades."[18] As he observes the three things that have unleashed this "storm of creative disruption" are "information technology, particularly the internet, financial markets and globalisation".[19]

In light of these developments, Australia cannot stay still. We need to take the decisions on further reform that will boost our productivity so that we can compete in the fast-moving world.

The Washington Consensus versus the Beijing Consensus

The neo-liberal policies that I have continually referred to in this book have been part of an accepted consensus amongst key economic policy-makers across the Western world since World War II. They have been adopted by international agencies such as the International Monetary Fund (IMF) and the Organisation for Economic Development and Cooperation (OECD). As the influential IMF is based in Washington DC this set of policies have often also been labelled the "Washington Consensus".

---

[16] Ibid.
[17] Joseph Schumpeter, (2003) *Capitalism, Socialism and Democracy*, Routledge, New York, (originally 1942).
[18] Adrian Wooldridge (2015), *The Great Disruption: How business is coping with turbulent times*, The Economist, London, 3.
[19] Ibid.

In contrast, at the 19th Communist Party Congress in October 2017 in Beijing President Xi Jingping declared that the Chinese state-centred economic model had triumphed and should be considered by all nations.

There has been quite a debate on this issue. The model that President Xi supports could be summarised as "a model of politics and state capitalism, with a strengthened one-party state at the centre of both".[20] It has also been described such that "whereas the Western ruler has a responsibility to insure the people have the right of political expression, assembly, and debate in the public square and the people have a duty to exercise those rights, the exact opposite is true in Confucian societies [ie China]. There the ruler has a responsibility to protect and support while the people have a duty to obey".[21]

Professor Stefan Halper of the University of Cambridge is concerned that the so-called Beijing Consensus has a strong chance of prevailing if the West does not counter with a strategy to argue the continuing relevance of its political and economic model.[22] Professor Martin Jaques of the London School of Economics argues that the "baton" has already been passed and that 2008 financial crisis marked the "fundamental shift".[23] In contrast respected *Financial Times* journalist Geoff Dyer strongly argues that the economic system of the West will prevail. He notes that "To win a bigger role in the world, it is not enough to be wealthy; a country also needs to secure trust. Without a political system that embraces a greater degree of pluralism, allows more dissent, and is rooted in the rule

---

[20] Roland Rajah (2017), "State capitalism is here to stay", *Australian Financial Review*, 1 November.
[21] Stefan Halper (2010), *The Beijing Consensus: How China's authoritarian mode will dominate the Twenty-First century*, Basic Books, New York, 250.
[22] Ibid., 251-252.
[23] Martin Jacques (2012), *When China Rules the World: The end of the Western World and the birth of a new global order*, Penguin Books, New York, 585.

of law, China will struggle to get the respect it needs to turn its economic weight into power and influence".[24]

Ironically, as Roland Rajah of the Lowy Institute has pointed out, President Xi's advocacy for "state economic power is at odds with the market forces that have brought his country's biggest successes".[25] And as he goes on to argue "The view that Chinese state capitalism is on the ascendancy extrapolates a situation that is both recent and unsustainable. It was only in the wake of the global financial crisis that China was forced to switch to state-led activity. That was useful for avoiding a disorderly adjustment. But imbalances it created are now the problem".[26]

My view is that, in the end, China's success is based on the standard economics of supply and demand. It cannot change that fundamental fact. I firmly believe that the Western model has been the reason behind its success (despite its continued heavy reliance on state intervention) and for Australia to abandon that model would be tantamount to lunacy.

This specific debate runs parallel to another debate about the failing of Western culture. Ironically, back in 1992 Stanford University political scientist Francis Fukuyama declared the "end of history", which was a catchy title to describe the serious proposition that Western political and economic thought had basically triumphed. Fukuyama now says "No one living in an established liberal democracy should ... be complacent about the inevitability of its survival. There is no automatic historical mechanism that makes progress inevitable or that prevents decay and backsliding".[27]

---

[24] Geoff Dyer (2014), *The Contest of the century: The new era of competition with China – and how America can win*, Vintage Books, New York, 277.
[25] Rajah 2017.
[26] Ibid.
[27] Francis Fukuyama (2015), *Political Order and Political Decay*, Profile books, London, 548.

Indeed, *Financial Times* columnist Edward Luce comes to the similar pessimistic conclusion saying that: "Can the West regain its optimism? If the answer is no – and most of the portents are skewing the wrong way – liberal democracy will follow. If the next few years resemble the last, it is questionable whether Western democracy can take the strain. People have lost faith that their systems can deliver".[28]

Former editor-in-chief at *The Economist*, Bill Emmott, is also concerned that the achievements of the past are again in danger. However with a note of optimism he concludes that: "Ultimately, the be-all and end-all of Western strategy in facing these challenges has to be a stark and simple one, the same as at many fragile and nerve-racking moments of the cold war: to rebuild economic and hence political strength. The two go together. The West's economic and political weakness in recent years has essentially been self-inflicted. It can therefore be self-cured".[29]

That leads into what I think is largely a false dispute between liberalism and conservatism.

When I talk about liberalism I am more talking about the classical liberal tradition, as I have previously outlined. I am not talking of the American version which can be associated with left-wing politics and for many US Republican politicians is simply a synonym for socialism. Indeed some Americans find it bemusing that Australia's Liberal Party is also considered its main conservative party.

In the Australian context there has been a clamouring argument over whether the present Commonwealth government is conservative "enough". Indeed many conservative commentators (like Andrew

---

[28] Edward Luce (2017), *The Retreat of Western Liberalism*, Little, Brown, London, 202-203.
[29] Bill Emmott (2017), *The Fate of the West: The Battle to Save the World's Most Successful Political Idea*, The Economist Books, London, 206.

Bolt and Alan Jones) argue that the current government is actually left-wing. I do not subscribe to that view and find it laughable.

So what is liberalism? In summary, as Professor Alan Ryan of the University of Oxford says, "the core of liberalism is that modern toleration is focused on the individual, it rests on a commitment to the sanctity of the individual personality and the inviolability of the individual conscience".[30]

What about conservatism? Put in an historical context conservatism is a "tendency" or a state of mind as opposed to being necessarily a set of philosophical positions.[31] To go back to the 18th century British politician Edmund Burke, the doyen of conservatism, it means retaining past practices that have been agreed to over decades or centuries and have stood the test of time. They should not be lightly abandoned.[32]

Indeed as Professor Alan Ryan says, conservatism in the United States today means defending what would be called classical liberal philosophical positions like limited government. In his words "temperamental conservatives are thus forced to be ideological liberals".[33]

Thus I claim that I am both a conservative and a liberal, and in particular I am an economic rationalist (which was discussed in chapter 2).

Finally, I cannot let a discussion on liberalism pass by without mentioning that I am distantly related to a lady who was born

---

[30] Alan Ryan (2012), *The Making of Modern Liberalism*, Princeton University Press, Princeton, 8.

[31] J.S. McClelland (2005), *A History of Western Political Thought*, Routledge, London, 716-717. Although others would not agree. For example Kieron O'Hara (2011), *Conservatism*, Reaktion Books, London, 5 describes it as an ideology.

[32] Leo Strauss and Joseph Cropsey (1987), *History of Political Philosophy*, University of Chicago Press, Chicago,692-693 and George H. Sabine (1960), *A History of Political Theory*, George G. Harrap & Co, London, 512.

[33] Ryan 2012, 28.

Harriet Hardy. She later married a man named Taylor and is better known as Harriet Taylor. However, more than that she was later also married to John Stuart Mill, who is the father of classical liberalism. I note that Mill put on the record on a number of occasions that his wife Harriet actually co-authored his seminal work *On Liberty* [34] and also contributed to his magnum opus on economics, *Principles of Political Economy*.[35] So in a very indirect way I am related to one of the authors of the bedrock documents in liberalism and mainstream economics. That is something I am very proud of.

The economic reform agenda

In essence the changes that I present in future chapters is the part of a productivity plan to sustain the Australian Settlement 2.0.

So what is to be done?

Gary Banks[36], identified three channels of policy influence that have been the focus of government initiatives over the years and compiled a to-do list of productivity policies that I think provides a very good point of reference.

Banks' list is compiled under the rubric of incentives, capabilities, and flexibility. The Productivity Commission characterises the incentive channel as a driver of productivity enhancement, whilst capabilities and flexibility are enablers.

In thinking about policies to improve incentives, we might focus on promoting competition, such as reducing barriers that inhibit international trade or new entrants to markets.

Policies to enhance capabilities might focus on the development

---

[34] John Stuart Mill (2006), *On Liberty*, Penguin Classics, (originally 1859), preface; and John Stuart Mill (1961), *Autobiography*, Dolphin Books, New York, (originally 1873), 148.
[35] Mill 1961, 181.
[36] Banks 2012, 10-20.

of human capital (like industrial relations reform), improving infrastructure and institutions to devise productivity-enhancing changes and provide an effective level of support.

And finally, there are policies to provide a more flexible regulatory environment and undertake a substantive regulatory reform agenda.

The channels are strongly interactive, and the key to optimising government's influence is to harmonise and coordinate the reform agenda across all three. Australia is already making some headway in this area.

The latest Productivity Commission shopping-list for reform was published in its extensive report in 2017 titled *Shifting the Dial*. The Productivity Commission lists a whole range of reforms that it believes should help boost productivity. Many of these are in the social welfare areas like health and the provision of welfare benefits.

There is also a lot to do on education and skills. There is also discussions on infrastructure pricing and how to fund road building. There are discussions about stamp duties and land taxes, and major changes to energy markets.

There is a very strong focus on Commonwealth-State relations, and the Commission argues for "A formal commitment and an institutionally-supported process [that] are both needed to sustain co-operation on reforms of this nature beyond any one term of government." And, that "The role of monitoring and reporting on an agreed Joint Reform Agenda should be assigned to an independent body, such as a revamped National Competition Council or the Productivity Commission".[37] Indeed I strongly agree with this and I look at some elements of Commonwealth-State relations reform in chapter 8.

Another area that needs to be looked at is large scale tax reform. Martin Parkinson, current secretary of the Department of Prime

---

[37] Productivity Commission 2017b, 182.

Minister and Cabinet (and former secretary of Treasury) has called for an increase in the GST as a shift away from direct (ie income) tax to more indirect (ie GST) taxation. Another former Treasury secretary Ken Henry has said the same thing.[38] I will explore this matter in depth in chapter 7.

There has also been a debate about the levels of immigration and that will be discussed in depth in chapter 12.

However, there are some proposals raised by otherwise eminent economists that I don't agree with. Professor Ross Garnaut[39] appears to be arguing that the solution to Australia's international competitiveness problems, including the high dollar problem, is direct management of the currency. He argues that the Reserve Bank of Australia should set interest rates to deliver a 20 to 40 percent real depreciation in the dollar. At the very least that would be a return to the interventionist policies of the original Australian Settlement that have been our downfall in the past. In its specifics it would be a mind-bogglingly disruptive policy proscription, with potentially severe impacts on inflation and incomes.

One area where I think the government has dropped the ball is on red tape reduction. The Coalition came to office in 2013 with a public commitment to reduce regulatory costs by $3 billion dollars over three years. And indeed they exceeded that target. In just over two years, they had made decisions to cut regulatory costs by $4.8 billion. This is the result of hard work – measure by measure, portfolio by portfolio. As a result of sustained efforts across the whole of government, in just over two years they introduced legislation to repeal almost 3,600 Acts.

Thus they have reduced the time and costs devoted by the

---

[38] Paul Kelly (2014), *Triumph and Demise, the broken promise of a Labor Generation*, Melbourne University Press, Melbourne, 222-223.

[39] Ross Garnaut (2013), *Dog Days: Australia After the Boom*, Redback, Collingwood, 122-129.

community to complying with Commonwealth regulations by an ongoing $4.8 billion per year. That's $4.8 billion this year, $4.8 billion the next, and so on.

When I was the Minister responsible for this process it was tweaked but was very much still in place. I am alarmed that since I left the portfolio in 2016 there has been no annual report published on any further progress. In my view it is very important that this focus on red tape reduction proceeds.

So in conclusion, there is much that can be done. However, whatever we choose to do we are constrained by the political system in which we operate. In the next section I discuss a very important constraint on implementing reform.

Democracy Paradox

Above we identify a number of key issues for the sustaining of the Australian Settlement 2.0. Unfortunately it is the "doing" that is very difficult, and yes, I agree it has become increasingly difficult.

People say that Prime Ministers Hawke, Keating and Howard were able to implement reform, but that since 2007 it has been a drought. Why are politicians now so hopeless, goes up the cry.

There is no doubt that the changing media market has made it so much harder to conduct reform. Things were very different back in the Hawke, Keating and Howard years in terms of media. The other day I was speaking to the Conservative Club at the University of Sydney. The audience were principally born at the time of, or just after, John Howard won his victory in 1996. At that time I was a senior executive in the NSW Cabinet Office.

My audience were shocked to learn that it was only around the time of the election of the Howard Government that my area of the Cabinet Office first got an internet connection. Only one officer had a connection on their personal desk computer and they were responsible for being trained up to use the World Wide Web for the benefit of all the staff in my division. Different days indeed.

Briefly put, this leads to the critical point that during the Howard Government, let alone Hawke and Keating, there simply wasn't the social media environment of today. Nor was there 24 hour news channels and continual television news updates.

Why is this relevant? I think it is crucial to understanding how much more difficult it is to do reform today. Basically social media makes it exceptionally hard to build and prosecute an argument.

Ten or fifteen years ago and earlier politicians and others could develop the arguments and lay the groundwork for reforms over a period of months or even years. Today ideas can be hijacked by social media within hours and the turbo charged negativity that comes with that social media can kill decent ideas for reform in as quickly as a 12 hours news cycle let alone 24, 36 or 48 hours.

The mainstream media, which is being eaten alive by social media, has perversely reacted to this challenge by embracing it. In my view the thing that the mainstream media have developed and sold over the years is quality control – even the ABC.

Social media has no quality control and is massively biased toward political correctness and groupthink. As we have heard often in recent times, from all parts of the political spectrum, social media propagates fake news and scare campaigns. And the mainstream media has exacerbated this by giving it an elevated platform.

So today we may see a policy idea propounded by a politician featured on the nightly news broadcast, and then it is accompanied by the reporting of a tweet from a no-name person who expresses a total opposition to the idea – often in vulgar terms. A flood tide of this then quickly leads to the end of the debate. Politicians in a democracy have few defences. Unfortunately the ideological opponents of economic reform who run groups like GetUp! are experts in this.

Hopefully main stream media will come to its collective senses and stop promoting this and focus on their comparative market strength which is quality control. If they do not then it is eventually goodbye to the news services that we have seen in the past as they simply will no longer be commercial.

All this leads to something I have been thinking about for a few years which is the identification of what I call a Democracy Paradox.

Democracy is the best form of government bar none. However, our forefathers and mothers knew there were limits. My Democracy Paradox states that: "not everything that gives people a bigger voice actually improves the state of the nation or improves our democracy". You would think that giving individuals a bigger voice is inherently more democratic, but is it better for the governance of a democratic state?

Thus social media highlights a modern dilemma. It is that social media which apparently increases people's say, can have a very destructive effect. It reinforces the reason we have over the centuries created a representative democracy where we put faith in elected representatives to argue through and legislate on our behalf but checked by the rule of law and periodic elections.

It is the same Paradox that we have lived with for centuries where we cherish freedom of speech but we also believe it is important to limit it to stop libel and slander – i.e., a paradox. I am not calling for an end to social media. In fact exactly the opposite. It's positives in my view do definitely outweigh its negatives. However we do face a dilemma.

Often in history identifying a problem allows us to develop new ways of doing and marketing things and I hope that what I call –

for want of a better term – the "Quality Press" is able to reassert its importance as a bulwark of democracy.

Of course I am not alone in diagnosing this problem. Famous philosopher A.C. Grayling[40] has written about it and even Prince William[41] and former President Barack Obama[42] to name but a few, have weighed into the debate. The fact is that it is a very serious issue which defies an easy solution.

Conclusion

So what is to be done? In my view an awful lot. There is an enormous amount that needs to be done on the economic agenda. In this chapter I have given pretty much a helicopter view. I have deliberately not gone into a lot of detail. That will in many cases be given in subsequent chapters where I discuss the key issues of taxation reform and industrial relations reform. I also discuss international relations, trade negotiations, and defence at length. These are all crucial issues for sustaining the Australian Settlement 2.0.

I note upfront that I have not written detailed chapters on a number of important policy issues. For example I have omitted a discussion at any length on environment policy and climate change. One of the most important short term problems facing businesses and the general public is rapidly rising energy costs. Suffice it to say here that I think there should be a pause in the implementation of targeting renewable energy levels[43] while Australia works through

---

[40] A.C. Grayling (2017), *Democracy and Its Crisis*, Oneworld, London.

[41] Tony Jones (2018), "Prince William slams 'fake' world of 'touched up' social media photos in conversation with school children", *The Mirror*, 8 February.

[42] BBC News (2017), "Obama warns against irresponsible social media use", 27 December.

[43] Although being replaced by a National Energy Guarantee, I note that the Renewable Energy Target was at a level of 17.3 per cent in late 2017 compared to the target of 23.5 per cent by 2020. See Clean Energy Council (2017), *Clean Energy Australia Report 2016*, Canberra, 6.

the balance between climate change obligations and economic necessity. There is no sense in destroying Australian industry and imposing unwarranted burdens on consumers. I certainly wouldn't be increasing the target to 50 per cent as is being proposed by people on the left. We should not let ideological extremism overrule balanced policy. Further, while I gave serious thought to including a chapter on education policy and the related topic of innovation, in the end I did not. The university and technical and further education sectors are in great need of reform. We need to do everything we can to prepare for developments in Artificial Intelligence, 5G (i.e., the fifth generation of wireless systems), robotics and the Internet of Things. I would have loved to have gone into these matters but there is just so much that can be sensibly covered in just one volume. After all, I am not seeking to replicate the 2014 National Commission of Audit that covered virtually every governance area there is. That report totalled 1,247 pages and had five volumes. My selections are based on what I consider to be the core issues for sustaining the Australian Settlement 2.0 – the core economic and social framework that Australian society is based on over the decades, as opposed to the more immediate political debates.

However, as we will see in the next chapter I don't immediately proceed to discuss economic policy. Instead, I canvas the running of our democracy and in particular parliament. The reason for that is that I believe – like most Australians – that something needs to done in these areas if we are going to be able to implement the economic reforms that we need.

5

PARLIAMENTARY REFORM

Introduction

As I said in concluding the last chapter, before we discuss the detail of what needs to be done in terms of economic reform I want to give some suggestions for reforming our democracy.

Here I want to focus on two particular issues, which are the role of the Senate and political fundraising laws.

The issue of reforming the Senate can be shaped by your views about a Government's mandate to see its legislative agenda pass the parliament. You will often hear the argument that a Government has a mandate by virtue of winning the election. However, in our system a Government does not actually have a mandate to *pass* laws whether they campaigned for them in an election or not.

In my view a political party winning an election and forming government did win a mandate. But strictly speaking it was simply a mandate to *try to implement* its policy agenda. Put another way it was simply a mandate to introduce the relevant bills into parliament. In a representative democracy every single elected official to Parliament – member or senator – has a mandate on the basis of their electoral success. So in the Senate, for example, the major and minor parties, and the independents have all secured a mandate to represent those people who voted for them – both in terms of primary votes and second and third (and so on) preference votes.

So a Government cannot expect the Senate to be a rubber stamp for its policies simply because it won a majority in the House of Representatives. If you accept the typically expressed mandate theory – that the Senate simply must accept a Government's legislative program – you are conceding that there is no justification for the Senate or its voting system. That is the radical and logical extension of the superficial and commonly expressed view on mandates. I don't subscribe to that conclusion and nor do I think would the bulk of the Australian public.

In the end it is up to the Government to convince the Senate, as a majority, to pass its laws. However, if over many years the Senate proves to be a chronic obstruction against government mandates on policy I believe we should look at reforming our system to ensure that there is an increased chance of doing so. The logical reason for this is that if democratically elected governments are continually thwarted in achieving their agendas then the population will increasingly come to the view that our democratic system is not working. That matter is discussed in the next section.

As to funding reform I know that as a former politician and federal minister the one thing that all my former colleagues and I felt particularly uncomfortable about was fundraising. I believe that there has been a collapse in voter confidence in the existing system and that it needs change.

Reforming the Constitution

There are many issues that are on the agenda for Constitutional reform. They range from issues like Constitutional recognition of indigenous people, recognition of local government and questions on whether or not we want a republic. However in this section I basically concentrate on one issue, which is the extent of Senate power.

Most Australians know we have adopted the Westminster system of government however that system evolved in significant ways since the 1890s when the Australian Constitution was being written. One of the biggest changes has been to the power of the upper house of parliament. In Great Britain's case that is the House of Lords. For Australia it is the Senate.

When the Australian Federation was being constructed the House of Lords retained all its ancient rights and was an immensely powerful Chamber. It had full rights to block any legislation and it often did so. However, it was not a democratic institution. Its members were not elected but held their seats as a matter of hereditary privilege. As a result when the Federation Fathers drafted the Constitution they looked around the world for alternative models. They latched onto the system in the United States where the Senate was selected by democratically elected state governments (direct popular election of US Senators didn't begin until 1913). The really appealing feature for the Australians was the link to the states and the fact that each state had the same number of representatives. It had the added bonus of the democratic link.

Fast forward from 1901 to only 1911 and Westminster radically changed its system. After a bitterly fought-over series of Budgets and elections between 1909 and 1910 the British substantially reduced the power of the House of Lords. In the *Parliament Act 1911* they legislated that the Lords could no longer reject (nor amend without agreement) a Budget (and only delay it for a month) and could only delay any other legislation for up to two years. In the *Parliament Act 1949* that delaying power was reduced to one year for most legislation. Thus the Lords could delay legislation, but not ultimately defeat it.[1]

And yet in Australia we have persisted with the model we have while the Westminster model on which it is substantially based was fundamentally changed over a 100 years ago. While our Senate remains immensely powerful the House of Lords no longer is.

---

[1] House of Lords, "History of the House of Lords", www.parliament.uk, 13 February.

Nonetheless the Australian Founding Fathers did recognise that on occasion the two houses of parliament would collide and created a mechanism for resolving deadlocks between the House of Representatives and the Senate. That is known as the Double Dissolution provisions under section 57 of the Constitution.

A Double Dissolution Federal Election is "triggered" when one or more pieces of legislation are rejected twice by the Senate given that there must be at least a 3 month gap between rejections. If after the subsequent election the same bills are reintroduced and again rejected by the Senate then the House of Representatives and the Senate meet in a joint sitting. Because Governments usually have majorities in the lower House this gives them an added chance of passing legislation because the House contains double the number of members as there are senators.

Particularly since World War II the Senate has rarely been won by the government of the day.

In 2004 the Howard Government established the Consultative Group on Constitutional Change[2] to examine the prospect of reforming the Senate to allow governments a better chance of passing key parts of their agenda.

In its final report the Consultative Group noted that the current arrangements contained in section 57 of the Constitution were rarely used and not particularly useful. It is noteworthy that while John Howard had double dissolution triggers for each of his subsequent re-elections he never used them. In contrast Malcolm Turnbull did use double dissolution triggers and barely won the 2016 election and because of the lower quota of votes needed for a Senator to be elected in a Double Dissolution (i.e., 7.7 per cent of the vote rather

---

[2] Consultative Group on Constitutional Change (2004), *Resolving Deadlocks: The Public Response*, Commonwealth of Australia, Canberra, March 2004.

than 14.3 per cent of the vote in a normal half-Senate election) he lost three Senate positions to small micro parties.

The Consultative Group noted that over the years the ability of a government to win a majority in the Senate had virtually disappeared even when they won a significant landslide in the House of Representatives. The fact that the Howard Government had a majority between 2005 and 2007 was actually a case of the "exception proving the rule". The last time such an event had occurred was for an equally brief period in the 1960s. A 40 year gap suggests that there is a problem here.

The Consultative Group noted that the ability of governments to win Senate majorities had become harder with the introduction by the Chifley Government of proportional voting in 1948 and the subsequent large increase in the size of the Senate in 1984 to 12 senators for each state, which was implemented by the Hawke Government. The result has decreased even further a government's ability to secure a majority.

The Consultative Group, upon the request of Prime Minister Howard, explored two principal options for reform.

The first option "would allow the Prime Minister to ask the Governor-General to convene a joint sitting of both houses to consider a bill originating in the House of Representatives which the Senate had rejected or failed to pass. The bill must have been put before the two houses twice during the life of the parliament with a three months interval between each attempt to gain Senate approval. In other words, the first option removes the requirement for the parliament to be dissolved and an election held to resolve the deadlock. Rather, it would be possible to move to the joint sitting after the trigger events have been reached".[3]

The second option "would allow the Prime Minister to ask the

---

[3] Consultative Group on Constitutional Change 2004, 7.

Governor-General to convene a joint sitting following an election in order to consider a bill that was the subject of disagreement between the two houses on two separate occasions in the previous parliament and was again disagreed in the new parliament. In other words, an option for a joint sitting becomes a standard feature following each general election of the House of Representatives and half the Senate or the House of representatives alone".[4]

After conducting a series of consultations across the country the Consultative Group concluded that the community had no appetite for reform. As a result the Howard Government never pursued the matter, not least because they were able to reach that remarkable milestone of a Senate majority in 2005.

I believe we should return to this matter. If indeed there is little community support we should do what is the bread and butter of politics and seek to educate the public on the necessity of reform. It will be, undeniably, a hard task. But again it is something that needs to be prosecuted.

Finally, can I just add that if this matter was dealt with it would then be feasible to increase the size of the House of Representatives. As a former MP for a rural seat I know that the geographic size of such electorates is becoming so large that they are actually almost impossible to service properly. If we were able to solve the Senate deadlock problem then the existing political bar to increasing the size of the House (namely the automatic proportionate increase in the size of the Senate and therefore reduction even further of the 14.3 per cent quota for election) would be less of a problem.

Fundraising Reform

What would appear nominally as a side issue for this book, but is actually a hugely important one, is the issue of federal political

---
[4] Consultative Group on Constitutional Change 2004, 7.

fundraising. I think it is clear that there is a case for reform and I think it is crucial.

I believe that what is emerging as a major threat to our democracy is best typified by the ACTU's intervention in the electoral system during the course of the 2004-2007 Parliamentary term. They spent an unprecedented amount of money opposing the Howard Government. The more conservative estimate is that they spent something like $30 million plus. However, some other estimates are $40 or $50 million and former Federal Treasurer Joe Hockey (and John Howard's last Workplace Relations Minister) has claimed is was as high as $100 million.[5] We don't actually know because the ACTU stated that the bulk of their expenditure did not fall under the definitions of the Electoral Act and so they have never fully disclosed what they spent. Nevertheless this magnitude of expenditure needs to be put in perspective. In a typical Federal election campaign major parties spend around $20 million each.

Some people claim that the ACTU's intervention was no different than the commercial banks supporting the Liberal Party in the run-up to the 1949 election, when they were petrified about nationalisation by the Chifley Government. There are some similarities no doubt, but after that election I understand that it was not long before electoral funding returned to normal patterns. What we are seeing in Australia today is a continuation of this ACTU intervention with a similar story in the 2010, 2013 and 2016 elections. We are seeing the institutionalisation of the ACTU model, to the massive detriment of the non-union aligned parties.

On the Liberal Party side the sources of money for fundraising have become narrower and narrower. Twenty or thirty years ago the Liberal Party was able to match or exceed the Labor Party in

---

[5] News.com.au, "ACTU denies $70m IR campaign", www.news.com.au, 17 March.

fundraising by getting funds from a significant number of large Australian corporations. As the years have gone by and shareholder activism has increased an equally significant number of those large corporations have simply stopped donating money altogether or give equal (small) amounts to both major parties. In many cases they have done this because Australian corporations have increasingly been taken over by multinationals that do not prioritise Australian politics, given their global interests. Additionally, many companies, particularly mining companies, have adopted strict codes of conduct banning political donations. These were originally designed to stop potentially corrupt payments in Third World countries, but nevertheless have an impact on mature democratic countries like Australia.

The result of this is that while the source of funds for the Liberal side of politics is drying up the Labour side can still rely on a huge amount of resources from trade unions. Whether you are a partisan supporter of either major party or not it is abundantly clear that over the long run this is not a good state of affairs. On one side it has the Labor Party increasingly the captive of the trade union movement despite that movements share of the private sector workforce falling to as low as only 10 per cent. On the other side you have the similar situation where the Liberal Party receives funding from an also diminishing supporter base and increasingly from high net-worth individuals. It has led to the unhealthy precedent of Malcolm Turnbull personally being the single largest donor in the 2016 election – i.e., he virtually had to self-fund his party's election campaign.

So what do we do? I suspect the best way to proceed is to adopt the model that former Premier Barry O'Farrell sought to implement in New South Wales after his election in 2011.

However, before I describe how things could be changed I need to quickly state the general rules for federal political fundraising.

In reality they are fairly simple and are governed by the *Commonwealth Electoral Act 1918* (as amended).[6] There are no limits on how much can be raised and basically no limits on who they can be raised from. However, there are reasonably strict disclosure rules with a limit of over $13,000 (which is indexed) above which the donor must be publicly identified. This data is then periodically published by the Australian Electoral Commission. Finally, a candidate or Senate group is eligible for election funding if they obtain at least 4 per cent of the formal first preference vote in their electorate.

In NSW, the outgoing Labor Government of Premier Kristina Keneally set strict limits on donations from people and other entities of only $5,000 (now $6,100) and limited expenditure in individual lower house seats to only $100,000 (now $122,900), and total expenditure for a party and third-party campaigners, such as trade unions, of $1,050,000 (now $1,288,500). They banned donations from property developers, tobacco, liquor and gambling interests. One could cynically observe that after those groups had previously poured huge amounts of money into Labor coffers prior to 2011 now that the electoral mood was changing, the outgoing government wanted to handicap the fundraising potential of the Liberals. Lastly, a major loophole for third party participants allowed large spending by trade unions on their own behalf.

Now I know that it ultimately failed, but before we get to that let's look at what Barry O'Farrell proposed in 2012. Faced with the issues I raised above he decided that rather than abolish Labor's stricter rules and return to the previous status quo (roughly similar to today's federal laws), he would go even further and seek more bans. Therefore he passed legislation that banned donations from all corporations and all trade unions and further increased

---

[6] Information sourced from Australian Electoral Commission (2018), www.aec.gov.au 13 February.

public funding. This would level the playing field and remove the incentives for increasing "arms race" on raising funds.

Unfortunately, in my view, this legislation was struck down by the High Court in *Unions NSW v New South Wales* saying that it contravened an "implied freedom of political communication mandated by the Commonwealth Constitution".[7] This position was later reconfirmed in *McCloy v New South Wales*.[8]

Following this the NSW Government established an independent panel to examine the issue, chaired by former senior public servant Kerry Schott.[9] They explored the possibility of a complete ban on private donations and a move to total public funding. They found that the cost would be exorbitant – $100 million in NSW alone[10] – and noted that they only found one democracy that had done this and it was Tunisia and only for a short period of time.[11] As a consequence they made various recommendations that would incrementally change the system left in place by the Keneally Government. One important reform that they support is the banning of foreign donations.

I believe that we should look again – but this time at the federal level – at the O'Farrell reforms. Equally I believe that something must be done in restricting third-party expenditure to deal with the ACTU model that I talked of in the beginning of this section. At the very least it should be restricted as occurs in the NSW legislation. Due to the High Court's decision in Unions NSW v New South Wales and McCloy v New South Wales it would appear that a

---

[7] Kerry Schott, Andrew Tink and John Watkins (2014), *Political Donations: Final Report Volumes 1 & 2*, NSW Government, Sydney, December, 3, 36-38.

[8] Martin Clark (2015), "McCloy v New South Wales", *Melbourne Law School Opinions on High*, Melbourne, 7 October

[9] Schott, Tink and Watkins 2014.

[10] Ibid., 2.

[11] Ibid., 3.

change to the Constitution might be needed to allow for this. I think that investigation is warranted.

Conclusion

Australia desperately needs to fix its democracy. A poll conducted by ANU Professor Ian McAllister found that "satisfaction with democracy slumped from 86 per cent in 2007 to 72 per cent" in June 2014.[12] Further, a 2016 poll commissioned by the Lowy Institute alarmingly said that only 42 per cent of Australians aged between 18 and 29 thought democracy was "the most preferable form of government".[13]

There are many issues about our democracy besides the ones raised in this chapter and I refer the reader to the parallel issue of the destructive effect of social media on our democracy that is discussed in chapter 4. As with the economic reform issues that I canvas in this book the topics for discussion in this chapter have been chosen because I regard them as issues that rise to the top of the pile when examining the sustainability of the Australian Settlement 2.0. They are by no means all of the key parliamentary and related reforms that need to be discussed.

I believe that changing the deadlock rules in the Senate are a vital change to our system. We need to alter the Constitution via a referendum to implement them. However they are that important.

Equally, while it is possible to change some fundraising laws via simple legislation I argue that if we need to also alter the Constitution to establish even better laws that should be done.

Thus in this chapter I offer a number of potential solutions to

---

[12] O'Neill (2014), "Poll data reveals Australia's waning interest in politics, decline in support for democracy", *ABC News online* www.abc.net.au, 12 August.

[13] Michael Safi (2016), "Have millennials given up on democracy?", *The Guardian*, 19 March.

help deal with an increasing lack of faith in our democracy. If we do not deal with this issue then everything that we have gained from the creation of the Australian Settlement 2.0 will be lost. It is predicated on a strong liberal democracy.

Finally, I note that following the discussion in chapters 2 and 3 the business community has a particularly important role to play in arguing the case for sustaining the Australian Settlement 2.0.

6
TAX REFORM PART A
(THE REFORM AGENDA AND COMPANY TAX)

Introduction

When I was at University studying economics I remember reading that "taxation policy is probably the most important function of federal government decision-making, short of deciding on an act of war"[1]. It was true then, it is true now. Due to that I have spent a lot of my career on taxation policy.

Earlier in my career I was one of the principal authors of the *Fightback!* package that was produced by John Hewson and Peter Reith when they were respectively the Leader and Deputy Leader of the Federal Liberal Party between 1990 and 1993. That package proposed a huge number of changes to the tax system. The centrepiece was the introduction of a Goods and Services Tax (GST). The principal reason for doing so was to fund other tax changes such as major cuts to personal income tax.

Later I was in charge of the Business Tax Section of the Federal Treasury. Ironically many of my staff had been involved in arming Prime Minister Paul Keating with data to help him destroy the *Fightback!* package as a political document.

Later, when I was at ACCI we drew up a comprehensive blueprint[2] for reforming the taxation system and in 2006, together with Dick Warburton, I co-authored an independent report for

---

[1] *The Australian* (1981), editorial, 24 February.
[2] Australian Chamber of Commerce and Industry (2004), *Taxation Reform Blueprint: A Strategy for the Australian Taxation System 2004-2014*, Canberra.

Treasurer Costello and the Howard Government on an international comparison of Australia's tax system.³

In my view, over 10 years later, the case for reform remains. There has been progress in recent years, but not enough. For example, University of Calgary economist Dr Jack Mintz has noted that: "Critics will not accept the inconvenient truth of the link between the tax burden on capital investment and economic growth from which every Australian would benefit."⁴

This chapter firstly describes the current state of the Australian taxation system and why it is in need of reform. It then proceeds to focus on reform of company taxation. In later chapters I turn to the issue of personal income tax cuts and the GST; and reforming state taxation.

State of play on tax reform

No one likes taxes and Australians are no different in this regard than citizens in any other country in the world. They have an additional right to dislike the way the Australian taxation system has been built up in an ad hoc way over decades.

I note that for a comprehensive, and relatively up to date overview of the Australian taxation system, a very good place to start is the *Re:think Tax discussion paper*⁵ from March 2015 produced for the Government by the Australian Treasury. For the purposes of this book I have heavily relied on the statistical analysis in that document.

Due to our federal system, taxation is split between two levels of government. At the Commonwealth level Australia's taxation system is made up of:

---

³ Peter Hendy and Richard Warburton (2006), *International Comparison of Australia's Taxes*, Canberra, 3 April.

⁴ Frank Drenth (2018), "Maxed out on taxes", *Daily Telegraph*, 1 February.

⁵ Australian Government (2015), *Re:think Tax discussion paper, monograph,* Canberra, March.

- Direct taxes, such as:
  - Personal income tax;
  - Capital gains tax (CGT); and
  - Corporate (or company) tax; and
- Indirect taxes, such as:
  - GST;
  - Excise taxes on alcohol and tobacco; and
  - Customs duties (ie tariffs on imported goods).

In addition, at the state level there are a number of other indirect taxes, such as:

- Payroll tax;
- Stamp duties;
- Gambling taxes;
- Business franchise fees; and
- Land taxes

Before the Howard Government's introduction of the GST in 2000, there had been many official inquiries into the taxation system with the three most important since the early 1970s being the 1975 Taxation Review Committee Report (the Asprey Report)[6], the 1976 Committee of Inquiry into Inflation and Taxation Report (the Mathews Report)[7] and the 1985 Reform of the Australian Tax System: Draft White Paper (the Draft White Paper).[8] There have also been numerous examples of reviews at the political level that have principally come to nought. The most famous being the 1991

---

[6] Taxation Review Committee (KW Asprey, Chair) (1975), Full Report, AGPS, Canberra.

[7] Committee of Inquiry into Inflation and Taxation (R Mathews, Chair) (1976), "Inflation and Taxation", AGPS, Canberra.

[8] Commonwealth of Australia (1985), "Reform of the Australian Tax System: Draft White Paper, Canberra, June.

Fightback! package of the Liberal and National Parties. There have also been a number of state government reviews. What these multitudinous studies have shown is that there are many problems with the current structure of taxation in Australia today.

The major problems with the taxation system in the 1990s were:

- Inconsistencies in, and non-indexation of, the income tax base;
- Excessive reliance on income tax with a bias against saving;
- Inconsistencies in the tax treatment of different types of investment;
- A bias against exports; and
- Excessive reliance on state taxes with high marginal deadweight losses.[9]

Not much has changed 20 years on. I will examine these matters in the following discussion.

And, concluding this section, let me note the size of the taxation burden that Australians have to deal with. Taking into account social security mandates (which, by the way, I strongly argued for when I worked with Dick Warburton on our "International Comparison of Australian taxes" report to Treasurer Peter Costello in 2006[10]) the total Australian tax burden as a share of GDP is 32.2 per cent. When taking account of economic size and trade that is higher than an OECD average of 30-31 per cent. So we are not a low taxed economy.

Recent tax "reform" picture

Over the last decade there have been a large number of taxation related changes. The highlights include:

---
[9] Robert Albon (1996), "An Overview of Australia's Taxation Structure", Paper commissioned by the Productivity Commission, AGPS, Canberra, 1.
[10] Hendy and Warburton 2006.

- The introduction (2012) and later abolition (2014) of the Carbon Pricing Mechanism more colloquially known as the Carbon Tax.
- The introduction (2012) and later abolition (2014) of the Minerals Resource Rent Tax.
- The introduction (2014) of the Temporary Budget Repair Levy on top of the existing personal income tax. It ceased application from 1 July 2017.
- The introduction of a separate (lower) small business company tax rate of 28.5 per cent.
- The introduction in 2015 of immediate deductibility for asset purchases by small business for up to $20,000, subsequently extended.
- The announcement of the 10 Year Enterprise Tax Plan in the 2016 Budget including:
    - Targeted personal income tax relief;
    - Establishing a Tax Avoidance Taskforce
    - Reducing the company tax rate to 25 per cent
    - A very large Superannuation reform package saving $2 billion over 4 years
- The announcement of a Major Bank Levy in the 2017 Budget.

It probably goes without saying, but not all these changes can necessarily be described as "reform".

Prioritising tax reform

There has been a recent debate in Australia over the relative merits of the economic benefits of company tax cuts compared to personal income tax cuts. Personally I believe that both should be done. However let's have a look at the issue in a little more detail.

The Government stated in the 2016 Budget[11] that the company tax reform contained in its 10 Year Enterprise Tax Plan would boost GDP by just over 1 percentage point per annum after full implementation.

How does this economic dividend compare with other tax reform options? Luckily we have a direct comparison. In February 2016 the Government released Treasury calculations that showed a GST tax mix switch focussed on personal income tax cuts would not result in any sizeable boost to the economy.[12] So that would appear to be case-closed on that then.

However, not so fast. It should be noted that the calculations were based on a package skewed to adversely impact on lower income groups and was unlikely to be the type of package that any government would announce.[13] I say more on the economic modelling implications of such a GST tax mix in the next chapter.

More widely the literature on the benefits of personal income tax reform alone is mixed, although in favour of reform. In a recent overview of the academic literature, former senior executive at the International Monetary Fund, the World Bank and the Australian Treasury, Robert Carling, has noted that "the case for reforming personal income tax rests on its harmful economic effects, the damage to incentives and the excessive dependence on it relative to other sources of tax revenue. ... All taxes do some economic harm, but personal income tax is among the more harmful, particularly a progressive income tax".[14]

---

[11] Australian Government (2016), *Budget 2016-17: Sticking to our national economic plan*, 3 May, 2.

[12] Malcolm Turnbull and Scott Morrison (2016), "Release of tax modelling", joint media release, 12 February.

[13] Ross Burgess (2016), "Scott Morrison's 'no-growth' GST plan was bogus", *The New Daily*, 12 February.

[14] Robert Carling (2016), *Taming the Monster: reforming personal income tax*, Research Report 12, Centre for Independent Studies, April, 11.

Helpfully, the Treasury calculated for the *Re:think* discussion paper the economic cost of different taxes. They measured the "marginal excess burden" of the taxes or put another way they measured some of the economic costs associated with a tax on the aggregate welfare of Australian households. Specifically they calculated the adverse monetary impact of raising an additional $1 of revenue on the economy. This is sometimes called the "deadweight loss".

Saunders[15] succinctly explains that deadweight losses arise:

> ... when individuals change their behaviour for another which would have been preferred had the tax increase not occurred. For example, if income taxes rise, some people might decide to work fewer hours, or they might conclude it is not worthwhile training for an additional qualification, or they might stay on welfare rather than look for a job, or be deterred from the risk of setting up a company of their own. Deadweight losses, in other words, represent the disincentive costs of tax. They are the value of all the work and output that we lose as a result of taxing people's incomes.

Chart 1 gives the Treasury results. The marginal excess burden imposed on the economy (or deadweight economic cost) of a hypothetical flat rate labour income tax is around $1.20 or 20 per cent.[16] That is 20 cents in the dollar extra burden on households across the economy. This is on their low baseline model and is roughly equivalent to the burden of a 10 per cent GST. In itself 20 per cent will strike the reader as a very high number. Nonetheless, the chart shows that there is by far a worse marginal excess burden for stamp duties on conveyances and company income tax. Thus it reinforces the argument that company tax cuts should be a priority issue at the federal level, and reform of stamp duties at the state level.

---

[15] Peter Saunders (ed) (2006), Taxploitation: The Case for Income Tax Reform, the Centre for Independent Studies, Sydney, xi.
[16] Australian Government 2015, 24-25.

Chart 1: Longrun modelling estimates of the marginal excess burden of some of Australia's taxes

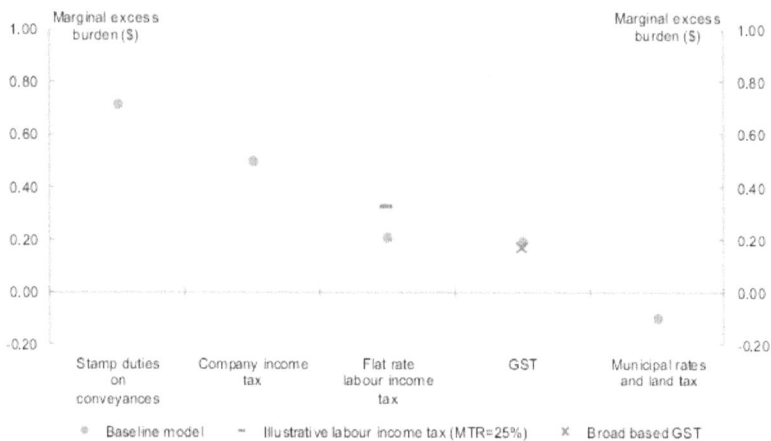

Note: Marginal excess burdens were estimated using a longrun CGE model of the Australian economy and tax system. Australian households are captured as a single economic unit in this model. The labour income tax is modelled as a stylised flat tax on labour income only. An outofmodel calculation for a marginal tax rate (MTR) of 25 per cent is presented as an illustration of an average taxpayer in 2011-12. Transfer payments are not captured in this model. Source: Treasury estimates.

Australian Government 2015, 25

Nonetheless, a higher rate of income tax e.g., 25 per cent was also measured to have an impact closer to 40 cents in the $1. Thus it would appear, a progressive tax would impose a higher burden which quickly surpasses the impact of other taxes like the GST. Personal income tax cuts then become an increasingly important economic reform.

Additional work by Treasury officers shows that "the incidence of major taxes is largely borne by workers through lower real wages caused by lower labour productivity".[17]

---

[17] Liangyne Cao et al (2015), "Understanding the Economic Efficiency and Incidence of Major Australian Taxes", *Treasury Working Paper* 2015-01, April.

Alex Robson[18] – who is currently the Prime Minister's Senior Advisor (economics) – also found that the deadweight loss for personal income tax in the United States ranged between 20 per cent and 40 per cent.

A 2006 Lateral Economics paper prepared for CEDA concluded that there were significant benefits to economic growth for targeted tax cuts. It noted that "the Australians facing the strongest disincentives to work are mostly on middle to low incomes. These people are also the ones most likely to respond to the incentive provided by tax cuts"[19].

More recently in 2017, Pascal Saint Amans, the Head of Tax Policy at the OECD has concluded that "tax cuts to low and middle income earners, in particular, can be an important way of supporting increased labour market participation and stronger growth".[20] In the OECD's *Taxing Wages 2017* report it notes that across the OECD there has been progress in reducing the income tax burden in recent years but it has been slow. The report goes on to say that "boosting the work incentives of low and middle income earners by reducing the tax wedge [i.e., net tax after taking account of welfare payments] on labour incomes continues to be an important way of encouraging inclusive growth".[21] By "encouraging inclusive growth" the OECD means decreasing inequality.

---

[18] Alex Robson (2006), "How High Taxation Makes Us Poorer", in Peter Saunders (ed) 2006, Taxploitation: The Case for Income Tax Reform, the Centre for Independent Studies, Sydney, 30-31.

[19] Lateral Economics (2006), *Tax Cuts for Growth: The impact of marginal tax rates on Australia's labour supply*, Committee for Economic Development of Australia, information paper 84, 1.

[20] Nasim Khadem, (2017), "OECD backs personal tax cuts to tackle rising inequality", *Sydney Morning Herald*, 15 September.

[21] OECD (2017), "OECD tax rates on labour income continued decreasing slowly in 2016", media release, 11 April.

Finally, a recent 2014 paper published by the Brookings Institution concluded that personal income tax cuts would have positive impact on economic growth but the net impact is uncertain and could generally be small depending on the way they are funded. They make the critical point that "the structuring and financing of a tax change are critical to achieving economic growth. Tax rate cuts may encourage individuals to work, save, and invest, but if the tax cuts are not financed by immediate spending cuts they will likely also result in an increased federal budget deficit, which in the long-term will reduce national saving and raise interest rates"[22].

So the conclusion is that company tax cuts remain a top priority while reform of personal income tax and state taxes rank very highly as well. In the remainder of this chapter I continue the discussion on company tax reform before turning to the other two matters in chapters 7 and 8.

Prospects for the passage of company tax cut legislation

Of key interest to the wider business community has been the Government's company tax changes.

At the end of March 2017 the Government was able to secure the passage of a large part of its 10 Year Enterprise Tax Plan. In particular this included a significant part of their company tax reforms passing through the Senate and subsequently being implemented. Despite trenchant opposition from the Labor Party and Greens the Government was able to secure just enough support from the Senate cross bench.

Companies with an annual turnover of up to $50 million will see their tax rate cut to 27.5 per cent, at a cost to the budget of $5.2

---

[22] William G. Gale and Andrew A. Samwick (2014), "Effects of Income Tax Changes on Economic Growth", *Economic Studies*, The Brookings Institution, September, abstract.

billion over the next four years, and eventually to 25 per cent at a cost of $24 billion over the medium term. That is a little less than half the cost of the package originally proposed by the government in the 2016 Budget.

The Federal Government's original plan, was to cut tax for all companies from 30 per cent to 25 per cent over 10 years, through to 2026-27.

To gain the passage through the Senate the Government had to make an obvious compromise on a ceiling of $50 million. There were also some side deals with Senator Nick Xenophon for a one-off payment of $75 to singles and $125 to couples who receive the aged, disabled and carers pensions, to cope with rising electricity prices, at a Budget cost of $260 million; and an agreement by the Government to provide a $110 million loan for a solar thermal plant in South Australia, and an agreement to examine the feasibility of constructing a gas pipeline from the Northern Territory to South Australia.

The prospects of further company tax cuts are very limited, certainly in this term of Parliament, which finishes in mid-2019.

The Labor Party have vigorously opposed any company tax reform except for companies at $2 million or less (and this has now been implemented). Nonetheless, if they were to return to Government it is not clear what their policy would be. When last in Government they repeatedly proposed company tax reductions. However, delivery was not forthcoming.

As it states in the 2016 Budget,[23] Australia's company tax rate is high by international standards and well above the average for OECD countries and those in the Asian region. If Australia is going to be competitive in the 21st century, we need a competitive tax system.

---

[23] Australian Government 2016, *Budget 2016-17 Overview*, 3 May, 10.

Charts 2 and 3 give a good overview of Australia compared to other countries, and the trends over time. And shows why reform is important. For example two countries we like to compare ourselves against are the UK and Singapore. The company tax rates are 19 per cent in Britain and 17 percent in Singapore.

Chart 2: Trend in company tax rates in selected economies

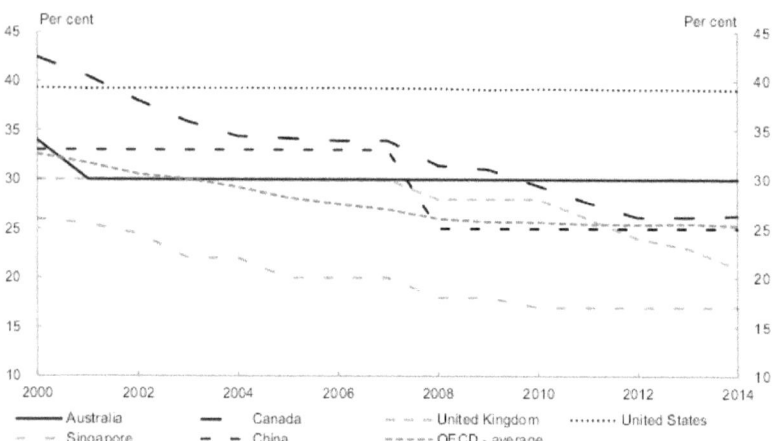

Source: Organisation for Economic Cooperation and Development (OECD) 2014, Tax Database — Taxation of Corporate and Capital Income, OECD, Paris, www.oecd.org; KPMG 2014, Corporate tax rates table, www.kpmg.com; and KPMG 2007, Hong Kong Tax Competiveness Series: Corporate Tax Rates, www.kpmg.com; KPMG 2006, KPMG's Corporate Tax Rate Survey, An international analysis of corporate tax rates from 1993 to 2006, www.lib.uwo.ca.

Australian Government 2015, 74

Reforming company tax rates

The biggest single event that has enhanced the argument for proceeding with the second half of Australia's company tax cut plan is what has been labelled the "Trump Tax Reforms" that occurred in the United States in the dying days of 2017. Although to be more accurate it was not President Trump's policy alone, but one jointly

adopted by the Republican Party, particularly US House of Representatives Speaker Paul Ryan.
The most important part of the reforms was a US$1.5 trillion

Chart 3: Company tax rates, selected trading partners, 2014

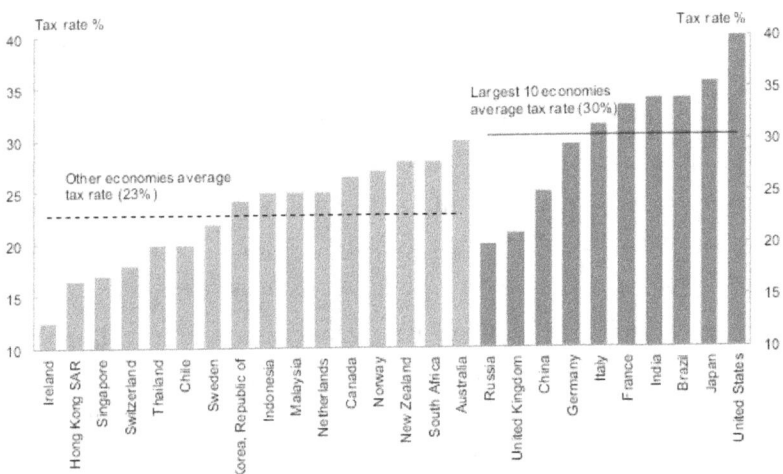

Note: Company tax rates in this chart are estimates as the effective tax rate can vary depending on the specific tax rules applied in each jurisdiction. Chart 5.2 uses a different data source to Chart 5.1 which may result in slight differences in the estimates. For example, the United States' company income tax rate is approximately 40 per cent. The estimate of this rate can vary depending on how company income taxes applied at the subcentral level (by state and local governments) are measured. The Indian Government announced in their 2015-16 budget that they would introduce a company tax cut from a base rate of 30 to 25 percent over four years, coupled with some reductions in tax concessions. The rate of 33.99% shown above includes various surcharges over the base rate.
Source: KPMG 2014, Corporate tax rates table, www.kpmg.com
Australian Government 2015, 75

cut in the company rate from 35 per cent to 21 percent.[24] The package also included a cut to the top personal income tax rate from 39.6 per cent to 37 per cent,[25] well below Australia's top rate.

The International Monetary Fund boosted world economic growth rate forecasts off the back of these changes from 3.7 per cent to 3.9 per cent, with US growth rate forecasts rising from 2.3 per cent to 2.7 per cent in 2018 and from 1.9 per cent to 2.5 per cent in 2019. Although it should be noted that part of this increase was attributed to another part of the tax reform package, namely to a temporary instant asset write-off for companies.[26]

As the chairman of the Australian Business Coalition for Tax Reform, Frank Drenth, has said: "If your most dominant business competitor permanently drops its prices, you have little choice but to follow suit if you want to remain in business."[27]

Indeed, Malcolm Turnbull has reconfirmed the importance of Australia's company tax cuts after the Trump legislation passed Congress. He said that: "With the US cutting company tax to 21 per cent, the need to remain competitive is more intense than ever."[28]

Although the Labor Party has been opposing these reforms it has not always played the populist card. In fact the Hawke and Keating Governments reduced company tax rates from 49 per cent to 33 per cent over their 13 years in office and as Leader of the Opposition, Bill Shorten, has previously stated when he was a

---

[24] Daniel Wild (2017), "Australia must match Trump to compete on tax", *The Australian*, 21 December.

[25] Cameron Stewart (2017), "Trumps High Stakes Gambit", *The Australian*, 21 December.

[26] Peter Martin and Eryk Bagshaw (2018) "IMF tick but break no sure thing" *Sydney Morning Herald*, 27 January.

[27] Drenth 2018.

[28] Benson, Simon (2018), "PM's tax cut drive for companies, workers", *The Australian*, 1 February.

Government Minister in 2012: "Any student of Australian business and economic history since the mid-80s knows that part of Australia's success was derived through the reduction in the company tax rate. We need to be able to make life easier for Australian business, which employs two in every three Australians."[29]

Finally, I note that a 2017 OECD report has stated "Lowering the effective rate of corporate income tax (as part of a tax shift) can deliver substantial income gains for all with few consequences for the distribution of income." The report goes on to say: "No statistically significant effect on the income distribution appears for company income tax."[30] As David Uren reported, "The OECD study, based on results in 34 advanced countries between 1980 and 2014, found that lower company taxes encouraged businesses to invest more in innovation to improve their returns."[31]

More radical change to company tax

The debate on reforming company taxation has not stopped with the question of the headline rate of tax. That issue is crucial but there is more to the tax system than that. For example I briefly noted in the last section that part of the economic benefits that will derive from the so-called Trump Tax Reform relate to the changes to the treatment of assets and depreciation.

For the purposes of this book I am not going to delve too far into the arcane area of company tax law. However, it is worth noting that there is a more radical change to the tax system that is currently being debated by tax professionals and economists. It is what has been labelled destination-based cash flow tax (DBCFT).

---

[29] *The Australian* (2018), "Cut Company tax to boost jobs", editorial, 12 January.
[30] David Uren (2018), "Company tax cuts benefit all, OECD", *The Australian*, 11 January.
[31] Ibid.

It has also been called a "consumption-based tax system". Out the outset of this discussion I would like to thank my old friend, Tim Beale – a leading taxation expert – for drawing my attention to this concept. He is one of, if not *the*, Australian expert on the issue. As he explained to me in an interview for this book: "The current system for allocating the rights to tax international profit is based on a compromise between the taxing incidences of 'residence' and 'source'. It is often argued that the conceptual basis for this compromise is weak and its implementation is flawed. One proposed option is to change the method of taxing companies by taxing consumption rather than income. Such an option requires the implementation of a destination-based cash flow tax. A DBCFT calculates a company's tax by taxing cash inflows while deducting cash outflows and so tax on consumption rather than income."[32]

This is a particularly relevant debate because the US Republican Party adopted it as part of their 2016 Election Platform and then proceeded to see if they could implement it through the course of 2017. In the end they decided not to pursue it after their protracted negotiations to get tax reform through the Congress. The Republican leadership announced at the time that "we are now confident that, without transitioning to a new domestic consumption-based tax system, there is a viable approach for ensuring a level playing field between American and foreign companies and workers, while protecting American jobs and the US tax base."[33]

What has brought this issue to the fore is the worldwide concerns of tax authorities – and ordinary tax payers, for that matter – about aggressive tax minimisation through profit shifting strategies of large multinational companies. Many analysts have come to the

---

32 Timothy Beale (2018), interview with author 23 January.
33 Paul Ryan; Mitch McConnell; Steve Mnuchin; Gary Cohn; Orrin Hatch; Kevin Brady (2017),"Joint Statement on Tax Reform", Washington DC, 27 July.

conclusion that the problem is rooted in the fundamental way we tax company income. As the various national systems become more complex the view is that the ability of companies to "write-off" expenditure in a way that minimises tax has become so problematic that the whole approach needs to be questioned. They argue that the clear alternative is to essentially tax "cash flow" or the "consumption" of companies.

It should be noted that the matter is not clear cut and there are lots of issues that need to be resolved if this matter were to be proceeded with. For example there is a big question mark over the implications for existing trade rules under the WTO. This has been raised by a number of commentators. In particular, the Productivity Commission has expressed concern.[34] That concern relates to what they term "related border adjustments" to the company income tax base whereby "revenue from sales overseas would be untaxed and the cost of imported goods would no longer be deductible in calculating taxable income. These adjustments would be equivalent to a subsidy for exports and a tax on imports."[35] They note that this matter has been "vehemently debated" but say that "ultimately these are empirical issues"[36]. Its conclusion, from an Australian point of view, is that if the US were to unilaterally proceed it "could have impacts on global trade even after compensating adjustments in the exchange rate. They would: lead to a small increase in US net exports; change the composition of economic activity in the United States, favouring exporters and firms that compete with imports, but their overall effect on real US GDP would be small [and] have little effect on economic activity in Australia and in most other US trade partners."[37]

---

[34] Productivity Commission (2017a), *Rising protectionism: challenges, threats and opportunities for Australia*, Research Paper, Melbourne, July, 43-53.

[35] Productivity Commission 2017a, 43.

[36] Ibid.

[37] Ibid.

There has been a vigorous debate in the United States about introducing such a system.[38] In Australia the Ralph Review looked at it and thought it had merit. The Henry Review also looked at it but did not think it was practical at that time to pursue it. However with the debate now reaching a legislative level in the United States more and more countries will look more seriously at the matter and I think it is well worth the Australian Government giving it more attention.

Other areas for reform

One area of the economy that is crying out for taxation reform is small business.

The ACCI pre-election survey for 2013 found that more than three-quarters of businesses expressed major and moderate concerns

---

[38] A.J. Auerbach (2010), "A Modern Corporate Tax", The Center for American Progress/The Hamilton Project; A.J. Auerbach and D. Holtz–Eakin (2016), "The Role of Border Adjustments in International Taxation," American Action Forum, available at www.americanactionforum.org; A.J. Auerbach, M.P. Devereux and H. Simpson (2010), "Taxing Corporate Income", in J. Mirrlees et al (eds.), (2010) Dimensions of Tax Design: The Mirrlees Review, Oxford: Oxford University Press, 837-893; Alan Auerbach, Michael Devereux, Michael Keen and John Vella (2017), "Destination-Based Cash Flow Taxation', WP 17/01 Oxford University Centre for Business Taxation, 6-7; Reuven Avi-Yonah and Kimberly Clausing (2017), 'Problems with Destination-Based Corporate Taxes and the Ryan Blueprint', Law and Economics Research Paper Series Paper No. 16-029 Michigan Law, University of Michigan; William B. Barker (2014), 'A Common Sense Corporate Tax: The Case for a Destination-Based, Cash Flow Tax on Corporations', 61 Cath. U. L. Rev. 955, 971; William B. Barker (2010), "International Tax Reform should Begin at Home: Replace the Corporate Income Tax with a Territorial Expenditure Tax" *Northwestern Journal of International Law & Business*, 647; Clemens Fuest, Christoph Spengel, Katharina Finke, Jost H. Heckemeyer and Hannah Nusser (2013), 'Profit Shifting and "Aggressive" Tax Planning by Multinational Firms: Issues and Options for Reform', October, Vol 5, Issue 3, *World Tax Journal*, 307; M.P. Devereux and R. de la Feria (2014), "Defining and implementing a destination based corporate tax", Oxford University Centre for Business Taxation Working Paper 14/07.

with company tax (79.7 per cent), compulsory superannuation levy (75.3 per cent) and personal income tax (78.1 per cent).

Further small and medium-sized firms rated the superannuation levy as one of their top five concerns, while large firms placed it well down in their list of concerns. As the ACCI commented "The concern of SMEs is understandable as the superannuation levy is one of the major on-costs for hiring workers and this on-cost will increase further following the increase of the levy from the current 9 to 12 per cent over the coming years". ACCI asked businesses which taxation areas needed further reform. It found that while small business ranked company tax reductions and personal income tax reductions as their first and second tax reform priority respectively; medium and large businesses rated payroll tax reductions and company tax reductions as their first and second reform priority.

Obviously I canvas changes to company tax and personal income tax in this book. Payroll tax is a state tax and while it is probably too large a revenue collector to get rid of, I will look at various aspects of Commonwealth-State taxation in chapter 8. I am not going to examine superannuation taxes in this book. It is an area where there has been large changes in recent years and I firmly believe there needs to be a moratorium on change so that industry participants can get over their reform fatigue. I believe that too many of the recent changes have simply been motivated by governments trying to increase their revenue take rather than enhance superannuation as a means to accumulate retirement benefits. Therefore at some stage it is an area that must be revisited.

Conclusion

Frank Drenth, chair of the Business Coalition for Tax Reform has noted that "The Henry Report in 2009 observed that company tax is a distortive and relatively inefficient tax that falls mainly on workers. Dr Ken Henry said at the time: 'The consensus of public finance theorists is that in Australia, if the company tax were to be cut, the principal beneficiaries will be workers'."[39]

There is a very strong case to continue to pursue taxation reform. In this chapter we focussed on changes to the company tax rate.

When a previous government cut the company rate to 30 per cent it was clearly a very competitive rate. However, many nations have gone well past that point. In recent times President Trump has led the charge on a major cut to company rates in the United States. At 21 per cent it put the Australian rate into the shade. Because of the potentially significant productivity boost to the Australian economy that would result I think it is essential that the Government continue to argue for further company tax cuts. Simply put it would be a reduction of taxation on badly needed investment.

Secondly, I think there is a case for examining the fundamental way we tax corporations. I have raised the recent debate in the United States on the destination-based cash flow tax for corporations and note that the Australian taxation authorities should have a closer look at this policy debate.

---

[39] Drenth 2018.

7
TAX REFORM PART B
(PERSONAL INCOME TAX REFORM AND GST)

Introduction

The last chapter gave an overview of taxation reform issues and gave a comparison between the priorities of cutting company tax and personal income tax. In this chapter we explore the personal tax system in more detail.

Where the GST comes into the equation is that its increase is a potential option for paying for reform of the income tax schedules. The chapter therefore also goes on to explore the GST in more detail. Finally it discusses the pros and cons of increasing the GST rate or expanding the GST base, as the centre piece of reform as opposed to some other form of tax reform.

Even mentioning GST changes can be highly controversial. However that doesn't mean they shouldn't be debated. As Professor Michael Spence of New York University's Stern School of Business and Senior Fellow at the Hoover Institution, a Nobel laureate in economics wrote: "Structural change can be simultaneously beneficial and disruptive. And policymakers have long had to strike a balance between the abstract principle of openness and concrete measures to limit the worst effects of change." He also notes that: "A significant across-the-board increase in investment may not fix all their [ie developed economies] distributional and adjustment problems. But it would help to spur growth and reduce economic and political frictions in their structural adaptations."[1]

---

[1] Michael Spence, (2017),"How to be an Open Economy", *Australian Financial Review*, 24 May.

How personal income tax rates compare

The Government made recent (modest) changes to the personal income tax. In the 2016 Budget the Government increased the 32.5 per cent tax threshold from $80,000 to $87,000. They stated that this measure would prevent average full time wage earners from moving into the second top tax bracket until 2019-20. Thus stopping around 500,000 taxpayers facing the 37 per cent marginal tax rate.[2] The changes can be seen by referring to tables 1 and 2.

Table 1: Personal Income Tax Scales prior to 1 July 2016

Threshold	Rate
$0 - $18,200	0%
$18,201 - $37,000	19%
$37,001 - $80,000	32.5%
$80,001 - $180,000	37%
$180,001 and over	45%

Australian Tax office 2017[3]

Table 2: Personal Income Tax Scales after 1 July 2016

Threshold	Rate
$0 - $18,200	0%
$18,201 - $37,000	19%
$37,001 - $87,000	32.5%
$87,001 - $180,000	37%
$180,001 and over	45%

Australian Tax office 2017[4]

---

[2] Australian Government (2016), *Budget 2016-17: Sticking to our national economic plan*, 3 May, 4.
[3] Australian Taxation Office (2017), www.ato.gov.au
[4] Ibid.

This modest tax cut cost a large $3,950 million across the four years 2016-17 to 2019-20.

Chart 4 gives an overall view of the average and marginal tax rates that existed before the recent changes.

Chart 4: Average and marginal tax rates, 2014-15

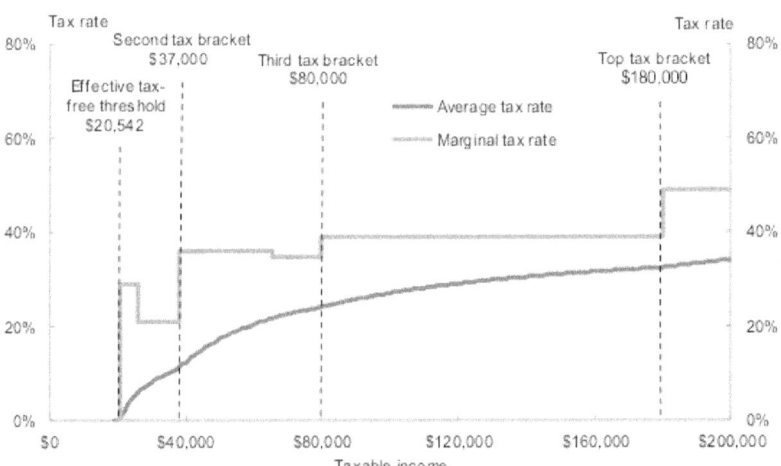

Notes: The rates shown are for a single person with no dependants who does not receive any Australian Government transfer payments. Marginal tax rates take account of the statutory rates shown in Table 3.1, as well as the Medicare levy of 2 per cent, the Temporary Budget Repair Levy (an additional 2 per cent on taxable income in excess of $180,000 per year) and the LITO. The LITO brings the effective taxfree threshold to $20,542. The 10 percentage point increase in marginal tax rates between $20,542 and $25,677 is due to the phaseout of the Medicare levy lowincome concession. The 1.5 percentage point increase in marginal tax rates between $37,001 and $66,667 is due to the phaseout of the LITO.

Australian Government 2015[5]

---

[5] Australian Government (2015), *Re:think Tax discussion paper*, monograph, Canberra, March, 37.

Chart 5 gives an overall view of the number a taxpayers in each income group and the significant burden placed on middle income earners in terms of revenue collection.

Chart 5: Who paid individuals income tax, 2011-12

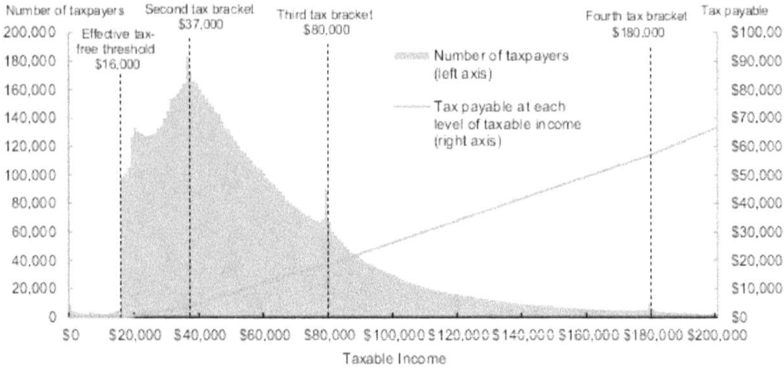

Note: The chart shows the number of tax filers who paid net income tax in thousand dollar taxable income brackets up to $200,000. Tax payable is calculated by applying the individual income tax rate scale, LITO and the Medicare levy to taxable income. Source: Treasury calculations using administrative data from 201112 tax returns for individuals.

Australian Government 2015, 40

Chart 6 shows that Australia is in the middle of the OECD pack when it comes to top marginal rates.

Chart 6: Top marginal tax rates comparison, OECD countries, 2013

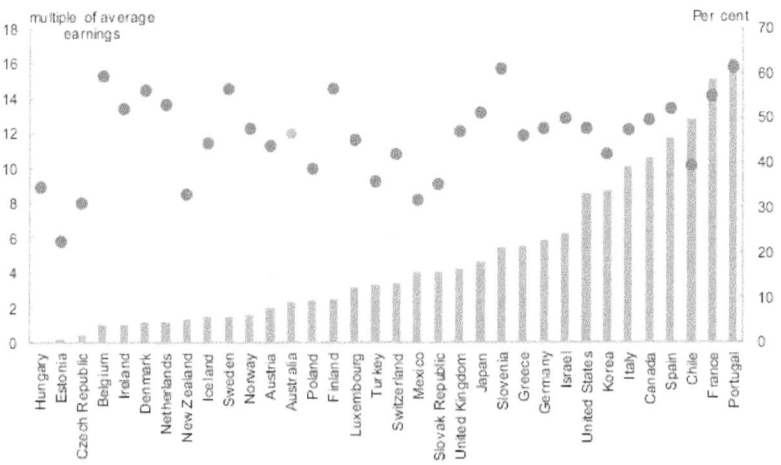

Note: Numbers for Australia are for 2013-14. Australia's top marginal tax rate for 201415 has increased to 49 per cent (45 per cent top statutory personal income tax rate plus 2 per cent Medicare levy plus 2 per cent Temporary Budget Repair Levy).

Source: OECD 2014, Tax Database — Personal Income Tax Rates, OECD, Paris

Australian Government 2015, 47

Table 3 shows that Australia's top rate of 45 per cent compares poorly against regional averages. Although it is important to note that the KPMG data in this table excludes state income taxes, such as in North America.

Table 3: Top Marginal Personal Income Tax Rates across the world 2017

Grouping	Rate
Global average	33.44
OECD average	42.47
Africa average	32.69
Americas average	34.29
Asia average	29.90
EU average	38.44
Europe average	34.87
Latin American average	34.11
North American average	36.3
Oceania average	40.00
South American average	34.11

KPMG 2017[6]

So, in spite of the most recent personal income tax cuts Australia's rates threshold compares very unfavourably with the countries that we would like to compare ourselves with.

Reforming personal income tax

In chapter 6 we saw that the reform of the personal income tax system represented a major economic reform opportunity to boost the Australian economy.

In this section we examine the major reform options for personal income tax. Given the debate in recent years it is reasonable to divide the analysis between reform with and without an increase in the GST.

First, while the general view is that major tax reform cannot proceed in the absence of an increase in the GST, that is not the

---
[6] Ibid.

case. There is the possibility of reforming the personal tax system without such a change.

One possibility is a change to the personal income tax to simply index the tax brackets (or thresholds) to end "bracket creep". Another reform option would see the income tax free threshold removed or reduced and replaced by an earned income tax credit system. I will examine these possibilities in detail in this section.

Another alternative is to deal with many of Australia's federal-state issues by creating a state income tax sharing arrangement. This will be examined in the next chapter.

In table 4 I give some rules of thumb on the cost of changing the marginal tax rates.

Table 4: Indicative impact of 1 percentage point reduction in Personal Income Tax

Threshold	Tax Rates		Indicative Revenue impact $m (2017-2018)
	Current	1% point lower	
First tax rate	19%	18%	-2,000
Second tax rate	32.5%	31.5%	-2,750
Third tax rate	37%	36.0%	-1,500
Fourth tax rate	45%	44.0%	-1,000

Australian Taxation Office 2017[7]

I note again that the recent modest tax cut in the last Budget cost $3,950 million across the four years 2016-17 to 2019-20.

Another way to come to grips of the potential costs of substantial reform is to simply note that, as table 5 above shows, to cut the rate at each threshold by one percentage point would have a

---
[7] Australian Taxation Office (2017), www.ato.gov.au

cumulative cost of $7.25 billion per annum. Alternatively to cut the top rate of tax from 45 per cent to 39 per cent would cost $6 billion per annum.

Indexing the tax brackets (or thresholds)

Bracket creep occurs when the personal income tax burden rises as average tax rates increase as thresholds are left unadjusted for the growth in average earnings. That is to say an individual tax payer's tax burden may rise from one year to the next because their nominal income increases and they move into higher tax brackets. This may occur even if real (ie inflation adjusted) income does not rise or even goes backwards. It is the direct consequence of a progressive tax system.

One option, frequently discussed over the years would be to simply fix the bracket creep problem by indexing the tax brackets. This would at least stop the marginal tax rate problem from worsening.

There would be an issue about what index would be used. For example would it be the CPI or another measure? Usually some variation on average wage earnings growth has been discussed.

Robert Carling from the Centre for Independent Studies has calculated that the cost of indexing the existing tax brackets to average earnings would be in the order of $12.5 billion a year if implemented in 2017-18.[8] So it is an expensive proposition.

Abolishing or lowering the tax free threshold

A number of countries, such as the United States, the United Kingdom and New Zealand have versions of an earned income tax credits (EITC) system. Instead of large tax free thresholds they tax earnings at lower levels than Australia, but to ensure a progressive

---

[8] Robert Carling (2016), *Taming the Monster: reforming personal income tax*, Research Report 12, Centre for Independent Studies, April, 12.

tax system they provide a system of rebates to lower income earners to supplement the welfare system.

While this can be criticised for churning money through the system it has the advantage of allowing lower marginal rates at higher income levels. This is because higher income earners no longer have the advantage of high tax free thresholds. Depending on any redesign to a personal income tax system these people may end up paying the same average tax rates. However, the distinct advantage is that for every extra dollar in earnings they make they are taxed at a lower marginal rate thus potentially incentivising their desire to earn more income.

Australia does not currently have an EITC system. Instead we have a high tax free threshold.

As seen above, for most Australians the tax free threshold is $18,200. This was increased to this level in the Carbon Tax Package as part of the compensation for its introduction. Prior to this the threshold was around $6,000.

However, in addition there is also a low income tax offset (LITO) which currently has a maximum value of $445. Together with the first marginal tax rate being 19 per cent, a LITO of $445 means that the *effective* tax free threshold is $20,542 ($445 divided by 0.19, added to $18,200). The LITO operates in a similar way to an EITC, but in Australia is very limited in its application.

For most taxpayers, the Australian tax free threshold and the LITO does not differentiate between sources of taxable income (for example, earned versus passive income).

In the absence of large expenditure cuts or an increase in the GST, the most likely design feature of an EITC, or expanded LITO, would be aimed at ensuring higher marginal rates are lower so as to encourage people to work, but that average tax rates are maintained so as to preserve the revenue needed to finance the federal government.

Taxing from the first dollar could potentially allow the drawing of the top rate from 45 per cent to as low as the 39 per cent or even lower. However, the cost of such a change would not be revenue neutral unless the Government wanted to create large numbers of losers at low income levels. Based on the latest data available the lowest threshold has in the order of 2.5 million people in it (see table 5).

Table 5: Individuals income tax by tax bracket, all individual tax filers, 2011–12

Taxable income band	Marginal income tax rate	Individuals — no.	Individuals — %	Net income tax — $b	Net income tax — %
$16,000 or less	0%	2,307,735	18.3	0.0	0.0
$16,001-$37,000	15%	3,453,310	27.3	5.3	3.7
$37,001 - $80,000	30%	4,745,935	37.6	47.4	32.8
$80,001 - $180,000	37%	1,836,900	14.5	54.0	37.4
$180,001 and over	45%	292,500	2.3	37.7	26.1
TOTAL	n.a.	12,636,380	100.0	144.4	100.0

Note: The effective tax free threshold in 201112 was $16,000, after including the lowincome tax offset. Totals are for those individuals lodging a tax return for that year.

Source: Treasury estimates using income tax returns for resident individuals for 2011-12.

Australian Government 2015, 41

A less ambitious proposal might be to strike a package that is closer to revenue neutral. Thus reducing the tax free threshold to say $10,000 (from an effective $20,542 today) and the increase of the LITO (and lowering its withdrawal rate) would potentially allow the reduction in rates for middle income earners in the order of 2 percentage points. While not spectacular change it could be the first step in a long term reform to the personal income tax that would increasingly lower rates over the years as (hopefully) Budget repair continued.

Helping to pay for personal income tax reform without a GST increase

In a total Federal Budget of $464 billion the amounts of money noted above are not necessarily huge. However, in times of Budget deficits ($29.4 billion in 2017-18) good economic management demands that they would need to be paid for.

Recent history shows that further expenditure savings are difficult to get through the Senate. However, the situation is not as completely hopeless as the media reporting would suggest. The Government's recent score sheet for getting expenditure savings through the Senate has been remarkably good. For example, the Treasurer noted on Budget Night 2017 that "since the 2016 election the Government has legislated around $25 billion in measures to help repair the Budget. This takes to more than $100 billion the budget repair measures implemented since the 2013 election".[9] It must be said however, that despite this rhetorical flourish, a significant part of this has been revenue increases and the Government has not returned to the huge spending cuts originally proposed in the 2014 Budget and they have been dropped as Government policy.

---

[9] Scott Morrison (2017), "Ensuring the Government lives within its means", press release, 9 May.

Nonetheless, the Government forecasts it will return the Budget to a surplus of $7.4 billion in 2020-21.

To help fund a personal income tax reform one of the last areas that has been left substantially untouched is work-related expense deductions. In total there is up to $5 billion per annum in such deductions. The introduction of a pared back system similar to that in the UK would potentially save $3 billion per annum. However, as with all other options it would be very hard to remove these concessions. As always the difference between the winners and losers creates a major headache for any politician proposing such a change.

The scope for more comprehensive tax reform with an increase in the GST

The obvious source of funds for funding really substantial personal income tax reform would be to raise the rate or expand the base of the GST.

Nothing that was said in the last section is excluded by looking at a package that would include an increase in the GST. It is a simple case of mathematics that an increase in the rate or base of the GST would fund a more substantive tax reform.

In recent years commentary has centred around two broad options. They are:

- to increase the rate of the GST from 10 per cent; and
- to broaden the base of the GST, thus raising more revenue.

Indeed the Federal Government seriously considered these options in late 2015 and early 2016 and held preliminary discussions with state governments on the matter. In the end the Federal Government decided not to proceed in February 2016.

Increasing GST collections

Many people advocate an increase in the GST and many people oppose it. However, it would be accurate to say that a large number of people on both sides of the debate are fairly unfamiliar with what exactly it is.

A GST is an example of a broadly based indirect or consumption tax.

There were two principal economic reasons for introducing the GST. First was the fact that the pre-existing indirect taxes (ie before 2000) like the wholesale sales tax were very inefficient because they taxed business inputs such that there was a cumulative cascading of taxes that added massively to business costs. This was particularly damaging to exporters and import-competing industries that were battling with businesses from overseas that were not suffering from the same handicap.

The GST or 'value added tax', which is its more economically accurate name, removed that double taxation burden. This was the principal economic reform and it meant billions of dollars to Australian businesses. However, it is a reform that is completed. It was long overdue but it is now done. The efficiencies and productivity benefits have already been booked many years ago.

The second big economic reason for introducing the GST was that it allowed for what became known as a 'tax mix switch'. That principally meant a reduction of the revenue burden on direct, income taxes to be replaced by indirect taxes. As we saw earlier in the previous chapter this is important as high marginal tax rates on personal income have a largely negative impact on economic activity, discouraging work and productivity improvements. In addition to the work that I have already referred to I note that the former Treasury Secretary (and now Secretary of the Department of Prime

Minister and Cabinet), Martin Parkinson, made similar observations in a 2014 speech.[10]

A tax mix switch was the key feature of the 2000 Howard-Costello tax changes. It was also the centerpiece of the Option C proposal of Paul Keating in 1985 when he was Labor Treasurer; and of the Fightback! package of John Hewson and Peter Reith.

However, the bottom line is that the Howard Government's tax mix switch has not had a lasting impact. At the time there were some substantial income tax cuts, but we seem to still have a heavy reliance on direct rather than indirect taxes in Australia. The reason for that is bracket creep on the income tax schedules and a heavy call on company income tax.

Increasing the GST rate

Increasing the rate from 10 per cent to say 15 per cent would raise large amounts of money. A sense of the magnitude can be given here.

An increase in the GST to 15 per cent would raise in the order of $35 billion. These "back of the envelope" calculations are nonetheless robust and can be treated with a reasonable degree of confidence. They could be further refined by formal economic modelling.

Such a change would be relatively straight forward to implement. There would be an increase in the rate on existing categories. Businesses, if they are GST registered (and they need to be if they earn more than $75,000) would be largely exempt from any direct impact as they receive credits for GST on business inputs. Of course there will be indirect impacts depending on the overall package. Thus if GST was raised to 15 per cent and no other

---

[10] Colin Brinsden (2014), "Tax experts back Parkinson's GST call", *Sydney Morning Herald*, 3 April.

changes were made this would have a large dampening effect on consumer spending and therefore business profits. That is not what is being proposed here. The principal purpose of the increased rate would be to fund large personal income tax cuts.

And to give readers an international comparison of a 15 per cent rate I note that the average rate in the EU is 20 per cent and it is 22 per cent in the UK.

Broadening the GST base

An expansion of the GST base to cover all food, water and sewerage would raise in the order of $15 billion. Of this the food change would probably be around $7 billion.

However, again we need to be very clear what we are looking at here.

Some people are claiming that these exemptions were all politically expedient decisions. Admittedly, the fresh food exemption was the price of getting the support of the Australian Democrats in the Senate to pass the original GST legislation. However, as for the other exemptions, they were not so much political decisions as tax administration decisions based on the difficulties of taxing these areas, especially given the heavy involvement of government in many of these sectors and the cross-jurisdictional issues in our Federation which could cause significant tax churning. They were not design flaws of the system but in fact design features deliberately taken for good, on-balance reasons.

Having said that all these issues need to be reexamined including the exemption for financial services. The reason is simple. Excluding these sectors of the economy from the GST base means that some of the fastest growing parts of the economy, particularly health and financial services, means that it is not truly a broad based consumption tax and is not the growth tax that was expected when it was introduced.

Comment on a GST package

A GST tax mix package would potentially fund sizeable personal income tax changes given potential increased revenues of $42 billion per annum. Of course any pragmatic government would have to ensure that social welfare recipients were not adversely effected and so a large amount of money would be absorbed in a "compensation package". The nature of that and its extent would necessarily depend on what the new rate and the new base was.

In discussing this topic there needs to be a bit of a reality check. In canvassing changes to the GST we must be wary of those who are simply arguing for bigger government, not a more efficient tax system.

For example we need to wary of those state Premiers who are calling for more tax revenue to fund massive increases in state expenditure which was promised by Prime Ministers Gillard and Rudd. They were always undeliverable promises and it was said so at the time of their announcements by many people. Those Premiers are being completely disingenuous on this issue. They want the Commonwealth government to wear the opprobrium of raising higher taxes so they get the applause for spending more money. It is one of the great dysfunctional aspects of Australia's federal system.

Which leads to another important point. For a GST tax mix switch to be implemented by the federal government the starting point would have to be that not all GST revenues go to the states, as they do today. Indeed new arrangements would need to be put in place so that any increase in GST collections were identified as federal revenue not state. It was on this basis that the tentative discussions between the federal and state governments were undertaken during 2015 and early 2016. It is understood, I believe, that after a period of grandstanding, that states would be in-principle prepared to accept these new arrangements. It is for this reason that there will be a need to look at other options to reform Commonwealth-State taxation. And it is something I will return to in the next chapter.

Of course it should be noted that the large revenues from a GST increase would almost certainly fund more economic reform than just a lower personal income tax and social welfare compensation. In addition it could fund the abolition of some inefficient state taxes (such as stamp duties on conveyancing), fund economic infrastructure and even pay for further company tax relief. The possibilities are numerous. Long term GDP boosts could range as high as 2.5 percentage points in the long term.

Such a reform is already supported by the ACCI,[11] the BCA,[12] the Australian Industry Group (AiG),[13] the Financial Services Council (FSC)[14] to name a few.

Although the Federal Government maintains its policy to fully implement the 10 Year Enterprise Tax Plan it would be fair to say that the potential for implementing the second half of the package has lost momentum. The Government has expressed unhappiness with the business community for its lack of support in seeking to implement this policy. Whether this is true in fact or not, that is the perception of most of the senior members of the Cabinet.

It is reasonable to assume that the Government will look at options for delivering further tax reform in the lead-up to the next Federal Election. It is interesting to note the growth in tax revenues as a share of GDP in the Government's Budget forward estimates

---

[11] Australian Chamber of Commerce and Industry (2015), *ACCI Submission: Re:think Taxation Discussion Paper*, June.

[12] Business Council of Australia (2015), *The Future of Tax: Tax White Paper Initial Submission*, 6 August.

[13] Australian Industry Group (2015), *AiG Group Submission: Response to the Taxation Discussion Paper*, June.

[14] Naomi Woodley (2016), "Increasing GST, slashing company tax could raise extra $36b for Government: FSC", *ABC News*, 18 January.

from 21.5 per cent of GDP in 2016-17 to 23.7 per cent in 2020-21.[15] It is not acceptable for this growth to continue indefinitely.

The business community may find that support for tax plans that actually encourage economic growth is a sensible short to medium term option in advancing sound economic policy. This is on the basis that some reform is better than none.

While company tax reform undoubtedly is directed to fostering greater investment and thus of direct benefit to the business community, personal income tax reform is also of substantial benefit. This can be listed as:

- business benefits due to more spending dollars in the hands of its customers;
- business benefits due to increased investment dollars in the hands of mum and dad investors; and
- business benefits from some easing in cost of living pressures on its work force due to larger take home pay.

In the current low wage growth environment (actually negative in the June quarter 2017 National Accounts and still flat in the December quarter)[16] the last point can be very important for relieving wage demands on business.

In recent decades it is actually the business community that has led tax reform arguments. Invariably success depends on building coalitions of mutual interest to create powerful third party endorsement to allow politicians the "cover" to proceed with sometimes controversial options.

---

[15] Australian Government (2017), *Budget 2017-18: Budget Strategy and Outlook*, Budget Paper Number 1 2017-18, Canberra 9 May, 5.5.

[16] Jacob Greber (2017), "Weak wages undercut economic growth pick-up", *Australian Financial Review*, 7 September; Geoff Winestock (2018), "Productivity falls for the first time in 7 years", *Australian Financial Review*, 8 March.

Simply advocating personal income tax cuts does not mean much. A politician does not have to be told that they are popular.

What is much more difficult is getting politicians to agree on the way the tax cuts are paid for.

Obviously increasing the GST or finding "savings" through cutting work related deductions are tough arguments. However, as even the most recent examples show, raising the tax levels on superannuation and cutting family benefits payments is possible and can be implemented despite a hostile Senate if the arguments are put effectively and enough people (or cross-bench senators) can be convinced. Usually wrapping up your policy proposals in a package of reforms enhances the chances of success. Of course, if Australia was able to reform its Constitution and reduce the ability of the Senate to indefinitely block reforms (as I argue for in chapter 5) then progress is more assured.

Through the 1980s the NFF (amongst others) argued for the introduction of a GST. While there was an amount of support around the ridges, both Paul Keating (in 1985) and John Hewson (1993) ultimately failed in their attempts to introduce one. There were powerful interest groups ranged against them and the business community was fractured in its support. It is arguable that the catalyst that allowed John Howard to successfully implement a GST was the ability of Graeme Samuel at ACCI in 1996 to build a coalition of support amongst the wider business community and win over the Australian Council of Social Services (ACOSS) to the argument. This was aided by holding the ACCI/ACOSS hosted National Tax Summit amongst these groups.

The AFR/The Australian National Reform Summit that was held on 22-23 September 2015 amongst business and community groups was a similar attempt. To a degree it worked and the Turnbull Government did react to its deliberations. Whether you regard it as good or bad the recent changes to superannuation stemmed directly from this initiative.

Another related aspect of the 1996 work of ACCI and others was the creation of the Business Coalition on Tax Reform (BCTR). In the early years this was chaired by John Stanhope who at the time was the chief financial officer at Telstra. It is still in existence but has limited profile or punch nowadays. The BCTR could be reenergised as a vehicle for pursuing reform. This would be a necessary early step.

Reforming the Capital Gains Tax

When I did my independent taxation review with Dick Warburton, the then chairman of the Board of Taxation, one of the areas we looked at was capital income taxation.

The review showed we had one of the heaviest burdens of those taxes in the OECD. The review noted:

> Capital gains are taxed in many different ways around the world. New Zealand does not impose [Capital Gains Tax] CGT and of those that have a CGT regime some have a stepped rate (as the holding period increases the tax rate decreases), some have a flat rate and others (such as Australia and Canada) use a discount system for taxing capital gains (only a proportion of the gain is taxable).[17]

The Review added: "For the short-term holding period, Australia's top marginal tax rate [on capital gains] … is the third highest of the OECD-10 [comparable countries] while for the long-term holding period Australia's rate … is the second highest."[18]

To say again, many countries have a stepped or tiered capital gains tax regime. Simply put the longer you hold an asset the lower

---

[17] Peter Hendy and Richard Warburton (2006), *International Comparison of Australia's Taxes*, Canberra, 3 April, 199.
[18] Ibid., 207.

the relative taxation burden on the capital gain. In many countries the tax burden falls to zero if it is a long term investment. Those countries recognise that is good for business investment and ultimately jobs. They obviously do not subscribe to the view of French economist Thomas Piketty[19] who has gained recent fame by arguing that in the long run capitalist economies result in higher and higher levels of inequality because the rate of return on capital is higher than the overall rate of economic growth. Thus the owners of capital simply get wealthier and wealthier to the detriment of the wider community. He uses this to argue for increased inheritance taxation. This analysis has many critics including prominent economist Professor Lawrence Summers[20] of Harvard University and Nobel Prize winner Joseph Stiglitz.[21] It is an interesting debate but I would conclude that Piketty's work is more political polemic than economic analysis.

The ACCI Tax Blueprint noted a 2004 pre-election survey showed that CGT was either a major or moderate issue for 61.7 per cent of businesses.[22] More recent surveys confirm this. The ACCI pre-election survey for 2013 showed that the level of concern had in fact risen to 68.4 per cent. Thus the ACCI had a policy that if you held an asset for 5 years the capital gains tax burden would be halved and then fall to zero if the asset was held for 10 years or more. This mirrored tax regimes in a number of OECD countries. The blueprint also proposed reforms related to CGT rollover

---

[19] Thomas Piketty (2014), *Capital in the Twenty-First century*, The Belknap Press of Harvard University Press, Cambridge.

[20] Lawrence Summers (2014), "Thomas Piketty is right about the past and wrong about the future", *The Atlantic*, 16 May.

[21] Joseph E. Stiglitz (2015), "Thomas Piketty gets income inequality wrong", *Salon.com*, 3 January.

[22] Australian Chamber of Commerce and Industry (2004), *Taxation Reform Blueprint: A Strategy for the Australian Taxation System 2004-2014*, Canberra.

provisions, carry-back of losses and franking credits.[23] I still believe that Australia should adopt that type of policy.

Conclusion

While in the past I have been sceptical about raising the GST rate or expanding the base I believe that most other tax reform options have been exhausted and that there is merit in returning to the issue. Indeed in hind-sight one of the biggest regrets of my time in Federal Parliament is not having pursued with gusto this change. I can say without reservation that I was worried about losing my marginal seat of Eden-Monaro. I was concerned that we could not sell the policy.

In the end I did lose the seat. In retrospect I strongly suspect the decision by Prime Minister Malcolm Turnbull and the Cabinet not to proceed with these type of changes severely affected the new Prime Minister's standing in the polls. It is clear that people do not like the idea of increased tax rates. That is very understandable. But what is apparent to me is that they nonetheless wanted to see major reform to deal with Australia's economic challenges and they simply weren't seeing enough of that. They collectively saw the failure to proceed with this tax reform as a massive lost opportunity.

The need to reduce the burden of personal income tax necessitates a return look at the GST.

A related issue is how the personal tax system is structured. In the first part of this chapter I examined the practicalities of a change to the thresholds. As we saw, taxing from the first dollar could potentially allow the drawing of the top rate from 45 per cent to as low as the 39 per cent or even lower. However, the cost of such a change would not be revenue neutral unless the Government wanted to create large numbers of losers at low income levels. Based on the

---

[23] ACCI 2004, 57.

latest data available the lowest threshold has in the order of 2.5 million people in it. Indexing the thresholds for inflation would be an alternative economic reform.

The 2018-19 Federal Budget – delivered on 8 May 2018 – made a start on some much needed reform to personal income tax. If the relevant legislation passes there will be some helpful changes to the tax brackets. The principal reform would be a change in the top threshold for the 32.5 percent tax bracket from $87,000 to (first) $90,000 on 1 July 2018; to $120,000 on 1 July 2022; and $200,000 on 1 July 2024. The existing 37 percent tax bracket will be abolished at this later date. The 19 per cent tax bracket will also increase from a top threshold of $37,000 to $41,000 in 2022. There are also changes to the low income tax offset to provide extra tax relief to low and middle income earners, starting in 2018.

As I say, these are welcome proposals and are in line with the comments in this chapter. Nonetheless, it remains the case that more substantive reform will require revisiting the issue of increasing the GST.

Lastly in this chapter I also discussed changes to the capital gains tax. Again this tax is an imposition on investment. I believe that there is a case for further reductions, not increases, in the capital gains tax.

8
TAX REFORM PART C
(FEDERATION TAX REFORM)

Introduction

In the United States they say that the states are the "laboratories of democracy".

What of course they mean is that a federal system, made up of a separate national government and numerous regional (state) governments, provides the opportunity for experimentation that hopefully optimises the chance for the best mix of policies for that region's population – e.g., in taxation, health and education provision, environmental protection and business development policies. That was the view of Alfred Deakin, Edmund Barton and Samuel Griffiths – Australia's leading Federation fathers. I hazard a guess it is generally supported by most Australians, even if they don't frame it in those intellectual terms but in the more pragmatic realisation that "Canberra" certainly doesn't always know what is best for their town or region.

However, that doesn't mean the federal system that we have today, nearly 120 years since it was set up, is ideal. Indeed it is far from ideal. It is in fact a sad mess. It has many "barnacles" on it, to use an expression of a former Prime Minister.

I have spent a lot of my career working on Commonwealth-State relations issues. I directly worked in that area of the Federal Treasury during the 1980s and then during the mid-1990s was a senior executive at the NSW Cabinet Office. This area a policy can be enormously frustrating with distorted motivations being constantly apparent because of the poor state of financial arrangements.

In this chapter I examine a quite radical change to federal arrangements in Australia.[1]

Federal-State relations reform shouldn't be about raising tax levels

There are many areas of overlap and duplication where we as a nation have been simply struggling to get right for decades. Some we have fixed, others we haven't.

One example of progress was in the industrial relations area where the union movement had callously, but rationally, gamed the parallel federal and state industrial relations systems for all they were worth by "forum shopping" to get the best deals for their members, but not necessarily for the community as a whole (I'm referring here to pricing people out of jobs and creating structurally high unemployment levels). This policy area was partly the subject of my doctoral thesis and it showed that there was essentially 104 years of this nonsense going on until John Howard largely fixed the inter-jurisdictional problem in 2005 by centralising the industrial system under federal jurisdiction.

Nonetheless there are many more federal-state problems. You don't need to go far to hear from people that the health and education systems are in need of drastic reform. Premiers complain that they do not have enough money to run these systems and thus are forced to beg more and more assistance from the federal government, which results in greater federal intervention. That is

---

[1] This chapter is heavily based on my previously published article Peter Hendy (2015), "Federal-State relations reform shouldn't be about raising tax levels", *IPA Review*, May 2015.

not necessarily a good thing. With industrial relations centralisation may have helped. However often the answer is to do the opposite. The duplication is enormous and most Australians will have heard that the federal government amazingly employs 1,868 education bureaucrats but does not own one school. There are almost countless examples across the portfolios where the federal government has its sticky hands involved in state decision-making because of the call on the Federal Budget. This is because the federal government raises more money than it directly spends and the states are in the opposite position.

However, don't be misled by the siren song from some premiers and self-serving lobby groups that this would be fixed with more tax revenues, preferably by increasing the GST rate or expand its base or both. There is currently a cacophony of individuals and groups making the case. As I described in the last chapter if the GST was to be increased or expanded it should principally go to funding personal income tax cuts and not increased spending (except maybe on infrastructure.

This chapter explores a different option for reform that has been considered before but in recent times (too readily) discarded. Many commentators dismiss it out of hand. However it is an option that has in the past had substantial support in both economic and political terms. Moreover it is an option that would not raise the overall tax burden.

I am speaking about an income tax sharing agreement between the federal and state governments.

The basic problem that needs to be addressed is clearly stated in the Government's March 2015 discussion paper on taxation reform[2] that notes that the states' revenue base is inadequate to fund

---

[2] Australian Government (2015), *Re:think Tax discussion paper, monograph, Canberra, March* 2015, chapter 8.

their spending growth responsibilities in areas such as health and education. Demand is outstripping supply.

A brief history of income tax is relevant. Up until 1942 states levied income taxes. Then due to World War II's funding demands it was mutually agreed to hand the tax to the federal government. After the emergency passed it refused to hand it back.

That is until 1977 when Prime Minister Malcolm Fraser proposed a "New Federalism" policy and passed legislation to allow state income tax surcharges (or rebates for that matter) to help states meet their funding needs. Unfortunately NSW Premier Wran waged a short-sighted scare campaign on the issue alleging this would lead to "double taxation" and the option was never taken up.

However, 14 years later Prime Minister Bob Hawke was inching towards reintroducing such a policy through a series of Special Premier's Conferences when he lost a leadership ballot to Paul Keating in 1991. Hawke had set up a "Working Party on Tax Powers" that reported on 4 October 1991 and noted one option for reform was the introduction of a State Income Tax Surcharge.[3] In response, all State and Territory leaders at the time signed a communique on 8 November 1991 calling for its implementation. They sought a 6 per cent surcharge in a broadly revenue neutral package of reforms, whereby the federal government would reduce income tax and also payments to the states. So it was recommended by experts and was politically doable. However the new Prime Minister Keating was personally against the proposal and it died there and then.[4]

Importantly, an income tax surcharge was recently recommended

---

[3] Australian Chamber of Commerce and Industry (2004), *Taxation Reform Blueprint: A Strategy for the Australian Taxation System 2004-2014*, Canberra, 43.

[4] Ibid..

by the National Commission of Audit (NCA) in its February 2014 report[5].

Many so-called experts will complain that reordering the intergovernmental share of income tax revenue would do nothing to fix the relative balance between direct (eg income) taxes and indirect (eg GST) taxes. That is the tax mix switch issue referred to above. There is truth to this.

To make it clear, the income tax sharing option I believe should be debated is not designed to raise more total revenue but to substitute federal taxes with state taxes, thus not increasing the reliance on income taxes. Indeed, in my opinion any possible economic efficiency benefits from reform would be lost if all that we are doing is locking in the deleterious effects of further increases in the overall tax burden.

Helpfully, the NCA didn't just raise the topic. They actually got the Treasury to do the economic modelling that shows how the figures would stack up.

Looking at the 2013-14 financial year the total transfer of funds (tied grants) from the federal government to the states, not including $51.2 billion in GST receipts, was $45.1 billion. The NCA notes that of this total $13.9 billion is for National Health Reform Funding; Specific education payments ($13.2 billion); payments for skills, disability and housing ($3.9 billion); and payments for 144 different National Partnership Agreements ($14.0 billion).[6]

As an option they proposed that 10 percentage points of the tax bracket base between incomes of $37,000 and $80,000 be allocated to the states. Currently that tax bracket attracts a tax rate of 32.5 per cent. So a change would mean that for taxpayers in that bracket

---

[5] National Commission of Audit (NCA) (2014), *Towards Responsible Government*, monograph, Canberra, February 2014.

[6] NCA 2014, Vol 1, Appendix 8, 149.

they would actually have a 22.5 per cent federal income tax and a 10 per cent NSW (insert other state names depending where you live) income tax.[7]

The Treasury calculated that this 10 per cent state income tax would raise $25 billion. The NCA shows that this would allow the federal government to completely withdraw from all education funding, public housing projects and a large number of National Partnership Agreements.

The NCA also recommended a possible change to the distribution of GST revenues to states. For example today Western Australia complains that it only receives 4.2 per cent of GST total revenues which is only 10 cents in the dollar generated in that state. According to the NCA the solution could be to largely scrap the existing Commonwealth Grants Commission formulas for dividing up the GST money between the states and substitute per capita grants based on population. However they note to do this either means taking GST revenue off subsidised states like Tasmania and South Australia or by increasing the pool. The NCA argues for the latter. It did the requisite calculation and so as to ensure that the currently subsidised states are not worse off it proposes that with a federal government "top up" of $4.9 billion on an annual basis (from non-GST tax revenues) this issue could be solved. The $4.9 billion would be divided between the subsidised states using the existing Commonwealth Grants Commission formulas. The NCA then goes on to argue that after this cross-subsidy is made all GST revenues should be distributed according to a per capita formula. It argues the $4.9 billion could be found from savings elsewhere in the Federal Budget and argues that the structural reform would be worth it. With that extra money all 144 of the National Partnership Agreements ($14.0 billion) could

---

[7] Ibid.

also go.[8] However, I wish to add here that as a commissioner on the Commonwealth Grants Commission I am not in a position to pass a public judgement on the GST distribution issue. I am only noting for the sake of completeness what the NCA stated.

So in summary the end result of implementing a state income tax would be to address the states' revenue problem, remove the federal government from a very large proportion of expenditure, and do it without increasing total revenues. That is a win-win proposition.

After the initial implementation you would allow states to vary their tax take. In a left-leaning state, where they seem to reward big spending governments, you might see the ALP raise the tax from 10 to 11 per cent. In NSW where a fiscally responsible Berejiklian government can deliver budget surpluses you might see a cut to 9 per cent if they thought it was sustainable. So be it, that is democracy.

We should thank Chairman Tony Shepherd and his NCA team for having the foresight to commission this modelling (see Table 6).

In conclusion, I have put forward the income tax sharing proposal as the basis of a long lasting reform of our Federation. It would not be a perfect solution but as with other options should be at least considered in the white paper process. Treasury has already done the first cut of the economic modelling. Let's widen the debate, forget about raising the tax burden, and get on with selling federal-state reform.

---

[8] Ibid.

Table 6: Illustrative impact of changes to the architecture of federal financial arrangements

	Current Architecture ($ billion)	Illustrative Architecture ($ billion)
GST Revenue and existing general revenue assistance	51.2	51.2
Commonwealth Grants to States		
National Health Reform Funding	13.9	13.9
School Specific payments	13.2	0.0
Skills & Workforce Specific Payments	1.4	0.0
Disability Specific Payments	1.2	1.2
Affordable Housing Specific Payments	1.3	0.0
National Partnership Agreements	14.0	0.0
Total Grants	45.1	15.2
Access to personal income tax base	0.0	25.0
Additional equalisation payment	0.0	4.9
Total Commonwealth transfers to States	96.3	96.3
Tied transfers	45.1	15.2
Untied transfers	51.2	81.1

Source: Mid-Year Economic and Fiscal Outlook 2013-14 and National Commission of Audit, February 2014.[9]

---

[9] NCA 2014, Vol 1, Appendix 8, 156.

Conclusion

Sustaining the Australian Settlement 2.0 means we need to fix the Federation. On 30 March 2016 Prime Minister Turnbull[10] raised the prospect of a state income tax option to deal with the problematic federal issues around taxation. At the time he correctly pointed out that "this is very big fundamental reform to federalism. ... The most fundamental reform to the federation in generations". He went on to say "this, we believe, is the only way that we can genuinely reform our federation. It will give the states real financial autonomy. He also noted that it would end "the depressing blame game where no one really knows who is responsible for what".

Unfortunately this was rejected by an overwhelming majority of Premiers and was dropped by the federal government. Personally, I believe that the collective Premiers were directly acting against the best interests of their constituencies. These changes would solve a lot of the issues they have been grappling with for many years. For the sake of – in my view – short term or partisan politics they have let slip a golden opportunity.

Despite this rejection, I think that a future federal government should return to this policy option.

There are problems begging to be fixed but will need maximum skills to achieve. I fully support the push for reform. Obviously the majority of state premiers will need to be on board for wholesale reform to occur.

The saviour for the states is not an increase in the GST. As I noted in the last chapter the economic case for increasing the rate or expand the base of the GST is to fund major personal income tax reform. That would mean that the federal government would need

---

[10] Lenore Taylor (2016) "Turnbull confirms state income tax plan and says it will fix 'core problem' of federation", *The Guardian*, 30 March 2016.

to keep most of the proceeds of the increased GST to provide that funding. My conclusion is that if the states want a sustainable and secure growth tax they need to revisit their opposition to a state income tax.

9
INDUSTRIAL RELATIONS REFORM

Introduction

After the last decade of change in industrial relations there needs to be a reordering to the sensible centre. This is always a controversial topic, and has been an ongoing debate since the beginning of Federation. As we saw in the first three chapters of this book, this debate was central to the rise and fall of the Australian Settlement and features in discussion on the sustainability of the Australian Settlement 2.0.

Most Australians are unaware that it was not the Labor side of politics, but ironically the Liberals, that originally introduced the unique Australian centralised wage fixing system over 100 years ago. It was at the time an arguable attempt to govern relations between employers and employees, reduce violent conflict, and at the same time provide a basic welfare system. Nonetheless it had fundamental flaws.

It has been the subject of much debate over the years and I have always agreed that the system needs to be balanced between the participants. Earlier in my career I helped, in a small way, the then Minister for Workplace Relations, Peter Reith, to implement a substantial reform agenda on the waterfront. It was a vital reform and a great achievement and I am proud that I was part of it. That was sensible reform against the opposition of a large number of left wing ideologues.

Indeed, to paraphrase Winston Churchill, the watchword for my stance on reform is that I am a member of the pragmatic centre.

Setting the context for reform

In his famous speech from 1942 Robert Menzies talked about the "forgotten people". He spoke of the: "… salary earners, shopkeepers, skilled artisans, professional men and women, farmers and so on". In summary he said: "… they are the backbone of the nation".[1] But they are not completely forgotten. Indeed the reason for continuing calls for industrial relations reform relate directly to these people. People who are neither protected by big business or big unions.

It is vital that we provide the strongest small business environment so that it can provide the job security that is so vitally needed.

Industrial relations is central to the productivity agenda to ensure jobs for the future.

Many Liberal politicians have shied away from talking about industrial relations reforms in recent years. However, it remains a legitimate area for debate. Let me say outright that the Howard Government's 2005 WorkChoices package was a big mistake and I acknowledge that. However as I have previously said we cannot ignore the fact that something needs to be done on a number of fronts.

A rigidified labour market does not help Australian youth find jobs.

To its credit the Abbott Government initiated a Productivity Commission review into this area but achieved very little reform in industrial relations. The Turnbull Government has undertaken a large amount of reform, but more needs to be done. I will have more to say on this below.

First, I just want to give a brief overview on industrial relations matters, without going over too much of the ground already covered in detail in the first three chapters.

---

[1] Robert Menzies (1943), *The Forgotten People and other studies in democracy*, Angus and Robertson, Sydney, 2.

Very quickly the salient features are that Australia's unique industrial relations system has its roots in the bitter industrial disputes of the 1890s. As a result a key component in the Federation negotiations during that decade was the treatment of industrial relations issues.

The Liberal protectionists who as a group dominated the Federation discussions came up with the idea of New Protection, which embodied both of their two policy pillars. In essence New Protection was to link high levels of industry protection with a centralised wage fixing system. In summary the argument went that the benefits for colonial industry, that would be able to grow strongly behind protective barriers, would be shared with the working man through the use of third party tribunals to ensure a "living wage" for everyone, thus controlling the frequency of violent disputes.

The business community was originally split in its support. As time moved on New Protection or as we have called it throughout this book – the Australian Settlement – came to be supported by the business community generally. However, as almost always happens with the business community it eventually got mugged by reality and as time moved from the 1970s into the 1980s they came to the view (or at least the majority did) that the system wasn't working in the national interest – that is, neither protection nor centralised wage fixing worked.

As far as the Labor Movement was concerned, they have stayed resolutely wedded to centralised wage fixing. To its credit the Keating Government did begin to understand the importance of enterprise bargaining and started to legislate for that, principally starting in 1993 with very much baby steps. And very importantly the Hawke and Keating Governments were instrumental in the dismantling of tariff protection as a principal pillar of Government policy. In 1995, despite the subsequent claims of their opponents that they have never had a mandate for industrial relations reform, the Howard-led opposition campaigned on industrial relations reform, particularly in relation to the waterfront, individual contracts (to be called Australian Workplace Agreements) and unfair dismissals.

On winning the election that mandate was not "respected" but they probably got 70 per cent of their agenda through the Senate, principally with the support of the Australian Democrats.

Finally after winning a Senate majority in the 2004 election the Howard Government moved further in: dismantling compulsory arbitration; the greater use of enterprise based agreements particularly individual statutory agreements; and on unfair dismissals. This legislative package was dubbed WorkChoices for marketing reasons.

As noted in the last chapter, probably the most significant long-term aspect of the 2005 legislation was the hostile takeover of state industrial relations systems using the Commonwealth's corporations power under the Constitution. This latter reform, the creation of a national industrial relations system, was thankfully left in place by the Rudd-Gillard Government. However, virtually all other aspects were dismantled during their six year government, including most of the other key reforms from 1996.

When you think back to 2008 when the Fair Work legislation was legislated by the Rudd-Gillard Government you could make the observation that no sane government would be re-regulating the industrial relations market in face of the worst financial crisis in 80 years and surging unemployment unless they had some primary motivation.

That motivation was, of course, easy to see. In the lead-up to the 2007 election campaign the ACTU effectively signed over a $30 million cheque (at least) to help the ALP get elected. The consideration for that little transaction was the implementation of the Fair Work legislation. As an aside I'd like to mention that Senator Nick

Xenophon, after extracting some minor changes to justify his deal-making, supported the legislation.

Major issues with the resulting legislation were:

- A significant increase in compulsory arbitration.
- Despite the denials, an unprecedented expansion of the opportunities for unions to indulge in pattern bargaining.
- An award simplification process that has massively increased cost pressures on small business – the penalty rates issue.
- Despite the sweet words about co-operation and reduction of red tape a new Fair Dismissals Code that is re-entrenching some of the worst aspects of the Keating Governments unfair dismissal regime.
- (And lastly) Expanded union rights of entry that do nothing if not give a legislated leg-up to union membership recruitment.

After 2007 Brendan Nelson became the Federal Leader of the Opposition and I was his chief of staff. I worked with him on resetting the Coalition's industrial relations policies. He declared that WorkChoices was dead and that AWAs were dead, he nonetheless very importantly went on to articulate that there remained four industrial relations policy pillars for the Coalition.

They were:

- Support for individual statutory contracts with a binding "no disadvantage clause" protecting worker rights.
- The continued support for a reducing red tape on small business imposed by the unfair dismissal laws.
- The right to freedom of association to either join or not join a union.
- Continued support for the retention of the Australian Building and Construction Commission.

Nelson's list was superseded by policy announcements for the 2010 and 2013 elections, and there was essentially silence on matters 1 and 2. This was the state of play when the Coalition won government in 2013.

After the 2013 election, the Abbott Government's Fair Work Amendment Bill 2014 dealt with union workplace access, individual flexibility arrangements and the removal of the ability to strike first and talk later.

In particular the Fair Work Bill sought to introduce amendments to provide clarity and certainty for employees around the use of Individual Flexibility Arrangements (IFAs). IFAs are not some diabolical invention of the Liberal Party. In fact they were introduced by Labor, by Julia Gillard (no less) when she was Workplace Relations Minister, with the intent of enabling employees and their employers to mutually agree on conditions that suit their needs, while ensuring that employees are better off overall compared to their underpinning employment instrument. The "better off overall test" was introduced with IFAs and the Coalition Government had no plans to change it. However the constraints on IFAs are very large and they are seldom used. In reality these were quite minor improvements and not all of them survived the Senate process. In my view more will need to be done in the area of IFAs, making them more attractive for employers and individual employees to use as individual contracts.

Prospectively, the really significant reforms were contained in the Fair Work (Registered Organisations) Amendment Bill and the Building and Construction Industry (Improving Productivity) Bill – which sought to restore the Australian Building and Construction Commission (ABCC). Unfortunately the Abbott Government had no appetite for progressing these matters and apart from introducing the Bills, hardly any effort was made to negotiate with the Senate, or devise a strategy to implement them. I will have a bit more to say on these bills below.

Further, the Abbott Government made no announcements on penalty rates under the award system or unfair dismissal. It was decided to leave these matters for the Productivity Commission to review.

In recent years a small number of key events have occurred and I will deal with each of them in turn.

First, after taking on the role of Prime Minister one of Malcolm Turnbull's top priorities was to advance the industrial relations agenda that had been left to wallow. He and the Cabinet made the crucial decision to advance the reestablishment of the ABCC and the setting up of the Registered Organisations Commission (ROC) as top priority issues. Indeed they became the formal legislative triggers for the Double Dissolution election that occurred in July 2016.[2]

The ABCC was a body set up during the Howard Government on the recommendation of the Cole Royal Commission into the Building Industry. That Royal Commission came to the conclusion that the building industry was so overwhelmed with corruption and crime that it needed a special industrial "policeman" to deal with it. It was one of the principal aims of the ACTU's support for the Rudd-Gillard Governments that this "tough cop on the beat" be removed. It took that Government some time but it was eventually abolished when Bill Shorten was the Workplace Relations Minister. The loss

---

[2] A Double Dissolution Federal Election is "triggered" when one or more pieces of legislation are rejected twice by the Senate given that there must be at least a 3 month gap between rejections. If after the subsequent election the same bills are reintroduced and again rejected by the Senate then the House of Representatives and the Senate meet in a joint sitting. Because Governments usually have majorities in the lower House this gives them an added chance of passing legislation.

to the Australian economy was enormous. Economic analysis had shown that the ABCC had seen a fall by 30 per cent in construction costs and now that was all being reversed.

The need for the ROC was based on the uncovered scandals in the union movement, such as the Health Services Union scandals involving Craig Thomson, Michael Williamson and Kathy Jackson. This was mainly to do with union officials ripping-off union members by raiding bank accounts for their own personal gain – such as expenditure on holidays, clothing and, in some cases, prostitution services. As a consequence the Coalition had vowed to take the regulatory function off the Fair Work Commission and give it to a separate organisation that would properly police allegations of misconduct. Understandably union leaders across the country hated this idea. Although I think it is clear that the rank and file union members may have had cause to support it.

After the election both these very important pieces of legislation were implemented. It is worth noting that while they had been the triggers for the Double Dissolution election it was not required that a Joint Sitting of Parliament be convened to see them passed. While the Labor Party continued to vehemently oppose the Bills, the cross bench in the Senate accepted the argument that these Bills were not about an ideological obsession of the Liberal Party but were about fighting corruption. It was a narrow majority but both Bills eventually passed. This was a significant achievement for the Turnbull Government. I like to think I played a part in this success, particularly in my role as Chief Economist in the Prime Minister's Office after the 2016 election, when I was also the senior advisor on workplace relations matters.

Another extremely important reform that occurred at this time was the passing of another anti-corruption measure in the form of the *Fair Work Amendment (Corrupting Benefits) Act*. This act makes it unlawful for union officials to be paid money that could not be identified as being in payment for direct services, such as the provision of training for the employees of a particular company. The Heydon Royal Commission into Trade Union Governance and Corruption found numerous incidents of unions receiving "kickbacks" that if they had occurred between company directors would be described as bribes and would be jailable offences. Thus the Royal Commission recommended the copying into the Fair Work laws of a whole series of clauses from the Corporations Laws to fight this behaviour. Again this Bill was able to pass the Senate with the help of the cross-bench in August 2017.

Together, the ABCC, ROC and Corrupting Benefits legislation are potentially huge reform. Indeed they could be the biggest reform to industrial relation in half a century.

Where to from here?

One area where the Turnbull Government has dropped the policy ball is articulating a forward agenda on industrial relations reform.

One of my biggest regrets after working in the job as Chief Economist in the Prime Minister's Office in 2016-2017 was that I was unable to get any internal support for implementing further industrial relations reforms, beyond the one's mentioned above.

Tony Abbott, Joe Hockey and Eric Abetz need to be commended for initiating the Productivity Commission Inquiry into the Workplace Relations. However, while that report was published on 21 December 2015 the Coalition Government has said nothing about how it will proceed. Equally the Labor Party has not articulated any detailed forward agenda on industrial relations.

The Productivity Commission's inquiry was a huge undertaking and it produced a report of 1229 pages. It made a number of key findings.

Overall its assessment was that: "Despite sometimes significant problems and an assortment of peculiarities, Australia's workplace relations system is not systematically dysfunctional. It needs repair not replacement."[3] I am not entirely comfortable with this conclusion but I concede that pragmatically it is a sensible observation given the restricted terms of reference. The Commission goes on to argue that reforms to the workplace relations system need to focus on "substance over procedure, rebalance some aspects of the system that have favoured some parties over others, and reform [the Fair Work Commission]."[4]

As a consequence the Productivity Commission made 69 recommendations in all. I won't go through all of them here. However, important proposed reforms related to unfair dismissal laws; general protections; enterprise bargaining; enterprise contracts; transfer of business, industrial disputes; right of entry; the Fair Work Commission and other institutions; policies for weekend penalty rates; and migrant workers.

Probably the Productivity Commission's most notable recommendations related to enterprise bargaining and penalty rates.

With respect to enterprise bargaining, there were two key recommendations.

The first relates to the no-disadvantage-test.

When companies or other employers negotiate an enterprise agreement with their employees they must be aware that they cannot force workers to take lower than "safety net" terms and conditions that have been determined in the various industry awards (by the Fair Work Commission). Formally employers are restricted by the "better off overall test" (or BOOT). The Productivity Commission found the existing rule too restrictive. They thought that the test

---

[3] Productivity Commission (2015), *Workplace Relations Framework*, Inquiry Report, Melbourne, 30 November, 4.
[4] Ibid.

should ensure that this no-disadvantage-test should apply to "each class of employee" working in the enterprise rather than to each individual. This had been a longstanding understanding with no-disadvantage-tests. However recent decisions of the Fair Work Commission had created an enormous amount of doubt. The upshot was that agreements negotiated in good faith by employers and unions could be overturned by one lone veto despite the overwhelming support of the workforce. However, this is a particularly sensitive issue because it was the removal of various no-disadvantage-tests in WorkChoices that had created a big backlash in the period 2005 and 2007. Coalition (and for the matter Labor) politicians have been shy ever since to even concede that the test should be reviewed, irrespective of the importance and evidence that reform is needed.

Second, the Productivity Commission also noted that the lack of satisfactory individual statutory agreements were a gap in the system. In line with what I referred to above, the Productivity Commission noted that they were also of the view that IFAs were inadequate and that in addition, common law contracts were also often subject to ambiguity.

To help deal with the issue the Productivity Commission proposed the introduction of "Enterprise Contracts". It is worth quoting the Commission in detail to explain this new concept:

> To meet the needs of such businesses, the Productivity Commission recommends the adoption of a new type of arrangement – the enterprise contract (EC) (figure 9). An EC would see employers vary awards for classes of employees (for example, casual employees or weekend employees), and this would allow employers to innovate at the firmspecific level in a way not otherwise available under awards. As with enterprise agreements, the EC could not include terms that disadvantaged employees relative

to the award. Employees would be covered by the NES, and their rights to take actions under unfair dismissal and the General Protections of the Fair Work Act would not be diluted. An EC could not go below the minimum wage.

Employers could offer it to all prospective employees as a condition of employment (a process no different from that of engaging a new employee under the set terms of an award or an enterprise agreement). No negotiation or employee ballot would be required for the adoption of an EC, nor would any employee group be involved in its preparation and agreement unless the employer wished this to be the case. Employers and individual employees could still negotiate IFAs as carve outs from the EC if they mutually agreed.

Existing employees would be able to choose whether to sign on or stay with their existing employment contract, but it would be unlawful to coerce them to do so. Employers and employees would need to sign the EC, and would be informed about any tradeoffs against the award (for example, a $1.50 increase in hourly wages in exchange for a new type of rostering arrangement). Tradeoffs that relate to the preferences of an individual employee should be addressed through an IFA.[5]

On penalty rates the Productivity Commission delved deeply into the issue. In the Australian award system it has been very longstanding practice that "loadings" (ie higher pay) are given to employees for working on weekends and public holidays. This is because of society norms that include encouraging better work-life balance. In particular the Productivity Commission found that community norms had changed over the decades and there simply was no longer the case for differential (higher) penalty rates for Sunday work compared to Saturday work. It therefore recommended that

---
[5] Productivity Commission 2015, 41.

the Fair Work Commission (the body that determines the level of penalty rates) make changes.

Many readers will know that this recommendation was partly reflected in a Fair Work Commission decision in 23 February 2017 to change the existing penalty rate rules across the system. The Fair Work Commission found that the existing system had an adverse impact on employment and should be changed. However, it was by no means a radical change and penalty rates were in no way "abolished" as many trade union people complained. In fact the reaction was hysterical. Nonetheless, it is the decision of the independent tribunal and stands – as reconfirmed by a failed Federal Court appeal by the union movement.

Personally my view is that many of these recommendations should be implemented. In particular I note the Productivity Commission's recommendation on the Enterprise Contract. While I initially was very lukewarm about the idea in the absence of any other "movement at the station" it should be worth considering. It directly offers a pragmatic solution that may be of particular assistance to small business that often fail to cope with the complexities of the award system. It is by no means perfect. However, there is an outside chance that a future government may be able to get it through the Senate.

Conclusion

There is definitely a case for reforming the industrial relations system. For those interested in reading more, a good starting point is the speech that former Fair Work Commission Vice President Graeme Watson gave following his dramatic resignation from the Commission in 2017. He lists example after example of the dysfunctional nature of the system.[6]

---

[6] Graeme Watson (2017), *Captured Courts and Tribunals: A Threat to Democracy*, an address to the Centre for Independent Studies, Melbourne, 21 March.

With an increase in what has been dubbed the "Gig Economy", whereby more and more people are working freelance on task by task jobs, industrial relations must keep up with modern developments. The answer isn't as the ACTU would argue, i.e., to increase regulation to force people into more traditional-type job relationships. The answer is to provide more regulatory flexibility to allow for more jobs while protecting people's employment rights.

The Productivity Commission has provided a solid agenda for reform over the next two decades. However, you can be sure that the union movement will not respect anybody's so-called electoral mandate to fix the industrial relations problems.

As I have said before, we can all wonder where the necessary courage will come from to make the reforms, especially in the political environment dominated by the social media – so ably manipulated by the union movement and their friends such as Getup!. But the history of this nation is that there are always people who will step up to the crease and do what is necessary in the public interest.

It is essential that the business community come to the fore and argue for further industrial relations reform. They have been relatively quiet in the recent years, relying too much on the favourable economic circumstances. They have been coasting. To sustain the Australian Settlement 2.0 they must become much more active. If not they stand to lose much of what they have come to rely on.

10
THE COUNTRY-CITY COMPACT

Introduction

As is abundantly clear if you have read this far into the book, I am an economist by profession. However as I have emphasised, I am not an ivory tower ideologue who simply cares between Right and Left. What is important is between right and wrong. You will also be aware that for a number of years I was the Federal Member for Eden-Monaro which is a seat that takes up the South East corner of rural New South Wales.

In this chapter I want to further discuss economic development policies for the regions. We saw in earlier chapters such policies were an important element of the original Australian Settlement. It needs to also be an important part of the Australian Settlement 2.0.

A pragmatic understanding of the difficulties rural and regional people are facing is particularly necessary. I am not here pleading for additional subsidies. Instead I am arguing for a clear headed understanding of the cost disadvantages that people in the regions face. It is also argued in the context of the cohesion of Australia as a nation. As was noted in earlier chapters the concept of a nation state has required a number of important pragmatic decisions to be made. For example in framing the Constitution the Founding Fathers established a powerful Senate that had as a defining characteristic the equal number of Senators from the original states, viz originally six each but now 12. While my calls for Constitutional reform in chapter 5 would somewhat diminish the power of the Senate it would not diminish the geographical representation of the body, ensuring that the legislative majority is geographically dispersed.

It is my belief that the Australian people would never collectively agree to changes to this fundamental bedrock of the Senate.

Equally the concept of Horizontal Fiscal Equalisation (HFE), while annoying to economic purists, is an important acknowledgement of maintaining the cohesion of the nation-state despite the diversity of demographics and natural resources across our large continent. Indeed it is the embodiment of Unity in Diversity. The recent Productivity Commission review into HFE has found a deep and wide-ranging support of the "fairness" of HFE across the Australian community.[1] In my view it is in this same context that I am proposing the reinvigoration of the Country-City Compact so as to deal sensibly with the feelings of neglect that regional and rural citizens feel. I would rather do this than leave those people to be the unwitting victims of populist drivel like that espoused by One Nation and the Shooters, Fishers and Farmer Party.

Regional policy

When I entered Parliament I said that I hoped to be a strong advocate who could both support good economic policy and the regions. And while I certainly believe in economic reform, I also noted that I believed in what I labelled the Country-City Compact.

The Country-City Compact – what I also call the "Triple C" policy – is something that has existed for the best part of 100 years in Australia.

Unfortunately it was a tragic victim of the reform agenda of the 80s, 90s and the 2000s. And while it is abundantly clear from earlier chapters in this book that I strongly supported that reform agenda, I did not agree with all the parts of it.

---

[1] Productivity Commission (2017c), *Horizontal Fiscal Equalisation*: Draft Report, Melbourne, October.

It sounds rhetorical, but rural and regional Australia deserves a fair go and the Country-City Compact needs to be revived, maybe in a different form, but it needs to be revived.

As we have seen throughout this book the Australian Settlement was a comprehensive social and economic policy. And as I have documented in laborious detail the bulk of the Settlement was rightly dismantled over the course of the last three decades by successive governments. However one aspect of that change was also the dismantling of another part of the Australian Settlement – the Country-City Compact.

In my view the Compact was a fundamental understanding of Australia's nation-builders that the country needed to have a fair share of attention and resources. The Compact recognised that there was an inextricable interdependence between the country and the city. It acknowledged that there was a mutual obligation that recognised the costs of living in the country.

Unfortunately, this has basically gone. And yet country regions remain vital to the nation. Almost all mining is in rural areas. And it remains the case that agriculture retains an important part of the national economy. Around 93 percent of the food eaten in this nation is grown in Australia.[2] In addition, some 30 per cent of Australians live outside the major cities.[3] Almost 40 per cent of those aged over 65 live outside major cities.[4]

Nonetheless, there is clear educational and health disadvantage. In educational terms retention rates in schools are in excess of 10 per cent less in rural areas.[5] In very remote areas 30 per cent of

---

[2] Commonwealth of Australia (2015), *Agriculture Competitiveness White Paper*, Canberra.

[3] Regional Institute of Australia (2015), *Population Dynamics in Regional Australia*, Canberra, January.

[4] Regional Institute of Australia 2015, 92.

[5] Independent Review into Regional, Rural and Remote Education (2017), Discussion Paper, Commonwealth of Australia, Canberra, July, 18.

children are not hitting the very minimal benchmarks for year 3. In health terms, life expectancy is lower by up to 7 years depending on remoteness. People are up to 4 times more likely to die from accidents. It is up to 2.6 times more likely for men to die from suicides in the bush.[6] Disability rates for rural males are between 20 per cent and 30 per cent higher.

So what does reviving the Country-City Compact mean?

In reality it means that priorities can be better set. However country people cannot just cry poor. They have been doing that for the last 30 years as their services and infrastructure have been increasingly run down.

Instead the intellectual case needs to be built so we can get that fair share. That is an intellectual case built around nation-building.

One of the important points that can be made is in the interaction of transport and regional development.

High speed rail and the Very Fast Train

In my view the time has come to accelerate the cause of the Very Fast Train (VFT) proposal.

I am strongly behind the VFT project because of its major implications for developing regional Australia. As a former Federal Member of Parliament in the "Capital Region" I have a personal interest in this because every major proposal put forward over the last three decades has nominated the Sydney-Canberra corridor as the first stage of any such project.

The Federal Government has rightly nominated infrastructure spending as a key to productivity growth for the nation. It is a central plank of our economic strategy for building our nation in the 21st century.

The Government has already committed $8.4 billion to proceed

---

[6] See for example Regional Institute of Australia 2015, 32-33.

with the Inland Rail project between Brisbane and Melbourne.[7] This is a freight rail project that when completed will substantially reduce the travel times (up to 25 per cent) between those two cities and by-pass the congestion on Sydney freight lines. The construction itself will take many years. It is a real nation-building project. Equally, however, greater attention should be given to the VFT.

Indeed it is disappointing that the Government announced in 2013 that it was abolishing the High Speed Rail Advisory Group. Happily, however, in contrast the Government subsequently announced that it is continuing to work with the NSW, Vic, Qld and ACT governments to protect the identified rail corridors to ensure that if and when the VFT proceeds it can do so in the least cost way.

Such a long term project will lead to development in the Capital Region that kills once-and-for-all Canberra's unhealthy dependency on the federal public service and concerns about being a "one company town". It will also help with wider regional development. Just making an economically stronger Canberra will help the region. But further, if a terminus came into Canberra airport it would be even more significant. The linkages with Moruya and Merimbula airports, and hopefully a revived Snowy Mountains airport (south of Cooma) could lead to huge economic spin-offs. Commuting from Goulburn to Sydney would become viable.

A detailed study for the Government released in April 2013 by AECOM consultants costed the VFT at $114 billion for 1,748 kms of track that would take until 2065 to build.[8] That would cover a route from Melbourne, via Canberra and Sydney to Brisbane (with 12 stops in regional Australia). Other researchers have estimated that it would cost between $63 and $84 billion and be built as early

---

[7] Darren Chester and Paul Fletcher (2017), "$20 billion investment in rail", joint media release, Canberra, 9 May.
[8] AECOM and associates, (2013), *High Speed Rail Phase 2 Report*, report to the Australian Government, 11 April, viii.

as 2025. The Sydney-Canberra link according to AECOM's higher costings would be $23 billion. Obviously these are substantial amounts of money.[9]

Overseas proponents are prepared to put private sector capital behind the project. There are Japanese and Chinese investors who are prepared to spend serious money. Indeed the completion of the recent trade agreements with China and Japan make the opportunities for such investment all the more attractive. In 2015 I inspected the Chinese VFT and participated in discussions at their Ministry of Railways. China, with its vast population, has a remarkably different economic equation to us for this transport mode. However the various studies recently done, including the AECOM report, show that it is viable.

Let me be clear, my support is not based on some pie-in-the-sky hope that the private sector can fully fund such a project. An objective reading of the research shows that even with private sector involvement there would be a heavy reliance on the public purse. But how is that different from the tens of billions of dollars being spent on urban infrastructure right now for which rural taxpayers see little commercial return to help them meet their cost of living pressures? Regional Australians don't begrudge taxpayer spending on urban infrastructure but are expected to cop it when it is used as an excuse for why they don't receive it in return.

And as a final aside, maybe the Federal Government's interest shouldn't stop there. On the basis that the Capital Metro light rail project in Canberra proceeds I think a cross-border spur line to the regional metropolis of Queanbeyan, with its 43,000 residents, should be added to the ACT Government's master plan for the project.

That is some food for thought on how we can grow regional

---

[9] Ibid.

Australia and attract population away from the choking megacities. We could have a Country-City Compact that produces win-win results.

Conclusion

This chapter may surprise some of my neo-liberal friends. It is arguing the case for country people in terms of economic development policy. However as I have said there is a case from an economic development perspective to pay special attention to the disadvantages placed on those who live in regional areas.

Governments should make decisions based on an analysis of cost and benefit. However, there is much more to nation-building than a simple financial calculation. They need to be comprehensive economic evaluations that include the social and cultural dynamic. The Australian Settlement and its successor the Australian Settlement 2.0 have always been more than just a financial policy framework. I believe that in the past too many cost benefit analyses have been too narrow. In the transport area they have not adequately calculated the economic opportunity costs of regional development versus overcrowded cities. We have to maintain and grow our regions for these reasons and also because a large proportion of our export success comes from these areas. It is a mutually beneficial dynamic that simply cannot be ignored.

I have given one example – the High Speed rail project – to give a concrete example of where I think rural and regional development could be boosted by a bigger thinking on economic development. The current government's Northern Australia Fund project is another example of the same thinking. I would include the Snowy Hydro 2.0 project as yet another example. Of necessity a focus is on infrastructure spending. However, governments will need to be careful that bigger thinking doesn't morph into boondoggles.

It has happened often over the years. That is why the proper cost benefit analysis should remain at the core of Government decision making.

11
TRADE DEALS

Introduction

As we have seen in foregoing chapters the way the government conducts policy on international trade is central to the Australian Settlement 2.0.

Over 100 years ago the adoption of protectionist policies was a key pillar of the original Australian Settlement or, to remind readers of its initial name, New Protection.

Equally, the abandonment of that protectionist policy in the 1990s was a key pillar of the new Australian Settlement.

This chapter looks a little more deeply into the current debate, not least the critical challenges that are looming as *President* Trump implements *Candidate* Trump's protectionist agenda. Donald Trump as a candidate: "has pledged to tear up 'horrible' trade deals, including the North American Free Trade Agreement and the Trans Pacific Partnership; declare China a currency manipulator; and slap a 45 percent tariff on Chinese imports."[1] He has also threatened to increase tariffs to 25 per cent for steel products and 15 per cent for aluminum.[2] That is a strong mercantilist agenda that would turn US trade policy since World War II on its head. A trade war would be catastrophic for Australia.

In the face of these challenges I also discuss the Australian Government's forward agenda on trade policy and the importance of the Trans Pacific Partnership.

---

[1] Stewart M. Patrick (2017), "Trump and World Order", Foreign Affairs, Vol 96, No 2, 55.

[2] Rosie Lewis and Cameron Stewart (2018), "Ryan threatens to block Trump's tariffs", *The Australian*, 7 March.

Setting the context

Let me also add the wider international perspective to the discussion of international trade.

At this stage I will first just say a few words about the economies of China, the United States and the European Union. I will have more to say in the next chapter on international relations and defence.

Firstly, when I was in Parliament I visited China on a delegation of the House of Representatives Standing Committee on Economics. It reconfirmed my deep concerns about the fragility of the Chinese economy. The debt levels of provincial governments is a black box, as is the true financial status of many state-owned enterprises. The shadow banking issue is a real, not a shadow, problem.

Why is this all so important? It is because 20 per cent of Australia's total two-way trade is with China. Further, some 36 per cent of all merchandise exports are to China.

Our exposure to this one country is enormous and, dare I say it, potentially dangerous.

Never since Australia was riding on the sheep's back and was so exposed to the vagaries of the United Kingdom's economy have we been so dependent on one other country. That is why proceeding with the free trade agreements with South Korea and Japan were so important. And it is why pursuing other free trade agreements are also so critical.

It is why the current Government has facilitated uranium sales to India and to talk up the possibility of a bilateral trade agreement with that country. It is also why the Government is placing a special emphasis on the European Union, Great Britain and Indonesia.

In respect to the United States I note that the recent economic news has been good. That has been contributed to by an unprecedented economic experiment known as Quantitative Easing – essentially printing money – which has been occurring over the period since 2008. The Federal Reserve are in the process of reversing that policy and moving into an era of raising interest rates after they have been effectively zero for years now. How the market reacts in the long run to these unprecedented polices is simply not known. The fact is neither the US Federal Reserve nor leading economists are in any agreement on the ultimate outcome. By definition that is therefore a huge area of uncertainty. There is the prospect that as events unfold there may be a massive boost to inflation. We simply are not sure. The sooner the experiment concludes the better.

In relation to the European Union economists are more relaxed today about the progress of the economies there. However, again it should be noted that no fundamental resolution has been arrived at in solving the private and public debt problems that are at the root of their economic problems. There is still a fundamental disconnect between the operation of the single currency – the Euro – and the absence of a combined fiscal policy for EU nations. That probably means another Euro crisis is inevitable. It is just a matter of when.

I probably don't need to mention that the Middle East remains a troubling issue. Disputes between Russia and the Ukraine likewise are serious. Closer to home Australia must deal with issues in the Asia Pacific region that could explode at any time. In Northern Asia there are very serious territorial disputes going on, particularly related to sovereignty in the South China Sea and separately in the East China Sea. I will have more to say about these issues in the next chapter. Suffice it to say here that the South and East China Seas contain essential trade routes. The South China Sea is one of the busiest seaways in the world, seeing twenty-five percent of the world's crude oil traffic alone. As one of the world's largest trading nations that means they are also Australia's essential trade routes.

And just to round off with a short anecdote. When I was

principal advisor on foreign affairs for Julie Bishop prior to the 2013 election she received quite a chilling warning.

I won't name the British statesman involved but when asked what kept him awake at night he said the possibility of a silly misunderstanding on the India-Pakistan border causing a nuclear war.

So some food for thought.

What that all means is a country like Australia needs to get its house in order now and not wait because we simply do not know when the next external event will overwhelm everything. It reiterates our need to diversify our trading relationships to maximise the sustainability or our prosperity.

The benefits of freer trade and the threats of its demise

In his book *Why Australia Prospered*,[3] Ian McLean of the University of Adelaide has charted the progress of Australia's economy over the years. Unlike myself he expressed the view that the protectionist policies of the past "did not significantly stall growth". He comes to the conclusion that "prosperity was primarily due to luck rather than human effort or wise decisions".[4] In this respect he points to a happy coincidence of resource endowments, commodity booms, and the institutional and cultural benefits inherited from the British Empire. Nonetheless, having said that he does acknowledge that Australia has benefited from its participation in the world trading system. I would argue that it has been critical.

The benefits of freer trade and the lowering of Australia's protectionist barriers have been central to our prosperity. In chapter 3 of this book I detailed the decades of struggle to achieve this policy outcome and the arguments made to justify it. I don't intend repeating them in this chapter. However, what may be useful is to

---

[3] Ian W. McLean (2013), *Why Australia Prospered: the shifting sources of economic growth*, Princeton University Press, Princeton.
[4] Ibid., 247.

give some contemporary analysis by the Productivity Commission on the economic implications of freer trade.

The Productivity Commission released a timely Research Paper in July 2017 entitled *Rising protectionism: challenges, threats and opportunities for Australia*. It concludes that "International trade and investment are vitally important to the Australian economy. Barriers to trade and investment pose a risk to economic growth and living standards".[5]

The Commission[6] succinctly catalogues the benefits to Australia of the freer trade regime since World War II and I reproduce them below:

Trade is vitally important to the economy.

- Trade (exports and imports) is a big part of the Australian economy, equating to about 40 per cent of GDP.[7]
- Trade has been an important driver of economic growth. Over the past 25 years, Australia's economy has doubled in size; exports have accounted for over a quarter of this growth.[8]
- Thanks to the trade liberalisation that occurred during the 1980s and 1990s, the average Australian working household was better off in 2009 by between $100 and $150 a fortnight.[9]

---

[5] Productivity Commission (2017a), *Rising protectionism: challenges, threats and opportunities for Australia*, Research Paper, Melbourne, July, 18.
[6] Ibid.
[7] Department of Foreign Affairs and Trade (2016), *Australia's Trade Since Federation*, DFAT, Canberra.
[8] R. Tuhin and J. Swanepoel (2017), *Export Behaviour and Business Performance: Evidence from Australian Microdata*, Research Paper, 7/2016, Department of Industry, Innovation and Science, Canberra.
[9] Centre for International Economics (2009), *Benefits of Trade and Trade Liberalisation*, paper prepared for the Department of Foreign Affairs and Trade, CIE, Canberra.

- Many Australian jobs rely on trade. About 1 in 7 workers are ultimately involved in the production of exports. Another 1 in 10 are involved in import related activity. All up, over 20 per cent of jobs are connected with trade.[10]
- Consumers are big beneficiaries of trade. Trade means access to a wider variety of goods and services at more competitive prices, boosting living standards. The price of audio, visual and computing equipment fell over 50 per cent in the five years to June 2014, for example, thanks, substantially, to imports from countries where it costs less to make those types of products.[11]
- Exporting firms are typically more successful. They are larger, more productive, pay higher wages and are more likely to survive than nonexporters.[12]
- Imports reduce Australian production costs and increase employment. Over half of all Australian imports are essential inputs that businesses use to produce goods locally.[13] If firms had to buy higher cost domestic inputs, rather than import them, they would be less able to expand and hire more workers.
- Exposure to competition from overseas compels Australian firms to innovate and adopt more efficient production methods. More efficient resource use boosts economic growth.
- Foreign direct investment helps fund the growth and development of industry in Australia. Foreign investment brings new technologies and services and connections to foreign markets, boosting growth and exports.

---

[10] Centre for International Economics 2009.
[11] Department of Foreign Affairs and Trade (2014), *Fifty Years of Australia's Trade*, DFAT, Canberra.
[12] Tuhin and Swanepoel 2017.
[13] Department of Foreign Affairs and Trade 2014.

However, the Productivity Commission did not stop there. It analysed the threats from the current rise in protectionist sentiment around the world. It, of course, noted the threatening language from President Trump. In addition it stated:[14]

> In the years since the Global Financial Crisis (GFC), the number of tradelimiting measures implemented by [Group of 20] countries has more than quadrupled, and these new measures now cover about 5 per cent of world imports.[15] Recently, for the first time since the GFC, G20 countries backed away from a commitment to reject all forms of protectionism. And in the last few years, growth in the volume of world trade (which had quickly recovered from a GFC induced dip), has remained sluggish, with the combined share of exports and imports in global GDP falling for several years running.

In chapter 4 of the Research Paper the Commission tries to economically model the impact of what they acknowledge would be an "extreme" but not unprecedented rise in protectionism. For its base-case it looks at what happened in the 1930s and have modelled an across the board increase in tariffs by 15 percentage points, which would result in average levels similar to that of a number of key developed economies during the Great Depression.

The results are dramatic and sobering.

Firstly, this level of tariffs would result in a world recession. It estimates that global trade would be 22 percent lower and that global output would be around 3 percent lower, which is the equivalent of more than a year of global growth at current rates. It estimates the global stock of capital would decrease by 5 percent.

---

[14] Productivity Commission 2017a, 10.

[15] World Trade Organization (2016), Report on G20 Trade Measures (Mid-May 2016 to Mid-October 2016), WTO, Geneva.

In context, every US$1 increase in tariff revenue would cost US$1.18 in global income.[16]

More specifically for Australia the Commission found that[17]:

> Australia would not escape unscathed. The Commission's modelling estimates that, in total, economic activity (GDP) would be more than one per cent lower in each year that the higher tariffs were in force – equivalent to removing about half a year of growth from the economy or, in employment terms, close to 100,000 jobs.[18] For every $1.00 increase in Australian tariff revenue, economic activity in Australia would fall by $0.64. National income would be about 1.5 per cent lower, and the purchasing power of that income (or Australians' living standards) would drop by 1.8 per cent. For the median household this would amount to an income cut of nearly $1500 a year. Australia's export sectors would be hardest hit, with exports falling by close to 15 per cent. Reflecting the high proportion of mining and energy in Australian exports, activity in the primary sector would be hit particularly hard – output would fall by over 5 per cent. And exporters that use imports as an input to production would see a fall in competitiveness as import prices rose with higher tariffs.

They are the broad macroeconomic affects. The Commission goes on to say that the impact on households would be startling:

> Overall, both workers and capital owners would be worse off. For workers, wages are estimated to fall by 2.5 per cent on average due to less efficient production and, in line with the shifts in the structure of economic output, people employed in the primary and services sectors, especially

---

[16] Productivity Commission 2017a, 62.
[17] Ibid.
[18] Australian Bureau of Statistics (2017), *Labour Force, Australia*, April 2017, Cat. no. 6202.0, ABS, Canberra.

lower skilled workers, would face a higher risk of redundancy. In the Commission's modelling, at least 1 per cent of lower skilled workers (or an estimated 50,000) and 0.7 per cent of higher skilled workers (or an estimated 46,000) would have to find a new job. These figures are lower bounds, as the modelling only picks up moves between sectors and misses moves within sectors which would add considerably to these estimates.[19]

It goes on: "For capital owners, the rate of return earned on their assets would fall. And close to 5 per cent of Australia's capital stock would be mothballed – equivalent to nearly half of the investment in the mining sector over the past ten years."[20]

Finally the Commission concludes:[21]

that global tariff increases would depress economic activity in Australia is in line with other research. McKibbin and Stoeckel[22] predicted that a 10 percentage point rise in tariffs globally would cause Australia's GDP to fall by at least 1.4 per cent. Dixon[23] predicted that larger tariff increases (a flat rate of 20 per cent on all trade, except for 45 per cent tariffs on US and Chinese imports from each other), would see Australia's GDP fall by about 4 per cent.

Monkeying around with tariffs can be disastrous!!

What needs to be done

We simply have to pursue more trade deals. Waiting for the World

---

[19] Productivity Commission 2017a, 63.
[20] Ibid., 64.
[21] Ibid.
[22] W. McKibbin and A. Stoeckel (2009), *The Potential Impact of the Global Financial Crisis on World Trade*, Policy Research Working Paper No. 5134, The World Bank, Washington.
[23] J. Dixon (2017), 'The impact on Australia of Trump's 45 per cent tariff on Chinese imports', *Economic Papers*, vol. Online Early View.

Trade Organisation (WTO) to do the work for us is to lose in the international competitiveness market. The WTO is broken and badly broken.

The WTO was created in 1994 but it is the on-going successor of the post-World War II General Agreement on Tariffs and Trade (GATT). GATT/WTO has been an enormously successful economic arrangement for the world over the decades. It remains incredibly important because it provides the rules that govern international trade – from the levels of tariffs and quotas permitted, to rules about the identification of the "country of origin" of products traded.

However, as I said above the WTO is broken. It no longer appears to continue the advance against protectionism – and there is still a lot to do. This book is not the place to write a dissertation on the myriad problems with the organisation. Probably the root cause of all the apparent failures is the consensus model on which it operates. Consensus essentially means that all members have to agree to proposals.

When the GATT was established in 1948 it only had 23 member countries. While somewhat unwieldy that number did not prevent enough consensus to emerge to allow the advancement of reform. However, while the consensus model remains the number of members has ballooned to 164 (out of 194 countries in the world). Some of the newer members are China (joined 2001), Saudi Arabia (joined 2005), Vietnam (joined 2007) and Russia (joined 2012). It is not the number of members that is the problem, the more the merrier. The problem is the negotiation rules that have become very outdated. This problem has been known – certainly for the best part of two or three decades. However it would be apparent that it is almost impossible to get a consensus to change the consensus model.

And certainly Australia cannot solve the WTO problem on

its own, although it employs its best endeavours to do so. As a consequence the pragmatic response is to pursue bilateral and regional agreements in the best interests of Australia.

What I call "Trade Purists" pine for the WTO system and seem to be in denial that anything can be "good" unless it is a wide-ranging multilateral WTO agreement. I note that in recent times my old organisation the ACCI have fallen into this intellectual trap, warning of a "noodle bowl" of trade agreements.[24]

And, although I very often quote their work with favour, and it pains me to say it, I believe that the Productivity Commission's view on this matter, which aligns with ACCI, is also wrong-headed.

Economic theory would tell you that the greatest economic benefit would come from comprehensive multilateral agreements. However it is also the case that a large trading nation like Australia extracts benefits out of lesser deals and the economic modeling for various free trade agreements show this. More would be gained from multilateral WTO deals but in their absence we cannot let the world pass us by.

In the last decade Australian Governments have pursued bilateral free trade deals and regional partnerships. The Coalition Governments have been more enthusiastic about these deals and over the years have signed the: Closer Economic Relations with New Zealand (1983); the Singapore-Australia Free Trade Agreement (2003); the Thailand-Australia Free Trade Agreement (2005); the Australia-United States free Trade Agreement (2005); the Korea-Australia Free Trade Agreement (2014); the China-Australia Free Trade Agreement (2015); the Japan-Australia Economic Partnership Agreement (2015); the Pacific Agreement on Closer Economic Relations (2017); the Peru-Australia Free trade Agreement (2018).

---

[24] Eryk Bagshaw (2018), "Trade deal risks a 'noodle bowl' of agreements, warns business", *Sydney Morning Herald*, 25 January.

Labor Governments, under the influence of Trade Purists like Craig Emerson and Ross Garnaut, have been decidedly less enthusiastic. No such new deals were secured during the Hawke-Keating years. However, during the Rudd-Gillard years the pragmatic bug must have bitten the ministry (and then Trade Minister Simon Crean) because they did sign off on: the Australia-Chile FTA (2009); the ASEAN-Australia-New Zealand Free Trade Area (2010); the Malaysia- Australia Free Trade Agreement (2013).

Most important of all is the Comprehensive and Progressive Agreement for Trans Pacific Partnership (TPP). This has been negotiated across the Rudd-Gillard, Abbott and Turnbull Governments.

The TPP began as a negotiation between 12 countries, viz: Australia, Brunei, Canada, Chile, Japan, Malaysia, Mexico, Peru, New Zealand, Singapore, the United States and Vietnam. Those negotiations concluded in October 2015. Initially all countries pledged to sign-on, but here was a very long process in ratifying the deal across all 12 countries. Unfortunately, in the United States the 2016 Presidential year was at hand and both major party candidates, Democrat Hillary Clinton and Republican Donald Trump, opposed the deal. This was particularly disappointing in Hillary Clinton's case because she had actually helped negotiate the agreement when she was Secretary of State in the Obama Administration. The bottom line is that Donald Trump won and his administration pulled out of the deal. As a consequence, for a short time, Canada also pulled out of the agreement. According to the original terms of the agreement the absence of the United States meant that it could not proceed.

The good news is that on 23 January 2018 it was announced that all countries but the United States had renegotiated the agreement and pledged to implement it. The deal will see the removal of 98 percent of all tariffs between member countries. For Australia industries to significantly benefit include beef sales to Japan; and the improved quotas on wheat and rice. Further there would be better access for sugar to Japan, Canada and Mexico and the end to tariffs on sheep meat, cotton, wool, seafood, horticulture, wine and manufactured goods.

It is reported that "the new-look Trans-Pacific Partnership would open up an economic zone worth almost $14 trillion".[25]

The Australian newspaper reported that ironically, "independent international modelling of the deal has revealed that the decision by US President Donald Trump to pull out of the original 12-nation agreement could deliver a greater trade boost to Australia than if the US had stayed in, countering opposition arguments that it is a hollow deal".[26]

The independent economic modellers had noted that the reason Australia actually had a better deal with the removal of the US was because it already has a comprehensive free trade agreement with that country, but Japan, New Zealand, Malaysia and Vietnam had no existing such deal and now weren't getting one.[27]

The report went on to note that: "The modelling report conducted by the Peterson Institute for International Economics, a US-based think tank, showed that Australia's economy would grow between 0.5 per cent and more than 1 per cent by 2030 under TPP 11, which has been rebadged as the Comprehensive Progressive Agreement on the Trans Pacific Partnership."[28]

It is a good deal for Australia.

Finally, the Turnbull Government is currently negotiating

---

[25] John Dagge (2018), "Australia home free with TPP", *Daily Telegraph*, 25 January.
[26] Simon Benson (2018), "Trade Pact to deliver GDP boost", *The Australian*, 25 January.
[27] Ibid.
[28] Ibid.

agreements with: the European Union; Gulf Cooperation Council; Hong Kong; India; Indonesia; the Regional Comprehensive Partnership; and Great Britain. They should pursue all these as a matter of priority.

Conclusion

The future success of the Australian Settlement 2.0 depends upon sustaining and building up on Australia's participation in the liberal world order and rules-based trading system.

Australia has been one of the great winners from the system that has been created since World War II and we have more to gain.

This is a policy area that has bipartisan support between the two main political parties, but the "consensus" stops there. The Greens are totally opposed to this agenda and the minor parties like One Nation are so-called economic nationalists at their worst.

In no other area is a reversal of policy of greater danger to Australia's future prosperity. To close our borders, even partially, will only reactivate the long term decline we saw with the original Australian Settlement. Nothing would more accurately describe it than the phrase I have previously used – sleepwalking to disaster.

12
INTERNATIONAL RELATIONS AND DEFENCE

Introduction

One of the key elements of the original Australian Settlement related to foreign affairs and defence – Paul Kelly labelled it Imperial Benevolence. And as we saw in chapter 2 one of the key reasons for Federation was defence issues. As such, a comprehensive analysis of how the Australian Settlement has evolved requires us to look at the topic of international relations before we conclude this book.

In my career I have worked in the Defence portfolio and in more recent years I was the principal advisor for foreign affairs and trade for the now Minister for Foreign Affairs, Julie Bishop.

Indeed, on 7 October 2001 I was the Chief of Staff of the Minister for Defence. That date is important because it was on that day that the final order was given for Operation Slipper to send Australian troops into Afghanistan after 9/11. In this case I was a small cog in the great military machine but nonetheless held an important position as the closest confidant of the Minister.

As the order went out it hit me – it physically hit me – that I was part of a decision-making process that would probably see the death and wounding of many brave Australian soldiers. In fact there have been some 41 operational deaths and 261 wounded in action. As you can appreciate these matters weigh heavily on a person. It is a salient example of where politics becomes a dreadfully serious endeavour. We all deeply respect the sacrifice of these brave men and women. And indeed I want to acknowledge the sacrifice and duty of the thousands of people from the defence community and veterans' communities.

Finally, it is worth noting that I have had the character building benefit of working overseas in the Middle East. I may not know how to fight a war in the field as former serving military officers can, but I do claim another, just as important skill set, which is a reasonable amount of expertise about international relations and defence strategy from a policy point of view.

We no longer rely on imperial benevolence for Australia's international relations and defence strategy. In this chapter I begin with an overview of Australia's strategic setting. I then make some observations about key challenges facing our foreign affairs and military planners. They relate to China, Russia, North Korea and Islamic terrorism. I discuss some of the current debates. Finally I offer some thought-provoking policy ideas on Australia's future strategy.

The strategic setting

In this section we start with a helicopter view of Australian defence strategy and international relations before discussing some of the main challenges.

Overview

To remind readers of the international relations aspect of the original Australian Settlement discussed in chapter 2, I note that Paul Kelly stated that an element of the Settlement was imperial benevolence. Kelly says very little about imperial benevolence, except to note that Australia, as part of the British Empire, relied overwhelming through the first half of the 20th century on the Empire for its defence and trading markets. As he noted "the Royal Navy was the guarantor of White Australia. British finance and trade preference underwrote Australian growth".[1]

Over the years that has substantially changed. The principal

---

[1] Paul Kelly (1992), *The End of Certainty: The story of the 1980s*, Allen and Unwin, Sydney, 11.

watershed was, of course World War II when the focus of our strategy turned from our imperial benefactor – Great Britain – to the United States. Famously, Prime Minister John Curtin stated on 27 December 1941, shortly after the bombing of Pearl Harbour, that: "Australia looks to America, free of any pangs as to our traditional ties of kinship with the United Kingdom."

Australia's international relations and defence strategy since that time has relied heavily on our defence treaty with the United States, namely the Security Treaty between Australia, New Zealand and the United States (ANZUS) signed in September 1951. Indeed it has been the bedrock of our strategy during and since the Cold War, when a principal protagonist was the Soviet Union (i.e., Russia and its then communist empire).

The other part of the strategy since World War II has been a cooperative engagement with Asia. Australia had begun diplomatic relations with countries such as China way back in 1921 during the Government of Stanley Bruce.[2] However the historic signing of a trade treaty – the Commerce Agreement with Japan in 1957, only 12 years after the horrors of World War II – was a vital and crucial development initiated by Menzies Government. Through the following decades, which included participation in wars in Korea and Vietnam and conflicts in Malaya and Indonesia, Australian Governments have focussed on building deeper and deeper relations with our region. The recognition of Communist China by the Whitlam Government was particularly important, as was the growing integration with the Chinese economy encouraged by the Hawke, Keating and Howard Governments. Recent governments have treated these matters as top priorities.

Thus, in this section I examine where we are today and the principal challenges.

---

[2] I.M. Cumpston (1995), *History of Australian Foreign Policy 1901-1991*, Cumpston, Canberra, 223.

Noted international affairs commentator Alan Dupont has commented:

> Australia has been the beneficiary, enjoying unparalleled growth on the back of East Asia's economic ascendancy. Many regarded this lengthy outbreak of peace and stability as the new normal, a signal that the region's bloody conflicts and fractious past had been consigned to the dustbin of history. However, history's real lesson is that rising wealth and power eventually lead to increased rivalry, competition and conflict.[3]

I could add, as the ancient Roman writer Publius Flavius Vegetius Renatus famously said "Si vis pacem, para bellum – if you want peace, prepare for war".[4]

When I joined Peter Reith in the Defence portfolio to be his ministerial chief of staff one of the early discussions was about the wider context of Australia's defence "posture" or preparedness. Probably every new defence minister for decades had been given a similar preliminary talk. We discussed the perennial challenge for Australian defence planners between the alternatives of "Defence of Australia" versus "Forward defence".

This has often been labelled the "Creswell-Foster Debate" as the early proponents that emerged in a series of "exchanges" in 1908 were Captain William Creswell, the then Director of Naval Forces and Colonel Hubert John Foster, the then Director of Military Studies at the University of Sydney.[5]

---

[3] Alan Dupont (2017), "Danger ahead as Asia's long peace ends", *The Australian*, 2 September.

[4] Quoted in Paul Cornish and Kingsley Donaldson (2017), *2020 World of War*, Hodder & Stoughton, London, 272.

[5] Michael Evans (2007), "Overcoming the Creswell-Foster divide in Australian strategy: the challenge for the twenty-first century policy-makers", *Australian Journal of International Affairs*, Vol 61, No 2, June, 193.

Generally speaking, the naval man, Captain Creswell, lined up with the Defence of Australia doctrine arguing that the prime (and some would say narrow) focus of the military was to secure the protection of mainland Australia and therefore there needed to be a heavy reliance of naval resources as opposed to land forces.[6] In the other corner Colonel Foster pointed out that as part of the British Empire, and because Australia's main security focus was really on off-shore maritime and trading interests, this "required an outward-looking defence policy with a clear expeditionary role for the army".[7]

It is a fascinating and very important debate. Basically Australian Governments have always worked with both doctrines and at times heavily weighted it towards the Foster view. Certainly this would be the view that predominates today.

From there I want to say a few words about the wider international relations strategy, beyond simply defence. This includes global governance, and Australia's role in the world.

I would say that there are three key elements pertinent to any discussion of our global politics: the UN, the US, and "US" – i.e., Australia.

Firstly the United Nations. Despite some United Nations naysayers I firmly believe that Australia needs to support effective action through the United Nations. Australia was a founding member of the United Nations and we have been a strong supporter for the seven decades since. Indeed, Australians played a leading role in one of the United Nations' first peacekeeping operations at Indonesia's birth as an independent nation. Further, Australia had the privilege of sitting on the inaugural UN Security Council in 1946. We filled that position again recently (secured by the Rudd Government) and few would argue with the great job performed by

---
[6] Ibid.
[7] Evans 2007, 194.

Foreign Minister Julie Bishop and permanent representative, Gary Quinlan. Since its inception, the United Nations has worked for three values: i.e., peace, prosperity and the preservation of human rights.

However, there is another arrangement that has also upheld these three values. Which brings me to the second key element – our great and powerful friend, the United States of America. That country has played a unique role since World War II. It has had an unparalleled burden placed on it, which over the decades has meant tremendous sacrifice at a terrible cost.

The role that the United States has played in establishing and maintaining the post-war world order has been uniquely powerful and pervasive. It is a role we should never take for granted. For if not the United States, then who? No other country has the capacity, the geo-strategic circumstance, the inclination, or the habit of upholding that world order. Absent that engagement – absent that leadership – the world would look very different than it does today.

Which brings me to the third key element – Australia's role.

Lowy Institute Director Michael Fullilove, caused quite a stir in 2014 when he called for a 'Larger Australia.' Dr Fullilove's argument is that far from 'punching above our weight' as is often claimed, Australia punches at, and sometimes, below our weight. He reminded us that Australia is the 12th largest economy in the world. We are the 5th richest people. We are not a superheavyweight, argued Fullilove, but we are certainly not a flyweight and should do more.[8]

This is true. However, before we decide what weight division we are in, we need to define the reason we want to be in the ring in the first place.

---

[8] Michael Fullilove (2014), "Time has come for Australia to step up", *Sydney Morning Herald*, 23 July.

For me, the answer is a simple, but extremely powerful one. It relates to the discussion we had in chapter 4, where we discussed the underlying philosophy of our economic and political framework. As Australians, we are the beneficiaries of centuries of hard-won liberal democratic thinking, institutions, traditions, and structures. The world order that has emerged from the horror of World War II has delivered unprecedented peace, prosperity, and freedom. In recent times, our role as a defender of those institutions – through our support of both the United Nations *and* the United States – has increased. But the false dichotomy of unilateralism versus multilateralism is a straw man – it has never been a reality. It has certainly never been a zero-sum choice of picking just the United Nations, or just the United States. The nuance-challenged binary presented by some (like those in the Greens who would be happy to see all our relations with the United States dumped) does not reflect the complexity and multiplicity of international action and international governance.

Australia can, has, and will continue to be a steadfast supporter of, and participant in, collective security through the United Nations. Australia can, has, and will continue to act in coalitions of like-minded countries to defend our common interests and common values. It is what we have done for decades.

But we do so in the face of new and as I said above, complex, challenges. Four of the big ones are set out in the following sections. However, first I want to give the formal government outline of Australia's international relations.

Government White Papers

In light of the threats and challenges that we face it is worth noting what the formal Government framework is in dealing with them. In this section I summarise the recent White Papers released by the government. In relative terms they are hot off the press. One is 122 pages (Foreign Policy) and the other, together with the two accompanying documents on industry policy and the integrated investment program, is 383 pages (Defence), so I will make this short and invite readers to do further research for themselves.

The 2017 Foreign Policy White Paper saw a move to redefine our position in the world away from simply the "Asia-Pacific" to the "Indo-Pacific", taking into account the importance to our strategic relationships in the Indian sub-continent.

The Government encapsulated five key objectives of "fundamental importance to Australia's security and prosperity", which were:

The Government will:
- promote an open, inclusive and prosperous Indo–Pacific region in which the rights of all states are respected;
- deliver more opportunities for our businesses globally and stand against protectionism;
- ensure Australians remain safe, secure and free in the face of threats such as terrorism;
- promote and protect the international rules that support stability and prosperity and enable cooperation to tackle global challenges; and
- step up support for a more resilient Pacific and Timor–Leste.[9]

Importantly on international rules and cooperation it notes that "We have entered a period of sharper challenge to the rules and principles that underpin international cooperation. Anti-globalisation, protectionism, changes in the balance of global power and geopolitical competition are testing the international order. ... It is

---

[9] Commonwealth of Australia (2017), *2017 Foreign Policy White Paper*, Canberra, 3.

difficult for countries like Australia, even working with others, to influence an international system that is predominantly shaped by the actions of much larger nations. At a time of challenge, we could choose to narrow our global vision and ambition. Such an approach would not, however, serve Australia's long-term interests nor align with our values."[10]

The 2016 Defence White Paper states: "The Government's policy is to align Australia's defence strategy with capabilities and resourcing, grow our international defence partnerships to support shared security interests and invest in the partnership with Australian defence industry to develop innovative technologies and deliver essential capabilities.[11]

The Paper states that the Government's defence strategy "will ensure that Defence is prepared to respond if the Government decides the pursuit of Australia's interests requires the use of military force. This strategy sets out three Strategic Defence Interests which are of fundamental significance for strategic defence planning."[12]

The three Strategic Defence Interests are:

- **Our most basic Strategic Defence Interest is a secure, resilient Australia.** The first Strategic Defence Objective is to deter, deny and defeat any attempt by a hostile country or non-state actor to attack, threaten or coerce Australia. The Government is providing Defence with the capability and resources it needs to be able to independently and decisively respond to military threats, including incursions into Australia's air, sea and northern approaches.
- **Our second Strategic Defence Interest is in a secure nearer region, encompassing maritime South East Asia and the South Pacific.** The second Strategic Defence

---

[10] Commonwealth of Australia 2017, 6.
[11] Commonwealth of Australia (2016), *2016 Defence White Paper*, Canberra, 13.
[12] Commonwealth of Australia 2016, 17.

Objective is to support the security of maritime South East Asia and support the governments of Papua New Guinea, Timor-Leste and of Pacific Island Countries to build and strengthen their security. In South East Asia, Defence will strengthen its engagement, including helping to build the effectiveness of regional operations to address shared security challenges, and the ADF will have increased capabilities to make contributions to any such operations. The Government will continue its commitment to strengthened regional security architectures that support transparency and cooperation. Australia will continue to seek to be the principal security partner for Papua New Guinea, Timor-Leste and Pacific Island Countries in the South Pacific.

- **Our third Strategic Defence Interest is in a stable Indo-Pacific region and rules-based global order which supports our interests.** The third Strategic Defence Objective is to provide meaningful contributions to global responses to address threats to the rules-based global order which threaten Australia and its interests. Australia will work closely with our ally the United States and other international partners to play an important role in coalition operations wherever Australia's interests are engaged.[13]

Amongst the strategic issues there were very important financial commitments and the Government announced that: "To deliver the capabilities set out in this Defence White Paper, the Government's long-term funding commitment provides a new 10-year Defence budget model to 2025-26, over which period an additional $29.9 billion will be provided to Defence. Under this new budget model, the Defence budget will grow to $42.4 billion in 2020–21, reaching two per cent of Australia's Gross Domestic Product (GDP) based on current projections."[14]

---

[13] Commonwealth of Australia 2016, 17-18.
[14] Ibid., 24.

China

What to do about China?

I am fascinated by that question and have recently been honoured to have been asked to participate in the *China Matters* dialogue, convened by renowned sinologist Linda Jakobson.

Indeed, China is the biggest single international relations issue for Australian governments. And there is no shortage of advice. Not least the debate that has been going on at the Australian National University between two well respected professors – both with extensive real world experience as defence strategists. I will come to this shortly.

China has been on the rise for many years now. It is now the principal trading partner with almost every country in the world.

However, in my maiden speech to Parliament I said:

> Having referred to China, may I say that I am not one of those starry-eyed analysts who look at that great nation with rose tinted glasses. We must be very pragmatic about China and note that we have differences as well as commonalities. We need to pursue friendship with China. But in my words it remains a "wary friendship.

As Prime Minister Malcolm Turnbull has said we must welcome China's economic success. Nonetheless, Australia must not resile from condemning any unilateral actions that for example jeopardise peaceful resolution of territorial disputes in the South China Sea and the East China Sea.

China's recent actions in the Asia Pacific region could explode at any time. In Northern Asia there are very serious territorial disputes going on that the Australian public is barely aware of. In particular there are serious clashes occurring over sovereignty in the South China Sea and separately of islands in the East China Sea variously called Diaoyu by the Chinese or Senkaku by the Japanese.

I fact Australia made a clear and deliberate expression of concern in 2013 about China's sudden announcement of a unilateral air-defence identification zone over the East China Sea. Foreign Minister Julie Bishop rightly protested and "called-in" the Chinese ambassador to add to the protest. The Minister said:

> The timing and the manner of China's announcement are unhelpful in light of current regional tensions, and will not contribute to regional stability. Australia has made clear its opposition to any coercive or unilateral actions to change the status quo in the East China Sea.[15]

In the South China Sea six nations are disputing sovereignty issues around the Spratly Islands. Arguably China has been the most aggressive claiming sovereignty over the whole area, and building artificial islands to consolidate that position. To be charitable the purpose of these islands is not entirely clear, but it is not entirely fanciful to consider them as China's unsinkable aircraft carriers.

As I noted in the previous chapter on trade deals, the South China Sea contains essential trade routes. It is one of the busiest seaways in the world, seeing twenty-five percent of the world's crude oil traffic alone. As one of the world's largest trading nations that means they are also Australia's essential trade routes. And one of the key themes emerging from the 2015 Shangri-La Dialogue in Singapore was the need for strategic certainty in the South China Sea. Defence Ministers from the United States, Japan, Malaysia, New Zealand, Germany, and the United Kingdom all expressed concern about strategic uncertainty in the Indo-Pacific.

At the time the Australian Minister for Defence and Secretary of the Department of Defence both made clear and deliberate statements articulating Australia's opposition to the extensive land

---

[15] Julie Bishop (2013), "China's announcement of an air-defence identification zone over the East China Sea", media release, Canberra, 26 November.

reclamation. In times of uncertainty this degree of clarity about what Australia values is extremely important. In fact, it is critical.

It is in that context that the Secretary of the Department of Defence, Dennis Richardson, voiced his concern at the unprecedented pace and scale of China's land reclamation activity in the South China Sea.

Mr Richardson said: "Over the last year alone, China has reclaimed nearly four times the total area of the other five claimant States combined." He went on to say: "The speed and scale of China's land reclamation on disputed reefs and other features does raise the question of intent and purpose."[16]

Further, the then Defence Minister Kevin Andrews, had this to say at Shangri-La Dialogue:

> We are particularly concerned at the prospect of militarisation of artificial structures. It is therefore important that countries agree as soon as possible on a substantive Code of Conduct for the South China Sea between ASEAN members and China.

He went on to say:

> Disputes must be resolved peacefully, and Australia urges all parties to exercise restraint, halt all reclamation activities, refrain from provocative actions, and take steps to ease tensions.[17]

This position has been maintained. More recently the 2017 Foreign Policy White Paper stated:

> Maritime and land border disputes are a growing source of potential instability in a more contested Indo–Pacific.

---

[16] Dennis Richardson (2015), "The 2015 Blamey Oration: The strategic outlook for the Indo-Pacific Region", address to the 3rd International Defence and Security Dialogue, Sydney, 27 May, 12.

[17] Kevin Andrews (2015), Address to 114th International Institute of Strategic Studies Asia Security Summit: The Shangri-la Dialogue", Singapore, 31 May.

> ... Like other non-claimant states, however, we have a substantial interest in the stability of this crucial international waterway, and in the norms and laws that govern it. We have urged all claimants to refrain from actions that could increase tension and have called for a halt to land reclamation and construction activities. Australia is particularly concerned by the unprecedented pace and scale of China's activities. Australia opposes the use of disputed features and artificial structures in the South China Sea for military purposes. We support the resolution of differences through negotiation based on international law.[18]

The White Paper goes on to say:

> Elsewhere in the region, Australia is concerned about the potential for the use of force or coercion in the East China Sea and Taiwan Strait. ... How India and China manage their relationship, including competing border claims, will also have important implications for regional stability. In all of these matters, it is vital that those concerned act with restraint and avoid actions that add to tensions.[19]

Similar sentiments were expressed in the earlier 2016 Defence White paper. Indeed it notes that one of the principal reasons for writing it related to China:

> Why now? ... Events during the three years since the release of the last Defence White Paper in 2013 demonstrate how rapidly Australia's security environment can change. The relationship between the United States and China continues to evolve and will be fundamental to our future strategic circumstances. Territorial disputes between claimants in the East China and South China Seas have created uncertainty and tension in our region."[20]

---

[18] Commonwealth of Australia 2017, 46-47.
[19] Ibid., 47.
[20] Commonwealth of Australia 2016, 30.

And why is this all so important?

Because, when tensions are high, the risks of miscalculation resulting in conflict are very real. Like others, I wish for a rising China to be fully incorporated into the rules-based world order that we all – China particularly – have benefitted from over the last several decades.

China cannot be allowed to unilaterally impose a solution. Attempts by any nation to establish a military presence with the intent of defending contested sovereignty claims or a unilateral Air Defence Identification Zone in the South China Sea is destabilising and dangerous. There is plenty of room for China to rise in Asia. We welcome it and benefit from it. However, provocative moves can play to the region's worst fears about China's rise, and endanger the rules-based order that we will all rise or fall by.

Prominent international specialist Professor Graham Allison of Harvard University argues that we are serious danger of the United States and China heading for armed conflict. He says that this is the result of falling into the "Thucydides Trap". As he states: "As a rapidly ascending China challenges America's accustomed predominance, these two nations risk falling into a deadly trap first identified by the ancient Greek historian Thucydides. Writing about a war that devastated the two leading city-states of classical Greece two and a half millennia ago, he explained: 'It was the *rise* of Athens and the *fear* that this instilled in Sparta that made war inevitable'."[21] Similar nightmare scenarios have been raised by other authors like retired British Army officers Paul Cornish and Kingsley Donaldson in their book *2020 World of War*.[22]

Nonetheless, there is reason to be cautiously optimistic. It can be argued that in the case of China and the other big strategic

---

[21] Graham Allison (2017), *Destined for War: can America and China escape Thucydides trap?*, Scribe, Melbourne, vii.

[22] Cornish and Donaldson 2017.

power, the United States, the typical structural forces that push major powers toward direct conflict are weak. Unfortunately, that is not to say that the risk of conflict in Asia is not real. It is very real. Particularly conflict between neighbouring countries that could potentially drag in the United States. A miscalculation arising from a secondary dispute, particularly in North Asia, could present the most likely catalyst for confrontation.

So what do the two professors at the Australian National University have to say?

Professor Hugh White in particular has put forward the challenging thesis that we do not have the luxury of "not having to choose" between the United States and China. He has written on this topic extensively in recent years with his latest comprehensive contribution being the 2017 *Quarterly Essay* monograph "Without America. Australia in the New Asia".[23]

He says that we do have to choose and sooner than most people anticipate. He warns that the United States will inevitably vacate the Indo-Pacific region and that this may happen precipitously. He argues that Australia is in danger of causing itself irredeemable harm by continuing to side with the United States.[24] Instead he argues we should be much more pragmatic and accept that our future lies in China's orbit. He also makes a number of policy suggestions that spin off this core analysis that I will address later in the chapter.

In particular White states that "For a long time Canberra's refusal to admit either that a great strategic contest is underway between our major ally and our major trading partner – or that the contest might not go as we'd like – has been symbolised by the bold assertion that "Australia doesn't have to choose between America

---

[23] Hugh White (2017a), "Without America. Australia in the New Asia", *The Quarterly Essay*, Issue 68, 2017.
[24] Ibid.

and China."[25] And he has stated that: "At the same time, Donald Trump's presidency has undermined Canberra's confidence both in America's future in Asia, and in Washington's regard for Australia as an ally."[26]

It is probably true to say that White goes further than virtually any other Australian analyst in arguing for abandoning our alliance with the United States and getting closer to China.

One of his key antagonists on this matter is his ANU colleague Professor Paul Dibb. Dibb begins by arguing with White's principal assumptions. They are, first, that China is economically and militarily superseding the United States. Second, that the United States will depart the region. And, third, that Beijing's motivations in the Asia pacific are benign.[27]

Dibb notes that "The US and its allies account for about 70 per cent of world military spending. And China's inevitable demographic future is that it will get old before it becomes rich and truly powerful."[28] He is referring to its rapidly ageing population, which is a result of the decades long "one child policy".

The 2017 Foreign Policy White Paper agrees with this assessment stating:

> Even as China's power grows and it competes more directly with the United States regionally and globally, the United States will, for the foreseeable future, retain its significant global lead in military and soft power. The United States will continue to be the wealthiest country in the world (measured in net asset terms), the world's leader

---

[25] Hugh White (2017b), "America or China? Australia is fooling itself that it doesn't have to choose", *The Guardian*, 27 November.
[26] Ibid.
[27] Paul Dibb (2017b), "Hugh White fails on China's rise, ANZUS demise", *The Australian*, 14 December.
[28] Ibid.

in technology and innovation, and home to the world's deepest financial markets.[29]

And the Defence White paper notes that "[t]he United States will remain the pre-eminent global military power over the next two decades",[30] adding, however, that "[w]hile China will not match the global strategic weight of the United States, the growth of China's national power, including its military modernisation, means China's policies and actions will have a major impact on the stability of the Indo-Pacific to 2035."[31]

The White Paper concludes:

> The Australian Government judges that the United States' long-term interests will anchor its economic and security engagement in the Indo–Pacific. Its major Pacific alliances with Japan, the Republic of Korea and Australia will remain strong. Most regional countries, including Australia, clearly consider a significant US role in the Indo–Pacific as a stabilising influence. Japan and India, major economies and military powers in their own right, are also playing stronger roles in Indo–Pacific security and political affairs and are seeking to influence the balance of the regional order.[32]

While in respect of Beijing's intentions Dibb observes:

> These are highly contentious judgments [by White] in almost every respect. There is every indication that China's President Xi Jinping sees an opportunity to export into our region his superior form of authoritarian state capitalism, which he claims gets things done much more efficiently than decadent Western democracies."[33]

---

[29] Commonwealth of Australia 2017, 26.
[30] Commonwealth of Australia 2016, 41.
[31] Ibid., 42.
[32] Commonwealth of Australia 2017, 26.
[33] Dibb 2017b.

I am in agreement with Dibb as I believe most commentators are. You could see this when the Obama Administration initiated a "pivot" to the Asia-Pacific. That was very important for Australia. And then most recently the United States Secretary of Defence, Jim Mattis, formally stated in the 2018 National Defence Strategy that both China and Russia were "revisionist powers" with "authoritarian" models[34] and "We will continue to prosecute the campaign against terrorists that we are engaged in today, but great power competition – not terrorism – is now the primary focus of US national security".[35]

However, whomever is correct – White or Dibb – China remains a major international relations issue for Australia.

So things are tense. However, for Australia the bottom-line is, as the Foreign Policy White paper says,

> The Government is committed to strong and constructive ties with China. We welcome China's greater capacity to share responsibility for supporting regional and global security. We seek to strengthen our Comprehensive Strategic Partnership for the benefit of both nations.[36]

The future of the region depends on co-operation not confrontation.

And let me conclude by wholeheartedly agreeing with a recent statement by former head of the Office of National Assessments, Allan Gyngell. He stated in a submission that "Australians of Chinese heritage should not have to fear being looked upon by their colleagues, neighbours or society at large as 'stooges' of the Communist Party of China … if they also feel proud of China's rich

---

[34] Paul Maley (2018), "Our strategy: all the way with USA", *The Australian*, 27 January.
[35] Daily Telegraph (2018), "China, Russia 'worse than terrorists'", *Daily Telegraph*, 21 January.
[36] Commonwealth of Australia 2017, 4.

cultural heritage".[37] Naturally they have a perfect right to be proud of their cultural heritage and their ancestral nation's strong growth after the previous period of international domination. We need to ensure that we do not discriminate against people because of their ethnicity.

Russia

Not since the end of the Cold War and the disintegration of the Soviet Union into the Russian federation has this nation loomed so large in Australia's international relations space. As the Australian Government has said:

> We will continue to engage the North Atlantic Treaty Organisation (NATO) on global security issues, including terrorism. In the face of Russia's destabilising activities, NATO – and strong transatlantic ties more broadly – is now more important to security in Europe than at any time since the end of the Cold War. Given its international role and reach, Russia's policies affect Australia both directly and indirectly. We will deal carefully with Russia to advance our interests where we see scope. Equally, Australia will work with partners to resist Russia's conduct when it is inimical to global security. Australia remains particularly concerned by the downing of flight MH17 and Russia's annexation of Crimea and intervention in eastern Ukraine.[38]

And the United States is taking a hard line. US Secretary of State Rex Tillerson said in December 2017:

> On Russia, we have no illusions about the regime we are dealing with. The United States today has a poor relationship with a resurgent Russia that has invaded

---
[37] Kirsty Needham (2018), "Students 'no stooges' in great brawl with China: ex-spy boss", *Sydney Morning Herald*, 17 February.
[38] Commonwealth of Australia 2017, 81.

its neighbours Georgia and Ukraine in the last decade and undermined the sovereignty of Western nations by meddling in our election and others.[39]

I well remember that in 2014 as a member of the Government's Foreign Affairs Policy Committee I attended a discussion with the Ukrainian consul-general in Australia. It was a closed meeting so I can reveal little of the discussion. Suffice it to say that the urgent concern for his country was that the recent annexation of the Crimean peninsula may have within days be followed by an invasion of the remainder of their country by Russia.

The then turmoil in Ukraine, and Russia's bullying approach, is well known and I will not go over it again in detail. I am more interested in discussing the international communities' reaction. Suffice it to say that on 22 February 2014 Ukraine's parliament deposed their president, Victor Yanukovich, and within a few days pro-Russian military forces began occupying the Crimea and after a world-record-breaking plebiscite, in terms of speed, this region was reabsorbed into Russia on 17 March.

A large number of press releases from world capitals condemning the naked aggression of Russia followed. The United Nations Security Council resolution reflecting that anger didn't pass as it was vetoed by Russia. Interestingly China abstained. As a member of the Security Council for 2013-15 Australia rightfully voted for the resolution. Subsequently on 27 March the UN General Assembly passed a non-binding resolution declaring the Russian-backed referendum invalid, with 100 nations in favour, 11 voting against, and 58 abstentions. Russia's supporters included those bastions of democracy and the rule of law Cuba, North Korea, Nicaragua, Syria, Venezuela, Zimbabwe, Sudan, Belarus, and Bolivia. Interestingly China again abstained.

---

[39] O'Malley 2018.

The United States expressed its genuine concern about developments. President Obama condemned Russia's actions and imposed sanctions in the form of travel and economic bans on certain key personnel in Russian President Vladimir Putin's government. Australia copied these sanctions. However, added together these sanctions and a non-binding resolution of the UN are hardly damaging consequences for Russia.

Why does this all matter to Australians? The first reason is that we are key member of the international community and it is vitally important that the collective community stops cross-border aggression wherever possible. These types of issues are always difficult to deal with in the UN system as two of the overriding principles in the UN Charter are non-interference in the internal workings of a nation state, while at the same time supporting the right of populations for "self-determination". On the other hand Russia contends it is simply supporting the self-determination of ethnic Russians.

However, strong messages have to be sent to transgressors. How far you go is always hard to judge. In the United States some have argued that the Obama Administration's unwillingness to engage in military options with respect to the on-going conflict in Syria had sent a clear signal to President Putin that he could get away with his actions in respect of Ukraine. Conversely, Jay Carney, President Obama's then press secretary, noted that if that was so obvious then how is it that Putin wasn't scared off from the 2008 invasion of Georgia despite the then recent invasion of Iraq led by President George Bush. These are certainly very difficult issues to deal with.

The 2016 Defence Policy White Paper nominates the "refusal to act in ways consistent with international law and standards of behaviour, such as Russia's coercive and aggressive actions in Ukraine",[40] as a major security concern. The Foreign Policy

---

40 Commonwealth of Australia 2016, 46.

White Paper goes even further and states that "it weakens global security."[41]

Turning its focus on the globally networked information systems, it notes:

> Cyber threats can range from unacceptable interference in democratic processes, such as the activities of Russian cyber actors during the 2016 US presidential election, to the theft and manipulation of information or disruption of government or commercial activity. At the extreme, cyber actors could attack critical national infrastructure such as power grids and financial systems.[42]

Alarmingly, Sir Nick Carter, the United Kingdom's Defence Chief of Staff, stated in a speech on 22 January 2018 that: "Our generation has become used to wars of choice since the end of the Cold War. But we may not have a choice about conflict with Russia. And we should remember Trotsky's advice that 'you may not be interested in war but war is interested in you'."[43]

Terrorism

The Foreign Policy White Paper warns: "The threat from terrorism will remain high and could worsen over the decade. There are now more Islamist extremists from more countries active in more places than ever before."[44]

Terrorism has loomed large in our collective consciousness for over 16 years now.

On one particular night back in 2001 (it was the 11th of September) when I was the chief of staff to the Minister for Defence, I was relaxing at home watching television at the very time that the

---

[41] Commonwealth of Australia 2017, 24.
[42] Ibid., 41.
[43] O'Malley 2018.
[44] Commonwealth of Australia 2017, 27.

terrorist event occurred. In fact, like so many Australians at the time, I was watching the US television drama "The West Wing". What else would you expect a political staffer to be watching?

Soon after the first plane hit the first tower at the World Trade Centre in New York, the television show was interrupted, and went to a live coverage from the twin towers. It was after 9 pm at night as I recall it so vividly. I was actually watching live via satellite when the second plane slammed into the second tower.

It was at that wrenching moment that we all knew that this wasn't just an aviation accident but something much more sinister and evil. It was soon after that I got a call from the chief of staff of the then Acting Prime Minister, John Anderson, requiring me to find the Minister for Defence, Peter Reith. In essence all hell broke loose.

We had Prime Minister John Howard in Washington and we needed to be concerned about his safety. A National Security Committee of Cabinet meeting was hastily arranged. When that occurred the next morning we were already discussing the invoking of the ANZUS Treaty with the United States for the first time.

I do not have to go through all the other events of the next few days. Terrorism had hit our country and many other countries.

Since then we have been living with the terrorist threat.

These attacks on 9/11, which saw 2,977 innocent people die including 11 Australians, was before the US or Australia ever went into either Afghanistan or Iraq. It was only after that event that these other actions occurred. Indeed before the 2003 operation in Iraq Australians were also subject to a further attack by Jemaah Islamiyah. A total of 88 Australians died in the 2002 Bali bombings.

This issue has been brought home to us because of the actions of extremists. We now face a continuing threat.

In more recent times we have dealt with the civil war in Syria and the ongoing conflicts in Iraq. It was estimated that some 60 Australians joined the fighting with terrorist groups in Syria and Iraq, and at least 100 Australians who supported them. And that more than 20 of these foreign fighters have returned to Australia.

The Australian connection does not stop there. We simply can't ignore statements of "Islamic State in Iraq and the Levant" (ISIL) when for example its spokesman Mohammed al-Adani stated in 2014:

> If you can kill an American or European infidel – especially the spiteful and filthy French – or an Australian or a Canadian, or any other disbeliever from the infidel fighters ... then rely upon God and kill them in any way possible.[45]

This is who we are up against.

There have been many terrorist events that have already occurred in Australia not least the Martin Place siege. There have also been a large number of events that have been thwarted by police like a potential gruesome beheading in Martin Place in Sydney, under the direct orders of ISIL.

They are atrocious barbarians. We cannot ignore that. We have to deal with the issue. But let me equally say that we need to be very careful about sweeping, rabble-rousing statements against Muslims generally.

I have lived and worked in the Middle East in the Gulf state of Bahrain. I was there with my wife, daughter and son. The Bahrainis are warm and hospitable people. I always felt safe and it was a very positive experience. I am proud of the fact that Bahrain has joined the Coalition to help fight ISIL.

People should be very careful about how they express

---

[45] Cindy Wockner (2016), "Islamic State says 'fill your cars with gas' as terror call targets Australia", news.com.au, 16 July.

themselves so as not to create unnecessary divisions when we need to all pull together in facing the current challenges. We need to talk in calm terms.

In conclusion as the Defence White paper states:

> The threat of terrorism and terrorist groups to Australia's security and our interests in a stable international order is growing. There are now more extremists fighting for terrorist causes in more countries than ever before. Terrorist attacks around the world increased by 35 per cent from 2013 to 2014. The United States State Department has estimated that more than 32,000 people were killed in terrorist attacks in 2014. The major threat we are currently facing is from violent extremism perpetrated or motivated by terrorist groups such as Daesh [or ISIL], al-Qa'ida and others that claim to act in the name of Islam. The anti-Western narrative of terrorists means that Australians will continue to be targeted at home and abroad.[46]

There may be very dark days ahead. Let us hope this conflict is not protracted. Unfortunately, I think it very well could be. Some military people have said it could take 15 years to resolve the issues. Maybe more. That is a daunting prospect. However from what we can see now and for the short future over the horizon we need to stay the course and commit our best effort to this ugly necessity.

North Korea

North Korea presents a genuine threat to Australia's security. Since the end of the war on the Korean peninsula in the 1950s there has been an uneasy truce between the combatants. Indeed the Cold War has never really ended on the Korean Peninsula.

---
[46] Commonwealth of Australia 2016, 46-47.

The greatest international threat comes from North Korea's dual development of nuclear weapons and missile technology. Over the years US administrations have adopted a position of strategic ambiguity on North Korea. In essence this has meant that they have continued to protest about the nation's development of threatening military technology, however they have been prepared to overlook active intervention for the sake of peaceful coexistence.

Nonetheless, now that North Korea has gone a very long way down the track to developed a capability that can potentially deliver nuclear weapons via missiles to hit the continental United States and the Australian mainland we all have cause to be very worried.

The Trump Administration has decided to confront the issue head on and the possibility of conflict has risen enormously. In January 2018 the *Economist* magazine warned that there was a significantly heightened threat of "great power" war not least because of the North Korean issues.[47]

In summary, as the Foreign Policy White Paper declares:

> North Korea's long-range missile and nuclear programs represent the region's most immediate security challenge. Any major instability or conflict on the Korean Peninsula would have severe strategic, economic and humanitarian repercussions. A North Korean attack on the United States would also trigger Australia's commitments under our ANZUS alliance. Australia will continue to work resolutely with our partners to bring increasing pressure to bear on North Korea to end its dangerous behaviour.[48]

This was confirmed by Prime Minster Malcolm Turnbull when

---

[47] Economist (The) (2018), "World on the brink of new era of state wars", *The Economist*, London, 27 January.
[48] Commonwealth of Australia 2017, 42.

he said in response to a question about an attack by North Korea that "if there is an attack on the US, the ANZUS treaty would be invoked" and that "in terms of defence, we are joined at the hip".[49]

A more independent foreign policy?

People often call for Australia to have a more independent foreign policy. In this section I offer some ways that this could come about.

I referred to above that the United States Secretary of Defence, Jim Mattis, has talked of both China and Russia as trying to "shape a world consistent with their authoritarian model"[50] and that "We will continue to prosecute the campaign against terrorists that we are engaged in today, but great power competition – not terrorism – is now the primary focus of US national security".[51]

The Australian reaction was somewhat confused. Defence Minister Marise Payne stated that "[i]t is for the US to determine what is of concern in relation to its national security, but I would note that Australia shares similar concerns".[52] However, Foreign Minister Julie Bishop argued: "We have a different perspective on Russia and China, clearly. We do not see Russia or China as posing a military threat to Australia".[53]

The first duty of any Australian Government is to secure our borders and that means ensuring strong defence capabilities and maintenance of strong, constructive and stable international relations.

As noted above a mainstay of our defence is the ANZUS treaty. It is a long standing position of the Greens that we pull out of that

---

[49] Katharine Murphy (2017), "Australia will back US in any conflict with North Korea, Turnbull says", *The Guardian*, 11 August.
[50] Hunter, Fergus (2018), "'Different Perspective' to US on China, Russia threat", *Sydney Morning Herald*, 30 January.
[51] *Daily Telegraph* 2018.
[52] O'Malley 2018.
[53] Hunter 2018.

agreement. Interestingly, former Prime Minister Malcolm Fraser[54] has also argued for a rethink. Further, Paul Keating has called for Australia to "cut the tag" with America's foreign policy[55], although he maintains that he never meant that the alliance "be junked".[56] Personally, I am amazed about their positions and simply say look at what they did in government as opposed to their more recent statements. When they had responsibility for the safety of Australians they fully supported ANZUS.

Thus I do not support any such radical changes as the cancelling of our US alliance. However are there other ways to go about increasing our foreign policy independence?

The most obvious way to boost independence is to enhance our military forces and rely less on our allies. This could simply mean increased spending on the type of things we already do. It could also mean going to more radical options like the setting up of a comprehensive missile defence shield, the adoption of nuclear powered submarines or even going one step further, the adoption of our own nuclear weapons.

Increased spending

Let us start this section with a bit of a note of realism.

Part of the reason the Australian Government needs to repair the Budget as soon as it is possible is because more than $25 billion was ripped out of defence between 2007 and 2013. Defence spending in 2012-13 alone was cut by 10.5 per cent. This was the largest annual reduction since the end of the Korean War in 1953.

---

[54] Malcolm Fraser and Cain Roberts (2014), *Dangerous Allies*, Melbourne University Press, Melbourne.

[55] Leigh Sales (2017), "Paul Keating says Australia should 'cut the tag' with American foreign policy", *abc.net.au*, 11 November.

[56] Troy Bramston (2017), "Keating blasts Australia for adopting US foreign policy", *The Australian*, 23 September.

The share of GDP spent on Defence in the 2013-14 Budget was just 1.59 per cent, the lowest level since 1938.

Thus the commitment of the 2016 Defence White Paper for the Defence budget to grow to $42.4 billion in 2020–21, reaching 2 per cent of GDP, is itself a big ask.

Recently, Paul Dibb and former senior defence official Richard Brabin-Smith produced a report titled "Australia's Management of Strategic Risk in the new era" arguing that the rise of China needed Australia to significantly increase spending. They note that in "the South China Sea, Beijing's construction of military facilities — including airstrips for fighter aircraft and longer-range strategic bombers — has effectively brought China's military presence more than 1200km closer to Australia's northern approaches".[57]

To directly quote a report on their paper:

> 'This ... in itself should be a matter of considerable concern for our defence planning,' they say. The authors say the Australian Defence Force's readiness needs to be sharpened through higher training levels to enable rapid 'surge' capabilities, increased stocks of missiles, more maintenance spares, a robust fuel supply system and modernised operational bases, especially in the north of Australia. To increase warning time, it will be vital for Australia to continue to have high levels of intelligence collection and analysis across the region.[58]

Greg Sheridan noted:

> Identifying China's military expansion and rapid territorial conquests in the South China Sea as a potential threat is brave, tricky, delicate and complex. As they rightly observe,

---

[57] Brendan Nicholson (2017), "Defence experts warn on strategy", *The Australian*, 15 November.
[58] Ibid.

it is wrong to assume China will be hostile to our interests. We should do everything we can to positively engage the Beijing government. But defence planning must deal with reality and it always plans against capabilities rather than avowed intentions.[59]

Senator Jim Molan, a former Army major general, has also called for a sizeable increase in spending. He has said that Australia needs to "address its vulnerabilities on fuel security and high-end weapons holdings. Without doing so, we could be reduced to impotence in less than a week."[60]

Added to these voices is Hugh White. Although he has a different attitude to China than other commentators he raises the possibility of increasing Defence spending to 4 per cent of GDP.[61] Ironically in a separate article to the one he wrote with Richard Brabin-Smith, Dibb points out this is an heroic ask:

> I agree with his desire for much greater defence self-reliance. But finding an additional $35 billion a year is a far from trivial task for the commonwealth's budget without a clear threat.[62]

As a variation on simply expanding expenditure the Coalition Government has decided to expand the export potential of the home-grown defence industry. With a 10 year program of over $200 billion in future defence spending in the pipeline, much of this is to be locally sourced. The Government understandably would like to see some of this rub-off into increased exports. In January 2018 it announced a $3.8 billion program of loan assistance and the setting

---

[59] Greg Sheridan (2017c), "Straight-talking plan to strengthen our military", *The Australian*, 15 November.
[60] Jim Molan (2018), "A stronger Australia can be more useful US ally", *The Australian*, 4 January.
[61] White 2017a, 72.
[62] Dibb 2017b.

up of a Defence Export Office to facilitate this.[63] Hopefully it will work. However, in the past such attempts have failed and there are a number of sceptics. Personally I think it is the correct call and should be attempted.

Missile defence

A discrete element of a possible expansion of military capacity would be a comprehensive missile defence shield, especially against incoming missiles – even inter-continental ballistic missiles.

There has been a debate about this in Australia. As Greg Sheridan points out:

> For reasons that are beyond the rational, the government keeps ridiculing the possibility of missile defence playing any role in Australia's security. Yet our allies the US, Japan and South Korea are working flat-out to develop ever more effective missile defences.[64]

Nonetheless there are sceptics. ANU international relations research fellow Benjamin Zala argues:

> ... it would cost so much and, even then, we're still talking about just the interceptors; you would have to select a site that would be fine to put a large military installation there and then secure it and there has to be the radar technology to go with it. There's an enormous amount of logistic support.[65]

And, Associate Professor in Strategic Defence Studies Stephan

---

[63] Robin Bromby (2018), "Defence industry challenged to export as $3.8b facility backed", *The Australian*, 2 February.
[64] Sheridan, Greg (2017b), "Bell tolls for our own missile defence", *The Australian*, 30 August.
[65] Rory Callinan (2017), "Air defence systems 'costly and unreliable'", *The Australian*, 11 August.

Fruhling said: "You would be looking at huge expenditure which would be above and beyond the priorities."[66]

The Defence White Paper would appear to acknowledge that this is a matter of importance. It states:

> While the threat of an intercontinental ballistic missile atIndeed, Prime Minister Turnbull has said that they are looking at the issue. However, it is reported that "the United States' billion dollar Terminal High Altitude Area Defence, or THAAD, which has been deployed in South Korea, is not suitable to Australia's needs, [Malcolm Turnbull] says".[67] Nonetheless, it is also reported that he has said that Australia is interested in "acquiring missile defence for its air warfare destroyers and the new anti-submarine warfare frigates". This would enable those warships "to engage threat missiles at long range".[68]

Worth noting is that former Prime Minister Kevin Rudd, who opposed such a roll-out when he was in government, "now believed Australia should arm itself with a missile shield as a defensive response to North Korea's increasing capability."[69] Paul Dibb[70] also argues that we should seriously look at this capability.

As Greg Sheridan asks: "But where are we heading in five or 10 years time? To a North Korea with perhaps hundreds of nuclear-armed intercontinental ballistic missiles and us with no capacity at all to provide any defence for any of our cities whatsoever ?"[71]

---

[66] Ibid.

[67] James Massola (2017), "Bolster to missile shield an option: PM", *The Sydney Morning Herald*, 9 July.

[68] Paul Dibb (2017a), "Our nuclear armament position is worth reviewing", *The Australian*, 24 October.

[69] Massola 2017.

[70] Dibb 2017a.

[71] Greg Sheridan, 2017b.

Nuclear submarines

Nuclear submarines have been something that have been raised as a possible solution to the long term naval requirements of Australia. Superficially it appears attractive.

While there are some who argue that submarines are an obsolete concept, like Professor Roger Bradbury[72] of the National Security College, others are convinced otherwise. The Australian editorialised that "[f]or all the controversy over the choice, it is absolutely in the nation's interests that the Collins-class replacement project is successfully completed in coming decades to ensure this island nation has a modern and effective submarine capability."[73]

Let me start this discussion with an anecdote. As I have noted, earlier in my career I was the chief of staff for the Minister of Defence. In that position I was heavily involved in work to ensure that the Collins Class submarine program remained on track and provided the best possible maritime defence capability that was humanly possible. It involved many hours of frustrating work. It was one of the most difficult policy and administrative issues I have dealt with in my career, which has spanned senior levels in both the public and private sectors.

Ensuring the Collins Class submarines operated at their maximum efficiency, were actually in the water doing their job, and were properly integrated in terms of combat, command and control systems was the task at hand. It appeared to be a particularly fraught issue. Unfortunately at the time, and here I am talking about 2001, the Minister was being bombarded with contrary positions from the Department of Defence and the uniformed experts. It got to such a stage that the Minister requested me to convene a special meeting in

---

[72] Roger Bradbury (2017), "New submarines or billion dollar coffins?", *The Australian*, 5 October.

[73] Australian (The) (2017), "Submarines are vital for defence of island nation", *The Australian*, editorial, 5 October.

his office of all the relevant internal stakeholders. I did so and all the relevant top brass, the department secretary, and the deputy secretaries were present. There were in fact seven of these people present.

Unfortunately as the meeting, chaired by the Minister, proceeded it was apparent that there were some seven different and conflicting views on how to deal with the issues at hand. Worse than that, it was apparent that the individuals would not be reconciled. This was the end result of years of bad decisions. It became very hard to extract ourselves from the vested interests, but in the end we did.

I would like to think that 10 years ago the Howard Government saved the Collins Class and its remediation policies have meant the submarines have been able to largely fulfil their assigned role.

However my point here is that I do not wish to see a similar result occurring in terms of the submarine program when we get to the replacement for the Collins Class.

I am very cognizant of Greg Sheridan's opposition to nuclear submarines, which I will discuss below.

However a champion of nuclear submarines is former Prime Minister Tony Abbott.

As he said in a June 2017 speech: "Not more robustly challenging the nuclear no-go mindset is probably the biggest regret I have from my time as PM."[74]

So why are people talking about this option. The main reason is that due to Australia's geographic location the ability for long distance underwater cruising is a paramount consideration.

The former Prime Minister notes that "Conventional subs need to surface frequently to recharge their batteries, need to refuel every 70 days, and can only briefly maintain a top speed of about 20 knots. These are major constraints."[75]

---

[74] Tony Abbott (2017), *Address to the Centre for Independent Studies*, Sydney, 29 June.

[75] Ibid.

A ramp-up of the domestic nuclear industry would be necessary for such a project and we would need to rely heavily on our nuclear allies like the United States, Great Britain and France for assistance. It would be enormously expensive and would take a long time to develop, but we are talking of national security and decades into the future.

Other potential supporters of the proposal are Hugh White[76]; well respected defence strategist Ross Babbage; and the Centre for Independent Studies, to name a few.[77]

In the opposition corner are those who point to the enormous cost and additionally those who argue that there is just no mileage in changing policy on submarine acquisition after the delays over the last decade. We just have to get on with our current strategy. Prominent amongst these critics is Greg Sheridan who notes that: "There is no doubt nuclear subs would be a much better option than the conventional subs we are committed to. But, … [it] is also completely unrealistic and, if it gains any traction, can serve only to inject yet new delay into the already insanely slow process of our acquiring new subs."[78] He further believes that the Labor Party would never permit an adult debate on the matter. Something that Tony Abbott clearly disputes pointing to long-standing bipartisanship on defence issues.

Nuclear weapons

Allied to the debate about nuclear powered submarines is whether, if they were introduced, they should have nuclear weapons.

Academic Wayne Reynolds wrote a particularly fascinating

---

[76] White 2017a, 72-74.
[77] Cameron Stewart (2016), "Questions asked of Australia's rejection of nuclear submarines", *The Australian*, 22 January.
[78] Greg Sheridan (2017a), "Idea of an Australian nuclear submarine fleet just won't float", *The Australian*, 1 July.

book, *Australia's Bid for the Atomic Bomb*, which examines the story behind the internal debates within the government of Prime Minister John Gorton during the late 1960s. The project never got off the ground, not least because Australia's US allies did not support the proliferation of the weapons.[79]

Writing for the Lowy Institute Peter Layton has argued that in the face of long term threats from North Korea (which he says could have as many as 60 nuclear weapons), and possibly China, Australia should turn to nuclear weapons as an option. As he says:

> For all nations in the modern era, the great equaliser is nuclear weapons. Without them, future nuclear blackmail of Australia is possible. Nuclear threats could be used to adversely influence our foreign or domestic policies. What alternative would we realistically have?[80]

Hugh White[81] has argued that nuclear weapons should be seriously considered to ensure an independent foreign policy and Paul Dibb[82] has written a very revealing analysis of the issue.

Dibb notes that in the early 1970s Australia delayed ratifying the Treaty on the Non-Proliferation of Nuclear Weapons because defence experts advised the Government "that it was important for Australia to 'maintain its freedom to reduce the lead time' for the development of a nuclear weapon capacity against a serious breakdown in the international order."[83]

According to Dibb the bottom-line is that:

> The scenarios under which Australia would have to review

---

[79] Wayne Reynolds (2000), *Australia's Bid for the Atomic Bomb*, Melbourne University Press, Melbourne, 218.
[80] Peter Layton (2018), "Why Australia should consider sharing nuclear weapons", *Lowy Institute*, www.lowyinstitute.org, 17 January.
[81] White 2017a, 72-74.
[82] Dibb 2017a.
[83] Ibid.

its confidence in the US's extended nuclear deterrence include North Korea using a nuclear weapon against South Korea or Japan and the US not responding because of the fear of losing Los Angeles. Such a situation could provoke Japan and South Korea to rapidly develop nuclear weapons of their own and thus raise the spectre of nuclear proliferation in our region.[84]

The Australian Strategic Policy Institute's Andrew Davies notes that the various analyses of Dibb, Brabin-Smith, and White theses lead to the question of nuclear weapons capability. He says "we have reached the end of a period during which defence was more or less an academic exercise when there was no credible threat" and that China's rise has "upended" previous considerations.[85]

If Australia were ever to contemplate moving down this path it would mean abrogating our membership of the Treaty on the Non-Proliferation of Nuclear Weapons. This would almost certainly require an extreme threat to Australia because of other countries in the region adopting such weapons in defiance of the treaty. We would essentially be forced into it.

Layton argues that one way to possibly meet the constraints of the treaty on non-proliferation is to undertake "nuclear sharing". He notes that as a legacy of the Cold War the United States shares nuclear weapons deployed on their soil in Germany, Belgium, Holland, Italy and Turkey. They involve a dual-key system with the United States retaining final control. He also argues that the new British *Dreadnought* nuclear submarines might be another option of sharing.[86]

---

[84] Ibid.
[85] Tony Walker (2018), "Going nuclear gets some traction", *The Sydney Morning Herald*, 13 January.
[86] Layton 2018.

But let us not forget the financial cost. It has been reported that the current 30 year nuclear powered and armed *Dreadnought* submarine program of Great Britain is estimated to cost in the order of $300bn.[87] It is a cost that is virtually inconceivable in Australia's current fiscal environment.

The Quadrilateral Dialogue

Interestingly, since the launch of the 2017 Foreign Policy White Paper the Coalition Government has pursued a very significant diplomatic arrangement with three other nations that has been titled the Quadrilateral Dialogue.

The Dialogue is between Australia, the United States, India and Japan and has been ramped-up since a meeting of senior officials in mid-November 2017. It is between democracies and ostentatiously does not include China. The Dialogue is about "a shared vision for increased prosperity and security in the Indo-Pacific region and to work together to ensure it remains free and open" and was about "upholding the rules-based order in the Indo-Pacific and respect for international law, freedom of navigation and overflight".[88]

It has a long gestation given that it was initially proposed by Japanese Prime Minister Shinzo Abe when he was last prime minister over a decade ago. The Howard Government had agreed to participate. However, Prime Minister Kevin Rudd dramatically pulled out, announcing that he was doing so in a joint press conference with the Chinese Foreign Minister.

Professor Rory Medcalf of the National Security College welcomed the initiative saying it showed the participants "confidently share their strategic assessments amongst each other

---

[87] Dibb 2017b.

[88] David Wroe (2017), "Safety in numbers as four-way security meeting hedges China", *Sydney Morning Herald*, 14 November.

regardless of what China says".[89] Greg Sheridan also regarded it as a positive initiative.[90] Although other commentators like Geoff Raby condemned it as "a very bad idea" given that "it is a potentially dangerous response to China's ascendancy and flies in the face of more than 30 years of Australian policy engagement with China".[91] However, I agree with Greg Sheridan that "to be ashamed even to talk to other democracies" is "a truly humiliating and contemptible outlook".[92]

New Colombo Plan

Finally, I want to note that the New Colombo Plan is a very important initiative in terms of soft power diplomacy as well as the obvious educational and skills benefits. It builds on Australia's projection as a culturally different and independent nation.

The New Colombo Plan harks back to the old Colombo Plan of previous decades (named after the Sri Lankan city where the plan was launched) when students from Asian members of the Commonwealth of Nations came to Australia to attend our universities. The goodwill created for Australia has been immense. Especially when many of these students grew up to be the leaders of their countries. It ended in the 1980s.

The new plan builds on that concept. However, instead this time it assists Australian students to study in Asian universities – again building very valuable networks. Indeed my son Patrick was very proud to have participated, going to a university in China.

I worked on it as a policy in Opposition with now Minister for Foreign Affairs Julie Bishop. I commend her for implementing it

---

[89] Ibid.
[90] Greg Sheridan, 2017c.
[91] Geoff Raby (2017), "Why joining the Quad is not in Australia's national interest", *Australian Financial Review*, 6 November.
[92] Sheridan 2017c.

as a priority whilst in government. It will be one of her lasting legacies. Everything should be done, within reason, to expand the program – maybe even to the Middle East.

Immigration and population size

As referred to earlier in this book I believe that we have to reopen the debate on immigration and population strategy, not least to deal with the housing affordability issue. Prime Minister Julia Gillard,[93] to her credit, tried to raise this matter but the factional hardheads in the Labor Party – who derive immense power from ethnic branch stacking in Sydney and Melbourne – stopped that debate stone dead.

Australia is a very generous country in terms of welcoming immigrants and as Prime Minister Malcolm Turnbull so often says we are the most successful multicultural society in the world. And Reserve Bank Governor Philip Lowe has stated that: "our immigration program I see as a source of national strength. To give that advantage up just so that we can take some pressure off housing prices, I find kind of problematic."[94]

However, as Prime Minister Gillard pointed out there is genuine anxiety amongst Australians about the pace of population growth.

One of her first acts as Prime Minister in 2010 was to appoint a Minister for Sustainable Population (Tony Burke) and ask him to develop a population strategy for a sustainable Australia. She said that she supported "sustainable population growth" and rejected "the idea that Australia should hurtle down the track towards a big population". She made the following very relevant observation:

> We are very roughly the same size as America and we are a great country like America – but we are not America. We

---

[93] Julia Gillard (2010), "Address to Lowy Institute", reprinted in *The Australian*, 6 July.
[94] Judith Sloan (2017b), "Big immigration fan club is devoted to growth myths", *The Australian*, 21 November.

do not have the inland sprawling plains, fertile soils and cities for that kind of population. 80 per cent of our population lives along our coast precisely because our continent is different.[95]

Further, Ms Gillard noted it was "a giant policy question for Australia. It is truly the mismatch of modern Australia: communities with too many people and not enough jobs and then other communities with too many jobs and not enough people. … It is a positive debate we intend to lead and one that must not be constrained by self censorship or political correctness."[96] Unfortunately this initiative came to naught and there has been virtually no systemic review of population strategy and immigration levels since.

Australia takes in a very large number of immigrants every year. In the last 4 years net migration has averaged 190,000 per year and represents 55 percent of total population growth which has been around 1.7 percent. As a consequence of this high population growth, while nominal GDP growth has been good (if not as good as it could be) – hovering in the 2 percent plus region – GDP per head of population has been negative. That is to say economic growth is not keeping pace with population growth. It partly explains why so many Australians are dissatisfied with the state of the Australian economy even though the headline growth numbers are good.

This high growth translates into over-crowding in our major cities – mainly Sydney and Melbourne where the vast bulk of immigrants settle. Potentially part of the solution to our housing affordability issues is to revisit immigration levels and reducing the yearly intake.

In particular, noted economist Judith Sloan has written extensively on this matter.

---

[95] Gillard 2010.
[96] Ibid.

She claims that the repeated Government statements that we are the most successful multicultural nation in the world is simply code for the continued support of a "mass-migration policy".

Sloan notes that there have been four phases in immigration between the beginning of the 20th century and today. Initially the population born overseas fell continuously until the end of World War II and those who came were from the British Isles. Second, a change of policy, driven by the maxim "populate or perish" saw a large increase in immigration this time including from wider-Europe and not just the British Isles. Then, third, there was a long period between the early 1970s and 2003 when there was a relative pause in the migration program with the annual average during this period being some 70,000 migrants. Lastly, and fourth, starting with the Howard Government in 2003, there has been a surge with the net overseas migration intake from across the world fluctuating between 150,000 and 300,000 people. That is "adding another Canberra in the space of a few short years, or another Adelaide in just a few more".[97]

However these people are not going to Canberra or Adelaide. In fact it would be great if they did. Instead they are almost overwhelmingly (more than 70 per cent) crowding into Sydney and Melbourne.

Sloan notes that one of the principal reasons given for maintaining higher levels of migration is the ageing of the population. However the Productivity Commission has examined this and disagrees stating that immigration "delays rather than eliminates population ageing. In the long term, underlying trends in life expectancy mean that permanent immigrants (as they age) will themselves add to the proportion of the population aged 65 and over."[98]

---

[97] Judith Sloan (2017a), "Do we really want a population of 40m?", *The Australian*, 18 July.
[98] Ibid.

As to the economic benefits of immigration, again the analysis is mixed. The Productivity Commission estimates that by 2060 "it is estimated that per capita GDP will be 7 per cent higher based on the continuation of our immigration program compared with zero net migration." However the Commission readily admits that "no account is taken of the costs that immigration imposes on urban congestion, rising house prices, loss of social amenity or environment impacts. And compared with no net migration, real wages and productivity are actually lower with ongoing mass migration. The economic gains are simply the result of the (assumed) higher employment-to-population ratio."[99]

Unless analyses are undertaken using per capita measurements, they can be very misleading.[100] Again, as Professor Sloan points out:

> [W]hat the best quality studies show is that the economic benefits of immigration are zero or slightly positive, with most of the gains being captured by the migrants themselves. Employers and incumbent workers with complementary skills gain, but incumbent workers who have similar profiles to new migrants miss out in terms of employment prospects and wages.[101]

And while a recent Government paper catalogues the virtues of immigration (which I do not disagree with) it does not make any comments about the appropriate level of growth and particularly points out the lack of detailed research on the costs of providing infrastructure and services for a larger population.[102]

---

[99] Ibid.
[100] Sloan 2017b.
[101] Ibid.
[102] Australian Treasury and Department of Home Affairs (2018), *Shaping a Nation: Population growth and immigration over time*, Commonwealth of Australia, Canberra, 35-48.

There is an urgent need to return to Julia Gillard's call for a proper review, not constrained by self-censorship or political correctness. As Judith Sloan styles the question: Do we really want a population of 40 million?

Finally, I note that former Prime Minister Abbott has also stated that: "In the coming year, we can take the pressure off housing prices and make it easier for locals to get jobs by perhaps scaling back immigration."[103] It is not often that Tony Abbott and Julia Gillard are on a unity ticket.

Conclusion

This is a long chapter and it deals with a large number of key issues.

As I noted in the introduction to the chapter a comprehensive look at the Australian Settlement 2.0 needs us to articulate what the international relations and defence element of it are. As we have seen the change from imperial benevolence to a dual focus on our alliance with the United States and our ongoing integration with the Asian region (or now more broadly the Indo-Pacific region) actually started over 75 years ago during World War II. So that element of the Australian Settlement 2.0 is very mature. However, it is forever changing and the chapter discusses that.

We have examined the critical challenges and maybe even dangers that the rise of China, the re-emergence of Russia, North Korean aggression and the scourge of Islamic terrorism mean for Australia.

I also present some very important policy debates in the defence area that, if we could financially afford them, would secure an even more independent foreign policy. Unfortunately the key phrase

---

[103] James Elton-Pym (2018), "Coalition should limit immigration to win the next election", *SBS News*, sbs.com.au, 22 January.

is "if we could financially afford them". It would appear that at present we couldn't afford the more radical options such as a comprehensive missile defence roll-out or nuclear submarines. The option of nuclear weapons, if we were faced with wholesale nuclear proliferation in our region, is an even more significant challenge. It reconfirms why a strong economy and financial position is vital for Australia's future.

Finally, I make some recommendations related to reviewing immigration and population policy. I think these are urgent and a vitally important economic question that impinges on our international relations and defence.

13
Conclusion

My direct family first reached Australian shores from England some 160 years ago in the 1850s. They first went to the Victorian Gold rushes but sadly didn't find any gold. They then moved north and settled on the coast of New South Wales and I believe became farmers in what is now heavily urbanised French's Forest in Sydney.

Over the generations my family – including many relations from Ireland, Scotland and Germany – were variously farmers, small business people, and teachers in New South Wales and Queensland.

My great grandfather, William Hendy, after whom my father is named, and I get my middle name, was one of the founders of the teachers union in Australia and was one of the first state general secretaries. I am very proud of that fact.

There were also citizen soldiers in my family, with my Great, Great Grandfather's younger brother Charlie – one of the original ANZACs – serving at Gallipoli and badly wounded at the Battle of Fromelles; Great Uncle Bill a veteran of the Battle of the Somme, amongst other horrors, and the winner of the Military Medal, and Uncle Jack who fought in Bomber Command in World War II and flew as a rear gunner over Nazi Germany, and amazingly survived that nightmare. Another Great Uncle, Alwyn, served in the jungles of Papua New Guinea in World War II. Their example and sacrifices inspire me enormously.

In more recent times two other people who have inspired me are my parents Bill and May. I am the proud product of a small business family. Both my parents were pharmacists and they owned a series of chemist shops over the years. They did it tough and built a good life for themselves and their three children. I never seemed to escape working in the shop at some stage during my school holidays. What you learn growing up in a small business family is: self-reliance; perseverance; and the value of hard work. And I hope that I have lived by those values in my adult life. That and my beliefs as a proud Christian. I have run my own small business and also been honoured to represent other small businesses as the chief executive of the ACCI.

So like any typical Australian I have a lot invested in the country. I want to see it succeed. Not just for my own children, but for the wider Australian family.

The rise and fall of the Australian Settlement and its replacement by the Australian Settlement 2.0 (or a neo-liberal consensus) in the 1990s was undisputedly, in my view, a great thing for this country.

Specifically this study began with an historical analysis that concentrated on the policy issues of tariff protection and centralised wage fixing, which were the core economic elements of the original Australian Settlement.

In fact it was a main contributor to Australia's "sleepiness"' over many decades. It answers the question posed in the title of this book: So why did Australia sleep?

It was because too much faith was put into easy answers. Time and again people thought the answer was in government regulations when actually it is often the problem that needed to be fixed.

It sometimes appears that when it comes to economic reforms what we see is a dance with the nation jerkily lurching two steps forward and one step back. There has definitely been a lack of political will to get things on a path of continuous improvement.

So in conclusion there are many policies that could be embarked upon that will increase productivity that will be a sustainable improvement for Australia. In the tax field I will state again that it probably is time to revisit the issue of radical income tax reform paid for by increasing the GST and implementing a tax-mix switch. It would be structural tax reform. But it is essential that the Commonwealth-State tax system be also massively reformed in the process. There is also more to do on company tax reform to ensure that the public is satisfied that multinational businesses are paying their fair share. Finally on tax we should reform capital gains tax – not to increase the tax but to reduce the tax to encourage more investment.

We should return to the issue of industrial relations reform and freer trade must remain a priority. We should also look at the relative disadvantage of regional and rural Australians. And we have to have a serious debate about immigration levels. The unquestioning acceptance of high annual in-takes cannot continue.

In a wider context we have to fix our democracy to make all this happen. Senate reform is vital and well overdue. A complete overhaul of campaign finance laws needs to be undertaken. We probably should increase the size of the House of Representatives.

In the area of international affairs and defence Australia faces many challenges. We almost certainly need to spend more money. Which is yet another reason to get our Budget back into order. And those spending demands could absolutely sky rocket if nuclear proliferation in our region continues and we have to seriously look at our own nuclear shield in face of an increasingly dangerous world.

Other things that need to be done. We need a Republic. It is long overdue for that change. It is not an elitist issue. It goes to the cultural identity of Australia. As an Australian with a heritage centred on the British Isles I have no innate problem with being closely linked culturally with Great Britain. However an incident when I was on a recent holiday in the United States caused me to again query the status quo. An old family friend we met up with, who worked at the US State Department and had served in their military, was absolutely staggered to find out in conversation that Australia was still a monarchy. He had never given the matter any thought prior to this, but naturally assumed that Australia had cut that link with Great Britain long before now. Equally, however, my view is that people could leave the flag alone given so many brave men and women have fought and died under it.

*****

So why did Australia sleep?

As detailed in this book it did so due to a whole range of complex reasons. The Australian Settlement was a uniquely Australian social and economic framework. Nominally it looked like a great success. However in the end it was a principal part of the problem. Its demise and replacement with the Australian Settlement 2.0 has been a lifesaver for Australia over the course of the last 30 years and has saved us from a lot of the economic and social dysfunction endured by our neighbours in the OECD.

However we are in danger of becoming a zombie nation if we reject the neo liberal policy framework.

As I said in chapter 1, this book's title is unashamedly a lift of the name of John F. Kennedy's book, originally published in 1940, called *Why England Slept*.

It is worth quoting again Kennedy's conclusion:

> At times it may appear that I have tried unjustifiably to clear the leaders of responsibility. That is not my view. But I believe, as I have stated frequently, that leaders are responsible for their failures only in the governing sector and cannot be held responsible for the failure of a nation as a whole.

So long as England was a democracy, a democracy with a Parliamentary system, so long as the leaders could have been turned out of office at any time on any issues, Parliament, and hence those who elect the Parliament, must all bear their share of the responsibility".[1]

Kennedy's observation is just as relevant to laying the blame for the fact Australia's potential has not been fulfilled. To repeat it again "Parliament, and hence those who elect the Parliament, must all bear their share of the responsibility". We all have a role in the future of our beautiful country.

In contemplating this I want to refer to something else Kennedy was famous for saying. In respect of the mission to the Moon he said "We choose to go to the Moon in this decade and do the other things, not because they are easy, but because they are hard; because that goal will serve to organise and measure the best of our energies and skills".[2] In 2018 the Australian of the Year, Professor (in quantum physics) Michelle Simmons, made a similar exhortation when she said "I believe that the things that are most worth doing in life are nearly always hard to do".[3]

And to follow on from the historic analysis in chapters 2 and 3, the Australian business community has a critical role to play in making the case for why the Australian Settlement 2.0 is good for the country – indeed its best option. It is incumbent on the business community to fully get behind any efforts to sustain the Australian Settlement 2.0.

*****

---

[1] John F. Kennedy (1962), *Why England Slept*, Mayfair Books, London, (originally 1940), 169.
[2] John F. Kennedy (1962a), "Address at Rice University", Texas, 12 September.
[3] Michelle Simmons (2018), "Quantum leap into limelight", edited version of Australia Day Address, *Sydney Morning Herald*, 27 January.

As I concluded in my valedictory statement to the House of Representatives when I departed after losing in the 2016 Federal election:

> So finally I note that Australia's economy is generally in good shape. However, as former Prime Minister John Howard use to state, economic reform is like a running race with an ever receding finish line. The task never stops.
>
> The Government has a large agenda piling up in respect of reforms that it has already announced. It is also going to return to the matter of taxation and industrial relations. They are both vitally important.
>
> One benefit of the current debates is that they will see people like myself, who hopefully have quite a few productive years left in the workforce, a solid agenda for reform over the next decade or so. Unfortunately there will be a lot to repair and it will take a lot of courage to do the things that need to be done.
>
> As I have previously said in a speech, we can all wonder where that courage will come from, especially in the political arena. But the history of this nation is that there are always people who will step up to the crease and do what is necessary in the public interest. At this stage we are probably looking for some dogged opening batsmen to build a long hard fought innings. Flashy players, with no clear commitment to reform, are not what we need right now.
>
> However, the arguments for reform need to be restated and the marketing job must continue ad infinitum.

INDEX

Abbott, Tony (and Abbott Government), 5, 148, 152, 238, 242-3, 245, 270, 307-8, 317
Adam Smith Institute, 11
Anderson, Bob, 79-80
Andrews, Kevin, 285
Arndt, Heinz, 73
Asprey Report, 185
Associated Chambers of Manufactures of Australia, 71, 73
Australian Council of Employers Federations, 71
Australian Chamber of Commerce, 71, 112
Australian Chamber of Commerce and Industry, 3, 71, 183, 219, 223, 230
Australian Industry Group, 114, 219

Banks, Gary, 156, 162
Barton, Edmund (and Barton Government), 26-7, 30, 35, 227
Beale, Tim, 198
Beijing Consensus, 157-8
Bell, Stephen, 35, 73, 78, 82, 94-6, 142
Bishop, Julie, 3, 262, 273, 278, 284, 300, 312
Blainey, Geoffrey, 116
Blandy, Richard, 103, 110

Brabin-Smith, Richard, 302-3, 310
bracket creep, 209-10, 216
Brigden Report, 72
Burke, Edmund, 161
Business Coalition on Tax Reform, 196, 201, 222
Business Council of Australia, 72, 95-6, 140-2, 219
Button, John, 94, 120-1
Bruce, Stanley Melbourne (and Bruce Government), 39, 74-6, 275

capital gains tax, 222-3, 225, 321
Carling, Robert, 188, 210
Carmody, Geoff, 108
Castles, Frank, 31-3, 38, 47-8, 52-3
Chifley, Ben (and Chifley Government), 40, 47, 77, 175-7
China, 136, 157-9, 256, 259-61, 268-9, 274-5, 283-93, 300, 302-3, 309-12
Clinton, Hillary, 270
Clough, Harold, 111, 122
company (or corporate) tax cuts, 187, 189, 192-3, 196, 202
Confederation of Australian Industry, 71, 87, 107
Copeman, Charles, 116
Costello, Peter, 3, 105, 115, 151, 184, 186, 216

Country-City Compact, 251-4, 257
Court, Ken, 91, 116
Curtin, John (and Curtin Government), 40, 275

Davis, Brent, 112-3, 127
Deakin, Alfred (and Deakin Government), 15-16, 26, 28-9, 33-5, 37-9, 42-4, 55, 57, 69, 138, 227
defence spending, 144, 303
Democracy Paradox, 165, 167
destination-based cash flow tax, 197-8, 200, 202
Dibb, Paul, 289-90, 302-3, 305, 309-11
Downer, Alexander, 91, 102
Draft White Paper 1985, 185
Drenth, Frank, 184, 196, 201-2
Dupont, Alan, 276
Dyer, Geoff, 158-9

Edwards, John, 109-10
Emmott, Bill, 160
Evans, Greg, 119-20

Fahey, John, 151
Fightback!, 5, 65, 133, 183, 185, 216
Fisher, Andrew (and Fisher Government), 38-9
Fraser, Malcolm (and Fraser Government), 28, 41, 62-3, 78, 86-7, 91-2, 230, 301

Freebairn, John, 110, 113-5
Fukuyama, Francis, 45, 159
Fullilove, Michael, 278

Garnaut, Ross, 62, 84, 118, 128, 145-6, 164, 270
Gillard, Julia (and Gillard Government), 144, 146, 148, 152, 218, 240, 242-3, 270, 313-4
Gorton, John (and Gorton Government), 36, 62, 79-80, 309
Grayling, A.C., 168
Greenspan, Alan, 151
Griffith, Samuel, 16, 18, 27, 29, 227
Gropp, Lisa, 36, 80-1, 84, 86-8, 117-20
GST reform, 137, 149, 164, 183-5, 188-90, 203, 208, 211, 213-9, 221, 224, 229, 231-2, 235-6, 321

Halper, Stefan, 158
Hawke, Bob (and Hawke Government), 8, 47, 60, 62-3, 65, 79, 86, 90, 93-7, 100-1, 117-8, 120-2, 126, 131, 133-4, 140-2, 145-6, 165-6, 175, 196, 230, 239, 270, 275
Hay, Andrew, 101, 104, 110, 115-6, 119
Henderson, Gerard, 103-4, 116, 125
Henry, Ken, 164, 202
Hewson, John, 5, 62, 118-9, 133, 142, 183, 216, 221

Index

Higgins, Henry Bourne, 34, 38
high speed rail, 254-7
Hirst, John, 12, 25
Holt, Harold (and Holt Government), 36, 41, 62, 119
Howard, John (and Howard Government), 40, 60, 62-3, 65-6, 90-1, 102, 105, 108-9, 116, 125, 130, 1322-8, 142-6, 151, 156, 165-6, 174-7, 184-5, 216, 221, 228, 238, 240, 243, 275, 296, 307, 311, 315, 324
Hughes, William Morris, 39, 75
Hyde, John, 103, 111-3

immigration, 6, 31-2, 40-1, 44, 52, 61, 164, 313-7, 321
industrial relations reform, 63, 110, 115, 131, 138, 150, 163, 168, 238, 240, 245, 250, 321, 324
Institute of Public Affairs, 111
International Monetary Fund, 157, 188, 196
Islamic terrorism, 274, 317

Jackson Report, 84, 86, 117, 120
Jacques, Martin, 158

Kasper, Wolfgang, 110-2
Keating, Michael, 64, 142
Keating, Paul (and Keating Government), 8, 47, 60, 62-5, 79, 90, 95, 109-10, 113, 117, 121-2, 129, 131-4, 141-3, 145-6, 165-6, 183, 196, 216, 221, 230, 239, 241, 270, 275, 301
Kelly, Paul, 5-6, 8, 29-35, 40-2, 44-9, 51-4, 59-63, 64-6, 68-9, 135, 139, 141, 164, 273-4
Kelty, Bill, 126, 131
Kerin, John, 120-1, 138
Keynesian, 30, 47, 54-5, 150-1
Kennedy, John F., 6-7, 322-3
Krugman, Paul, 153

Layton, Peter, 309-10
Lynch, Philip, 88
Luce, Edward, 160
Lyons, Joseph (and Lyons Government), 36

McKnight, David, 63, 67-8
McLachlan, Ian, 115-6, 119
McLean, Ian, 7, 262
McMahon, William (and McMahon Government), 36, 62, 79-80, 119
Makin, Tony, 147-8, 151
Mathews Report, 185
Mattis, Jim, 291, 300
Mauger, Samuel, 33
Melleuish, Gregory, 6, 8, 42, 44-5, 47-9, 57-8, 65
Menzies, Robert (and Menzies Government), 8, 36, 47, 60-3, 73, 77, 111, 238, 275

Mill, John Stuart, 162
missile defence, 299, 301-2, 304-5, 318
Molan, Jim, 303
Morgan, Hugh, 115
Morrison, Scott, 152, 188, 213

National Commission of Audit, 134-5, 169, 231, 234
National Farmers Federation, 106, 116, 119
Nelson, Brendan, 241-2
New Colombo Plan, 312
New Protection, 24, 30, 32-3, 37-9, 41, 44, 47, 59, 65, 69, 134, 239, 259
Noakes, Bryan, 106, 109, 125-6
North Korea, 274, 293, 298-300, 305, 309-10, 317
nuclear, 150, 262, 299, 301, 305, 307-11, 318, 321
Nurick, John, 103, 112

Obama, Barak (and Obama Administration), 168, 270, 291, 293-4
O'Farrell, Barry, 178-80
O'Neil, Robert, 110, 181

Parbo, Arvi, 96-7
Parkes, Henry, 16-18, 26
Parkinson, Martin, 164, 216

payroll tax, 201
Peacock, Andrew, 4
Piketty, Thomas, 223
political fundraising, 105, 171-2, 177-9, 181
Polities, George, 95-6, 103-4
Porter, Michael, 108, 113, 115
Productivity Commission, 119, 135, 153-4, 156, 162-3, 166, 199, 238, 243, 245-8, 250, 252, 263, 265-7, 269, 315-6

Quadrilateral Dialogue, 311-2

Ralph Review, 200
Rattigan, Alf, 72-3, 80, 82-4
regional development policy, 254-5, 257
Reid, George (and Reid Government), 18-19, 26, 38
Reith, Peter, 119, 136, 183, 216, 237, 276, 296
Renewable Energy Target, 169
republic, 44, 64, 172
Richardson, Dennis, 121, 285
Robb, Andrew, 119
Robson, Alex, 191
Ross, Iain, 131
Rudd, Kevin (and Rudd Government), 144, 146, 148, 152, 218, 240, 243, 270, 277, 305, 311

Index

Russia, 261, 268, 274-5, 291-5, 300, 317
Ryan, Paul, 195, 198

Samuel, Graeme, 221
Sawer, Marian, 30, 45, 55, 58
Schott, Kerry, 180
Schumpeter, Joseph, 157
Senate reform, 171-6, 181, 321
Shepherd, Tony, 233
Sheridan, Greg, 116, 302-5, 307-8, 312
Sloan, Judith, 313-7
Spence, Michael, 203
Spicer, Ian, 96, 123, 125, 127-8, 133
state paternalism, 6, 31, 41, 43, 48, 51, 63-5
state income tax, 150, 207, 209, 230, 232-3, 235-6
Stiglitz, Joseph, 223
Stokes, Geoffrey, 6, 8, 31-2, 45-6, 48-55, 58, 64, 69
Stone, John, 46, 62, 83, 101, 106, 115
Summers, Lawrence, 223
superannuation, 68, 201, 221-2

Taylor, Harriet Hardy, 162
Tillerson, Rex, 292
trade agreements, 135, 144, 150, 256, 260, 269
Trans Pacific Partnership, 259, 270-1
Trebeck, David, 109, 119
Trump, Donald (and Trump Administration), 194, 196-7, 202, 259, 265, 267, 270-1, 289, 299
Turnbull, Malcolm (and Turnbull Government), 148, 152, 174, 178, 188, 196, 221, 224, 235, 238, 243-5, 270-1, 283, 299-300, 305, 313

Vernon Report, 72-3

Walsh, Cliff, 64, 108, 113, 115
Warburton, Richard, 183-4, 186, 222
Washington Consensus, 157
Watson, Graeme, 249
White Australia Policy, 6, 31, 40-1, 44, 48-9, 60-1, 65, 274
White, Bob, 97
White, Hugh, 288-9, 303, 308-9
Whitlam, Gough (and Whitlam Government), 9, 61-2, 78, 80-6, 91, 121, 275
World Trade Organisation, 122, 268

Xenophon, Nick, 193, 241
Xi, Jingping (and Xi Administration), 158, 290

www.ingramcontent.com/pod-product-compliance
Lightning Source LLC
Chambersburg PA
CBHW070013010526
44117CB00011B/1550